Reglobalization

This book charts the way towards a better, repurposed globalization, which it calls 'reglobalization', and shows how this can be built, incrementally but realistically, via reforms to the partial and fragile existing structures of global governance.

In making this argument, the book firmly rejects the new fashion for a politics of deglobalization, which has appeared of late in both left-wing and right-wing variants. Instead, it suggests that a reformed Group of 20 (G20), for all its current inadequacies, can still provide the critical coordinating function that the management of a process of reglobalization requires. The book argues that globalization is too important to be lost; rather, it needs to be saved from its capture by neoliberalism and rebuilt around different values for a post-neoliberal era. The emergence of a global pandemic as an issue only goes to emphasize the necessity, importance and urgency of the reglobalization project.

Reglobalization is essential reading for anybody living in the era of globalization – which is all of us – and anybody worried about its many economic, social and political problems – which is a growing number of us.

The chapters in this book were originally published in the journal *Globalizations*.

Matthew Louis Bishop is Senior Lecturer in International Politics and Associate Fellow of the Sheffield Political Economy Research Institute (SPERI) at the University of Sheffield.

Anthony Payne is Emeritus Professor of Politics and Founding Co-director of the Sheffield Political Economy Research Institute (SPERI) at the University of Sheffield.

Rethinking Globalizations

Edited by Barry K. Gills, University of Helsinki, Finland and
Kevin Gray, University of Sussex, UK

This series is designed to break new ground in the literature on globalization and its academic and popular understanding. Rather than perpetuating or simply reacting to the economic understanding of globalization, this series seeks to capture the term and broaden its meaning to encompass a wide range of issues and disciplines and convey a sense of alternative possibilities for the future.

Multiplicity
A New Common Ground for International Relations?
Edited by Justin Rosenberg and Milja Kurki

Rising Powers, People Rising
Neoliberalization and its Discontents in the BRICS Countries
Edited by Alf Gunvald Nilsen and Karl von Holdt

Reglobalization
Edited by Matthew Louis Bishop and Anthony Payne

Unity on the Global Left
Critical Reflections on Samir Amin's Call for a New International
Edited by Barry K. Gills and Christopher Chase-Dunn

The Interface of Domestic and International Factors in India's Foreign Policy
Edited by Johannes Dragsbaek Schmidt and Shantanu Chakrabarti

Questioning the Utopian Springs of Market Economy
Damien Cahill, Martijn Konings and Adam David Morton

Between Class and Discourse: Left Intellectuals in Defence of Capitalism
Boris Kagarlitsky

Challenging Inequality in South Africa
Transitional Compasses
Edited by Michelle Williams and Vishwas Satgar

For more information about this series, please visit:
www.routledge.com/Rethinking-Globalizations/book-series/RG

"*Reglobalization* is a timely and trenchant intervention in contemporary debates about the challenges and possibilities of building a more humane form of globalization. Bishop and Payne have put together a first-class line-up of scholars who explore the many different ways in which we could and must move beyond the neoliberal form of globalization that is so clearly failing us today without giving up on the more progressive possibilities of a genuinely global political and economic way of life."

Jacqueline Best, *University of Ottawa, Canada*

"As globalization retreats, *Reglobalization* not only accounts for its pathologies, but, more importantly, charts potential trajectories out of its crisis. Reminding readers that its current form is not given, the book issues a rallying cry to save globalization by going beyond its neoliberal nature. Surveying a wide range of global issues, including tax, inequality, trade, climate and migration, the authors lay out a comprehensive blueprint for a re-embedded, post-neoliberal reglobalization. This book will be essential reading for those looking to save globalization from itself before it is too late."

Tom Chodor, *Monash University, Australia*

"Seeking to separate its discussion from the policies and practices of neoliberalism, this important and compelling book asks us to rethink the case for globalization. It looks toward future possibilities, reimagining globalization in terms of its progressive potential in a post-neoliberal context. As the diverse chapters make clear, 'reglobalization' is no easy task; but it is a project that serves to reanimate debates about the 'global' within International Political Economy, one that recognizes how scholarship has an active role to play in rethinking, reimagining and reforming the global economic order."

Juanita Elias, *University of Warwick, United Kingdom*

Reglobalization

Edited by
Matthew Louis Bishop and Anthony Payne

Routledge
Taylor & Francis Group
LONDON AND NEW YORK

First published 2021
by Routledge
2 Park Square, Milton Park, Abingdon, Oxon OX14 4RN

and by Routledge
52 Vanderbilt Avenue, New York, NY 10017

Routledge is an imprint of the Taylor & Francis Group, an informa business

British Library Cataloguing in Publication Data
A catalogue record for this book is available from the British Library

ISBN: 978-0-367-63930-3 (hbk)
ISBN: 978-0-367-63931-0 (pbk)
ISBN: 978-1-003-12135-0 (ebk)

Typeset in Minion Pro
by Newgen Publishing UK

Publisher's Note
The publisher accepts responsibility for any inconsistencies that may have arisen during the conversion of this book from journal articles to book chapters, namely the inclusion of journal terminology.

Disclaimer
Every effort has been made to contact copyright holders for their permission to reprint material in this book. The publishers would be grateful to hear from any copyright holder who is not here acknowledged and will undertake to rectify any errors or omissions in future editions of this book.

Contents

Citation Information

The chapters in this book were originally published in *Globalizations*, volume 18, issue 1 (January 2021). When citing this material, please use the original referencing for each article, as follows:

Chapter 1

The political economies of different globalizations: theorizing reglobalization
Matthew Louis Bishop and Anthony Payne
Globalizations, volume 18, issue 1 (January 2021), DOI: 10.1080/14747731.2020.1779963

Chapter 2

Creating a race to the top in global tax governance: the political case for tax spillover assessments
Andrew Baker and Richard Murphy
Globalizations, volume 18, issue 1 (January 2021), DOI: 10.1080/14747731.2020.1774324

Chapter 3

The IMF, tackling inequality, and post-neoliberal 'reglobalization': the paradoxes of political legitimation within economistic parameters
Ben Clift and Te-Anne Robles
Globalizations, volume 18, issue 1 (January 2021), DOI: 10.1080/14747731.2020.1774325

Chapter 4

Reglobalizing trade: progressive global governance in an age of uncertainty
James Scott and Rorden Wilkinson
Globalizations, volume 18, issue 1 (January 2021), DOI: 10.1080/14747731.2020.1779965

Chapter 5

Towards a feminist global trade politics
Erin Hannah, Adrienne Roberts and Silke Trommer
Globalizations, volume 18, issue 1 (January 2021), DOI: 10.1080/14747731.2020.1779966

Chapter 6

Reforming global climate governance in an age of bullshit
Hayley Stevenson
Globalizations, volume 18, issue 1 (January 2021), DOI: 10.1080/14747731.2020.1774315

Chapter 7

Philosophies of migration governance in a globalizing world
Antoine Pécoud
Globalizations, volume 18, issue 1 (January 2021), DOI: 10.1080/14747731.2020.1774316

Chapter 8

Steering towards reglobalization: can a reformed G20 rise to the occasion?
Matthew Louis Bishop and Anthony Payne
Globalizations, volume 18, issue 1 (January 2021), DOI: 10.1080/14747731.2020.1779964

Notes on Contributors

Andrew Baker is Professor of Political Economy in the Department of Politics and International Relations at the University of Sheffield.

Matthew Louis Bishop is Senior Lecturer in International Politics and Associate Fellow of the Sheffield Political Economy Research Institute (SPERI) at the University of Sheffield, UK.

Ben Clift is Professor of International Political Economy at the University of Warwick, UK.

Erin Hannah is Associate Professor and Chair of the Department of Political Science at King's University College at the University of Western Ontario, Canada.

Richard Murphy is Professor of International Political Economy and Practice at City, University of London.

Anthony Payne is Emeritus Professor of Politics and Founding Co-director of the Sheffield Political Economy Research Institute (SPERI) at the University of Sheffield, UK.

Antoine Pécoud is Professor of Sociology at the University of Sorbonne Paris Nord (France), Research Associate at CERI/Sciences Po and Fellow at the Institut des Migrations.

Adrienne Roberts is Senior Lecturer in the Department of Politics at the University of Manchester, UK.

Te-Anne Robles is Teaching Fellow in East Asian Politics in the School of Government and International Affairs at the University of Durham, UK.

James Scott is Senior Lecturer in International Political Economy in the Department of Political Economy at King's College London, UK.

Hayley Stevenson is Associate Professor in the Department of Political Science and International Studies at Universidad Torcuato Di Tella in Buenos Aires, Argentina.

Silke Trommer is Senior Lecturer in the Department of Politics at the University of Manchester, UK.

Rorden Wilkinson is Professor of International Political Economy and Pro-Vice-Chancellor for Education and the Student Experience at the University of New South Wales, Sydney, Australia.

Foreword

We met nearly twenty years ago as student and lecturer, brought together by an undergraduate module at the University of Sheffield entitled 'Development'. We subsequently became entwined in the taxing marathon that is the researching, writing and supervision of a doctorate and stayed in close contact as Matt launched his academic career at the University of the West Indies in Trinidad and Tony was drawn into senior university management (but finding continuing research trips to the Caribbean a very necessary diversion). We worked together, at a distance, on a couple of minor research projects, but were given an opportunity to collaborate properly after Matt returned to the University of Sheffield as Senior Lecturer in 2016. By this time, Tony was one of the Directors of the new Sheffield Political Economy Research Institute (SPERI) and Matt was immediately drawn into its activities as joint leader, with Tony, of the Institute's 'Development and Globalization' strand.

SPERI was an innovation amongst research centres in the social sciences in the United Kingdom in that its mission was not only to carry out novel academic research of high quality, but to use this research to make and disseminate explicit policy proposals designed to bring about economic and social benefits in the real world. This edited book is a product of that ambition. It began as a series of posts on the SPERI blog, grew into a special issue of the academic journal *Globalizations* and now finishes its journey in traditional form as something that can be pulled off the bookshelf as needed. In the book, we certainly seek, along with our various colleagues, to contribute to a better understanding of the contemporary condition of the global political economy and its governance at the beginning of the 2020s. But, above all, we hope that we have helped to start a debate about how globalization might be re-made for the future in ways that deliver more of what the peoples of the world want and need.

In getting to this point we have incurred many debts that we must acknowledge: to our distinguished contributors and diligent referees; to Barry Gills, Editor of *Globalizations*; to Caroline Church at Routledge and Faye Gardner at Newgen; to SPERI colleagues, past and present; and, of course, to our respective partners, Merisa and Jill, who have always encouraged and supported both our friendship and our professional collaboration.

Matt and Tony
July 2020

The political economies of different globalizations: theorizing reglobalization

Matthew Louis Bishop and Anthony Payne

ABSTRACT

Globalization remains contested, and often misunderstood, with damaging real-world consequences. We make four interlinked contentions in this regard. First, globalization is here to stay: although critics might wish it away intellectually, and populists might attempt this practically, the scale of contemporary global integration renders these aims implausible and even undesirable. Second, by viewing neoliberal globalization as a distinct variant rooted in a particular time and place and born of a particular constellation of contingent social and political forces, we can conceive of, and ultimately construct, 'different globalizations'. Third, emergent forms of both right- and left-wing 'deglobalization' do not provide meaningful routes out of the crisis of a decaying neoliberalism. Fourth, only a repurposed form of 're-embedded post-neoliberal reglobalization' can deliver this. By conceptualizing the challenge in these terms, we provide the theoretical underpinnings for the special issue which addresses the potential for reglobalization in practice across the global political economy.

Introduction: we need to talk about globalization, again

It may seem strange to suggest, even in the subject's eponymous journal, that we must consider once more what we really mean by 'globalization'. Notwithstanding the immeasurable number of words already devoted to the explanation of this ubiquitous term – indeed, has any concept ever been subject to quite so much scrutiny from such a range of disciplinary vantage points? (James & Steger, 2014) – globalization as a phenomenon remains widely misunderstood. Yet it is too important for the argument to be left where it mostly sits in the general discourse of politics and political economy, particularly during our era of profound (and profoundly disorientating) global upheaval.

The core problem can be simply expressed. Globalization is treated too often as if it has a kind of pre-ordained technological inevitability that has huge political consequences, but is, at the same time, beyond political explanation. However, it cannot be sensibly said to *cause* anything (Hay, 2001). This way of thinking has the effect of turning it into an actor in the drama, propelled to the centre of the stage by some celestial will or force of nature. To be precise, it is to reify globalization – to make it into a thing that of itself can act and bring about outcomes. This does not really stand up to scrutiny since the concept refers to a highly complicated *process* of economic, social and political change that unfolds at a global level and, arguably, is distinctive and important precisely because it does unfold at that level.

This was the insight that underpinned the classic definition offered during the late 1990s in *Global Transformations*, a brilliant overview of the early debate by Held et al. (1999). They argued that globalization should be thought of as nothing less, but also nothing more, than 'the widening, deepening and speeding up of worldwide interconnectedness in all aspects of contemporary social life, from the cultural to the criminal, the financial to the spiritual' (Held et al., 1999, p. 2). Two decades on, all that needs to be added to this still-relevant definition is the qualification that counter-processes to 'worldwide interconnectedness' could nevertheless be mobilized at any time. The point we are making here is not a merely academic argument about conceptual precision; it is rather that the reification of globalization as a thing that can exercise intention, the framing of it as some sort of external actor bearing down on all of us, actually obscures, elides and therefore implicitly absolves of blame the social and political forces – the real actors in the great game of the new globalizing political economy – which have pushed every country in the world to live and make their way in a global context that is structurally different from that which prevailed, broadly speaking, from 1945 to the mid-1970s.

Moreover, we know who these actors are. Without wishing to appear excessively conspiratorial, it is clear that the big global corporations, the political leaders of the major Western states, the formers of opinion in the global media, think-tanks and in some leading universities, have collectively built and defended ideologically the theory and practice of global neoliberalism that has been, and still broadly remains, the ruling framework of governance within which Britain and so much of the world has been enmeshed for so long (Payne, 2016). Put starkly, it has been global neoliberals, understood as real actors with interests that they have pursued, who have knowingly driven forward and defended the new behaviours that have, over time, come to constitute globalization, thereby reproducing and refashioning the very structures that condition the parameters of action within that context. Equally, it was real politicians who subsequently argued, as did Tony Blair, the former British Prime Minister, in his valedictory speech to the Labour Party conference in September 2005, that we should not bother to 'stop and debate globalization', because 'you might as well debate whether autumn should follow summer' (Blair, 2005).

Yet, today, globalization is actually being debated more than ever. It has, for many, gone too far, reached too deeply into too many areas of social life, undermined democracy and led to severe economic dislocations, the costs and benefits of which have been grotesquely maldistributed. The backlash against the kind of depoliticized technocracy that Blair and other 'Third Way' leaders represented has been fierce. There is no shortage of critical literature that emphasizes the many problems with which these shifts are associated: among the voluminous literature on the subject, numerous recent (or recently revised and updated) books have examined the detrimental outcomes for, *inter alia*, the reproduction of racial and neo-colonial logics of accumulation and exclusion (Bhattacharyya, 2018; Shilliam, 2018), development (Selwyn, 2017), inequality (Bourguignon, 2015), authoritarian forms of marketization (Tansel, 2017) and the horrifying militarization of society (Enloe, 2016). It is certainly true that 'more globalization' – or, as we would have it, 'better globalization' – is a hard sell in inauspicious times characterized by enduring economic stagnation and decaying social security in much of the West (Gamble, 2014, 2016; Hay & Wincott, 2012), unprecedented and extreme imbalances of power and capital (Piketty, 2014, 2020) and a looming environmental crisis of historic scale (Klein, 2014).

However, it is crucial to stress again that globalization itself did not – indeed could not – cause these ruptures of its own volition; they derive instead from the aggregate decisions of powerful actors, underpinned by particular ideas about the world, and, within that context, the everyday actions of billions of people, some more influential than others. Furthermore, the challenges we face remain genuinely global in scope and their magnitude demands a planetary response. Any political posture that advocates backing away from globalization is delusional, since it takes aim at the wrong target based on a problematic analysis; rather, the urgent task is to build a variant *of* globalization which is geared towards finding solutions to those truly global challenges. Tony Blair was thus surely correct, in an ontological sense, to argue that *the fact* of globalization is undeniable, but he was evidently wrong, epistemologically speaking, since its nature and consequences – including the contours of the politically possible for dealing with it – are very much up for grabs. As Matthew Watson and Colin Hay (2003, p. 289) suggested at the time, by disingenuously invoking 'the image of globalisation as a non-negotiable external economic constraint' underpinned by a 'logic of no alternative', Blair and his contemporaries were able to 'render contingent policy choices "necessary"'. Yet there are, in fact, many possible globalizations, and the orthodoxies that prevailed before 2008 have never been more fiercely challenged (Hunt & Stanley, 2019).

Consequently, key political actors, especially those of the left, have a duty to shape policy actively at both the domestic and international level in socially beneficial ways, rather than passively bowing to the presumed inevitability of market forces. In light of the difficulties we face in grappling with these processes – including contesting those accounts which advocate, as we describe it, a 'deglobalization' approach – we make four interlinked contentions in this article. These reflect the organizational architecture for each substantive section, and they also underpin our broad agenda in the special issue as a whole. First, globalization cannot be wished away, much as many of its most trenchant critics would like it to be. It is here to stay in some form and cannot be wound back in any fundamental fashion. Consequently, vacating this terrain is an abdication, since globalization can be resisted, reshaped and repurposed, as well as more rigorously managed, just not demolished entirely. We need, in other words, to recognize that the globalization we currently have, including the backlash against it, reflects a political construction born of a particular phase in history.

Second, we need therefore to recognize the essentially neoliberal character of 'actually-existing' globalization (Harvey, 2005; Peck, 2011). This has brought with it a great many problems, and it has palpably extended too far – or at least too far too quickly, with insufficient and insufficiently democratic governance – in certain spaces of the global political economy. But it has also brought great benefits in some areas and has not extended far enough into others. Indeed, it is at least arguable that many of the pathologies we can identify today – not least the racialized forms of populism that are increasingly evident in many countries – might be *even worse* were it not for the scale of global integration hemming in nativist, nationalist projects. Contemporary critical accounts, from both right and left, which argue against globalization in general, discount this reality to an unacceptable degree: there is, put crudely, a real danger of throwing out the baby of globalization with the bathwater of neoliberalism.

Third, the major challenges we face are inherently transboundary in nature. There is no getting away from this simple reality, and it seems absurd, even fatuous, to have to reiterate it. Some of the most obvious difficulties include: the emergence of digital monopolies and their continued accretion of power; the destruction of domestic tax bases, debasing of work conditions and accentuated poverty; regional instability, weapons trafficking, wars and ongoing refugee crises; declining biodiversity, the destruction of natural patrimony and emergent pathogens which can lead to pandemics; and, of course, global heating and the rapidly accelerating climate emergency. No single state has the power to deal with any of these problems itself. But it is also unclear whether collective answers can be found by the international community. Nevertheless, what is certain is that those answers *will definitely not be discovered* via a retreat inside national borders. The only plausible solutions are global ones, requiring a global response by actors operating via institutions at the global level.

As such – and this is our fourth and final point – the only real thing worth debating when it comes to globalization nowadays is how it should, and could, be better organized, managed, democratized and reoriented to serving society. Consequently, in the final substantive section of this article we shall set out the case for seeking collectively to build a new and different globalization, which we call 'reglobalization', structured around different 'post-neoliberal' ambitions and values. To envision this in practice is an undeniably thorny challenge. However, in this special issue we present a series of pieces that seek precisely to envision just such a future in some of the primary policy areas of global governance. In our conclusion here we briefly introduce them as illustrations of what we call 'reglobalization in action'.

Separating globalization from a decaying neoliberalism

Globalization is a highly political process, and we should not be misled by the myth of its technological inevitability. It is important, too, to understand that the form of it that we have experienced up to now has been distinctly *neoliberal* in character. To deploy again the phrase of Held *et al.*, 'the widening, deepening and speeding up of worldwide interconnectedness' that has occurred over the past four decades progressed on specifically neoliberal terms and gained all of its social and political character from the major political shift towards the hegemony of neoliberalism that was initiated in the West in the early 1980s and rolled out thereafter.

In other words, globalization could *in theory* have been done differently. At its heart, the term connotes only a spatial expansion of the terrain on which political economy functions. It was the neoliberal project that coloured globalization, propelling it forward to become the 'actually existing' variant within which we live at the start of the 2020s. There has not been created the fully-blown 'hyperglobalization' or 'borderless world' envisioned by some liberals like Kenichi Ohmae (1990, 1995) wherein the market completely triumphs over states. This is partly because the binary distinction between 'markets' and 'states' can only ever be analytical, given their co-constitution and consequent existence in a relationship of deep interdependence. The global financial crisis of 2007–8 certainly demonstrated that finance had been steadily unleashed to a point where it was no longer properly under control and threatened the stability of the whole global political economy (Tooze, 2018). However, it was states that came to the rescue. In sum, the particular type of globalization that has emerged is historically specific and distinctive to its times, and we must not make the mistake of forgetting this.

We must not make another mistake either, which is to think that neoliberal globalization has been all bad. The deleterious aspects are much discussed and obvious: the endemic instability (as above), the deepening trend towards inequality, the divisions enforced in societies between 'winners' and 'losers' in the process, the distorting pressure placed on local and national identities by homogenizing global cultural artefacts (Pieterse, 2020). But there have been other more satisfying aspects that need to be recognized in the balance – in general, the new opportunities opened up to so many people to live, work and love across borders and, specifically, the extraordinary economic growth and consequent escape from mass poverty attained by China, India and other 'emerging' countries over the past three decades (Bishop, 2016). Reflecting on 'humanity's greatest achievement', John Lanchester, the British journalist and author of *Whoops!* (2010) – one of the best books on the global crisis written for a popular audience – proposed that this was the World Bank's announcement that 'the proportion of the planet's population living in absolute poverty … had halved from 1990 to 2010' (Lanchester, 2013). We know that the models of development pursued in China and India have not really been neoliberal in nature (Hopewell, 2016; Muzaka & Serrano, 2020). But this massive reduction in global poverty happened on neoliberalism's watch, so to speak, and it is hard to imagine that those two gigantic countries' economic take-off could have happened so dramatically outside of the framework of a neoliberal globalization within which they had ready access to massive export markets (Bishop & Murray-Evans, 2020).

What all of this suggests to us is that there can indeed be 'different globalizations'. If, as we have argued, the neoliberal variant has been a political construction born of a particular political moment and possessed simultaneously of negative and positive aspects, then it must be possible to move on from it by addressing the former and seeking to maintain and even improve the latter. The reality is that neoliberal globalization – not to mention neoliberal*ism* – has also changed over the different phases of its history in myriad ways too. The key point is that, in the final analysis, politics is always contingent on which economic and social forces are active and effective in any era. In this context, it has been striking that alternative models of globalization have lately begun to be advanced. We call these 'deglobalization from the right' and 'from the left'. In the next two sections of this article we examine these would-be global political economies and argue that both represent dead-ends.

Deglobalization 'from the right'

Amongst many prior fashions, deglobalization has become 'the new buzzword' of our times, according to Ruchir Sharma, the Indian author and chief global strategist at Morgan Stanley. He first used the term in a newspaper article in *The Guardian* in July 2016, just a month after the vote for Brexit in the British referendum (Sharma, 2016). He argued that this event moved the world into what he dubbed 'the AC era – after the crisis of 2008'. Brexit was, though, seen less as a cause than a symptom of a situation he described as 'a manifestation of global forces unleashed by the 2008 global financial crisis, including slower growth, rising inequality, and a widening backlash against open borders and incumbent leaders'. The consequences of this would be rising protectionism, falling global capital flows and reduced numbers of economically-dynamic migrants. Accordingly, Sharma's conclusion was stark: 'globalization as we know it is over'.

Yet, notwithstanding this acute analysis of the 'anti-establishment revolt' that had spread across the major democracies since 2008, it remained the case in mid-2016 that there had yet to be articulated a specific ideology of deglobalization. Indeed, the erstwhile British government led by Theresa May that subsequently took charge of negotiating Brexit claimed to want to move in the opposite direction towards the vision of a new 'Global Britain' (Lidington, 2018) in which the supposedly 'great island-nation' would somehow again be able to roam the trade routes of the world as if Queen Victoria were still on the imperial throne. Much has been written about the amnesiac neo-imperialist delusions of this way of thinking (Barnett, 2017a; Koram & Nisancioglu, 2017; Von Tunzelmann, 2019; Younge, 2018), including consideration of whether such critiques might be exaggerated or misplaced (Saunders, 2019; Siles-Brügge, 2019), and we will not expand on these debates here. It was instead Donald Trump's victory in the Presidential election in the United States (US) in November 2016 which marked the end of global neoliberalism in its ideological sense and inaugurated what Mark Blyth (2016) has called the era of 'neonationalism' (which we are describing here as 'deglobalization from the right').

The basis of Trump's approach to engaging with the global political economy was unequivocally established in his inaugural Presidential address in January 2017 in which he outlined the new economic nationalist agenda of the US:

> From this moment on, it's going to be America First. Every decision on trade, on taxes, on immigration, on foreign affairs, will be made to benefit American workers and American families. We must protect our borders from the ravages of other countries making our products, stealing our companies, and destroying our jobs. We will follow two simple rules: buy American and hire American. (Trump, 2017b)

From this mind-set there has subsequently flowed US withdrawal from the Trans-Pacific Partnership (TPP), the renegotiation of the North American Free Trade Area (NAFTA), the imposition of punitive tariffs on various categories of Chinese, Mexican, Canadian and European Union (EU) imports into the US and the rhetorically-charged ambition to build a wall along the whole of the US border with Mexico.

As a package, it is not difficult to follow and few have felt it necessary to elevate Trump's globalization policy to a sophisticated theoretical level. What is interesting and important, though, is the extent to which it has come about in response to a particular reading of China's conduct under neoliberal globalization. The key author of this interpretation is Peter Navarro, a former business-school professor from the University of California, Irvine, whom Trump appointed Director of the Office of Trade and Manufacturing Policy (Lowrey, 2018). Although not speaking Mandarin or spending much time in China, he had previously produced several hawkish books (Navarro, 2008, 2015; Navarro & Autry, 2011) and one infamous documentary (called *Death by China*) which argued that the country had in effect cheated its way to global pre-eminence via the deliberate deployment of lax labour standards, environmental degradation and currency manipulation. He contended that it had effectively been engaged in an economic war with the US for 25 years and was winning hands-down at the expense of American jobs.

Trump reiterated precisely this view when he addressed his hosts in the Great Hall of the People in Beijing during his first visit as President in November 2017, adding only the rider that he did not 'blame' China for building up a huge trade surplus, but rather gave it 'great credit' for 'being able to take advantage of another country for the benefit of its citizens' (cited in Phillips, 2017). His response, however, was not to seek to level the playing field by imposing new multilateral, or 'plurilateral', rules via arrangements such as the TPP, from which China had been deliberately excluded in any case (Bishop & Zhang, 2020). It was, instead, to take China on in the old game of 'dog-eat-dog' power politics. Up to a point, Trump's analysis made sense, not least in being sceptical of the virtues of ever-freer trade for its own sake (Wade, 2017). Yet these days President Xi, China's head of state, tends to endorse globalization, as he did at Davos in January 2017, knowing that it strikes an appealing contrast with Trump's declaratory economic nationalism (Jinping, 2017).

We should be wary, though, of drawing simplistic binaries, since there is no straightforward distinction between American 'free markets' and Chinese 'statism'. Free trade and protectionism are not absolute, but relative. They are also two sides of the same coin: all countries intervene *in order to* stimulate markets and sectors, and they often protect to develop and defend them too. China's extraordinary economic growth over the last 30 years has certainly been achieved by means of high levels of state control and intervention within its economy (Lin, 2014; Lin et al., 2003). But this was undertaken with the express purpose of developing a market-based economy that has liberalized significantly in recent years (Breslin, 2017). As regards the global political economy, China has undoubtedly engaged, but carefully and on its own terms, even if it is now seeking to play a more influential role – albeit one with differences of emphasis and intensity of action – in global economic governance (Chin & Thakur, 2010; de Graaff, 2020; Zhang & Keith, 2017). Nonetheless, Xi's defence of globalization is hardly surprising: like trade superpowers of yesteryear, China's contemporary posture reflects its preponderant economic power in open global markets that it increasingly dominates

(Hopewell, 2019) and remains considerably more 'selective' than its pro-openness rhetoric implies (Weinhardt & Ten Brink, 2020).

Trump's attacks on the global trading system also do not reflect a damascene conversion to developmental forms of statism. In fact, he has not called for a scaling-back of existing levels of openness as such, although he has condemned the multilateral regulation of the system itself. He has rather couched his demands in terms of *even freer* trade, based on the teleological belief that it is an end-state that can be reached if everyone liberalizes as far as the US supposedly has (Bishop, 2018). This view misreads what free trade is: i.e. something that can only ever be realized relatively, rather than absolutely, because states always retain defensive interests in the most sensitive sectors. The contemporary conjuncture – in which aggregate goods tariffs are at their lowest in modern history and behind-the-border services regulation is as advanced as ever, albeit deeply contested (Siles-Brügge, 2014) – is both the 'freest' trade has ever been, but also the point at which it has become most contentious. This is partly a consequence of the extent to which attempts at further opening rub up against those sensitivities and influential domestic lobbies, but also reflects the fact that many now have a clearer idea of who has paid the unequal distributional costs of global liberalization so far (Rodrik, 2017). So, where Trump sees other countries 'cheating', he misses the reality that their continued protections in certain sectors mirror the US's own defensive posture in others.

In any case, there is nothing misguided *per se* with deploying state power assertively in national economic management (Bishop, Payne et al., 2018). The key distinction is whether those powers are used largely in a positive, developmentalist way to build economic strength nationally before entering into global competition and accepting the reciprocity underpinning trade agreements, *or* in a largely negative fashion to fight global trade battles in crudely protectionist ways. Trump is a nationalist in this latter sense. In his other economic policies, he is pro-business (meaning corporate big business and rentier finance), pro-marketization, pro-rich and likely to do little economically for those who voted for him having lost their jobs in the de-industrialized parts of the US. He is, in essence, a hyper-neoliberal at home and a neo-nationalist abroad. That is a contradiction, to be sure, but not one that would worry him since so much of his power and style derives directly from his clever manipulation of contradictions. Although much commentary has focused on the follies of the trade war with China, a great irony of Trumpism and its strange mix of libertarian and nativist ideology is that, by attempting to emasculate the state's capacity to engage in economic governance, the Trump administration has increasingly come to undermine American interests and the country's external trade balance (Hopewell, 2017).

What does all of this mean? The upshot of Trump's 'deglobalization from the right' is to leave the global political economy dangerously vulnerable to 'strong man' games, as Will Hutton (2017) described them following the president's visit to Asia. Hutton noted as well that Trump moved on from Beijing to Da Nang to attend the Asia-Pacific Economic Cooperation (APEC) summit where in his speech he railed hard against the World Trade Organization (WTO) for its weakness and failure to 'protect' the US from 'abuse' of global trade rules by China (Trump, 2017a). Nor was this just for the road, because Trump has not backed away from more of these types of attack. The Canadian Group of 7 (G7) Summit in 2018 was another case in point (see Bishop, 2018), whilst he could hardly have been plainer than in saying to the United Nations (UN) General Assembly in September 2018: 'We reject the ideology of globalism' (Trump, 2018). Although this remark apparently generated derisive laughter amongst other world leaders (Borger, 2018), it is not funny at all. In the end, rightist deglobalization will probably not be pursued by any state hard enough or long enough to destroy globalization. But it has already pushed the global political economy towards a dangerously unstable new mercantilist era in which countries fight each other for economic advantage with no sense of a greater common good. As such, it is a *cul de sac* that threatens to undermine even the limited forms of multilateral global governance that have been constructed over the past 70 years. We should seek to retreat from it at the earliest opportunity.

Deglobalization from the left

Although many on the centre-left in the West have effectively found themselves defending a *form of* globalization about which they might have been more sceptical, there were plenty of others on the wider left who always stood defiantly against neoliberalism. They drew on a long history of critique of global capitalism that has again resurfaced. For 'deglobalization from the right' is matched these days by an analogous variant 'from the left'. It advances a progressive left-wing, rather than a regressive right-wing, nationalism, and yet the conclusion reached is much the same. The broad argument runs that globalization needs to be pared back via a retreat behind domestic borders, the difference being that this process should ostensibly serve progressive ends, such as the re-creation of national industrial capacity and the building of a 'green state'. There is a lot to agree with in this analysis: we share the concern about preserving domestic policy space, especially for poorer countries, and states clearly do need to be re-tooled in developmentalist ways if we are to chart a strategic course out of the economic and ecological crises in which we find ourselves (Bishop, Payne et al., 2018).

It is, moreover, an important intellectual and political development that needs to be taken seriously, principally because it challenges one of the supposed 'lessons of history' for the left. The Mitterrand experiment in France, which ran from May 1981 to March 1983, was the last time a full-throated socialist programme was attempted in an advanced capitalist country. As Jeffrey Sachs and Charles Wyplosz (1986) noted some years ago, unemployment quickly rocketed to 10 per cent and growth collapsed. The emergence of European and global financial markets, as part of incipient neoliberal globalization, meant that capital could easily flee. France's trade deficit widened precipitously, generating a major currency crisis in 1983 and an immediate political retreat by Mitterrand – the notorious '*tournant de la rigueur*'. By 1985 the French left had imposed even harsher austerity than the right-wing regime that preceded it.

Like many others, Arthur Goldhammer (2016) concludes that Mitterrand's programme was 'rooted in a faulty diagnosis of the evolving global economy in the 1980s'. In consequence, a new orthodoxy was forged on the left in Europe: namely, that socialism was impossible 'in one country' under neoliberal globalization. This of course explains in part the fateful embrace of it by the European centre-left in the late 1990s and early 2000s. Yet this totem is now questioned by progressive nationalists, albeit often under the guise of criticizing the perceived hold of neoliberalism upon the EU, rather than the neoliberal nature of globalization *per se*. The painful irony, as Goldhammer notes, is that the French architects of the Maastricht Treaty, many of whom had served in the bitter end-days of the Mitterrand experiment, were so scarred by the experience that they designed many EU treaty frameworks (and later the Eurozone) in more inflexible ways than otherwise might have been the case.

The new left critique of globalization takes many forms and has actually had the greatest impact in Germany and Britain, rather than in France. Jean-Luc Mélenchon's left-populist party, *La France Insoumise* (France Unbowed), calls for a new global economic regime based on ecological planning and 'protectionism with solidarity' (Stetler, 2017). Mélenchon's European platform commits to renegotiating, or simply ignoring, the EU's 'neoliberal' treaties, and has become increasingly wary of a putative 'Frexit' which is associated with the hard right. In Germany, by contrast, there has emerged a distinct intellectual position, sometimes dubbed the 'Cologne School', associated with the writings of, amongst others, Wolfgang Streeck (2017), Fritz Scharpf (2017) and Martin Höpner (2018). Its central claim, as Streeck (2016) has pithily put it, is essentially that the EU is 'a non-democratic non-state without demos' and this undermines both its legitimacy and capacity to confront the challenges it faces (and *vice versa* in a kind of vicious circle). Consequently, it is now lost to progressive causes and the fight-back against neoliberalism can only be built from 'retained' nation-states. These arguments have had a significant influence on the new 'party-movement' recently formed in Germany, *Aufstehen* or 'Rise Up' (Weisskircher, 2018).

However, the most striking illustration of this supposedly progressive nationalism is the case that has been made in Britain for a 'Lexit' (or left exit) from the EU, for which support exists in parts of the Labour Party too. Some have dismissed 'Lexiteers' as the 'useful idiots' of a disaster-capitalist coup who are guilty of reproducing the 'embarrassing' sovereigntist arguments and nationalist tropes favoured by the hard-right forces guiding Brexit itself (Worth, 2017, 2018). It would, though, be unfair to caricature this literature: it draws on a substantial intellectual base and offers a critique with a degree of inherent credibility. As advanced by its most sophisticated exponents – Christopher Bickerton and Richard Tuck (2017), Costas Lapavitsas (2019), Lee Jones (2016), Richard Seymour (2016) or the late anti-imperialist scholar, Samir Amin (2016) – the Lexit argument is also that the EU has become too distant and anti-democratic, such that governance needs to be 're-scaled' back to the national level. As Jones puts it: 'the EU emerged through the rescaling of governance to inter-elite networks insulated – by design – from popular control, which lock in anti-democratic and conservative policies'. Typical in this view are the horrors of the Greek debt experience, which understandably looms large in much Lexiteer analysis.

There is undoubtedly something in this critique. The EU, as presently constituted, does suffer from a democratic deficit that has lately allowed deflationary German 'ordoliberal' hegemony to become firmly institutionalized, tendencies that have certainly intensified during the post-crisis 'emergency' era (White, 2015). Moreover, there is a degree of persuasiveness to the broader argument that the supranational character of the EU is less the problem *per se*, than the fact that its technocratic remoteness can serve to undermine domestic democratic processes without giving citizens adequate channels of participation at the European level. This, it is argued, permits domestic politicians to depoliticize (and therefore de-democratize) arenas of policy that should be subject to meaningful contestation, as well as providing avenues for private actors to challenge democratically legitimate decisions that run counter to their pecuniary interests (see Lapavitsas, 2019).

Yet the conventional Lexiteer reading of the EU is too partial. It does not always accurately distinguish the EU from the Eurozone, it says little or nothing about 'social Europe', EU pre-eminence in global climate-change diplomacy, or its various initiatives to try to tax global financial transactions. It also paints the EU as fixed in stone, impervious to change politically, even though it argues, correctly – yet inherently contradictorily – that the EU *embraced* neoliberalism as a result of conscious decisions made by political actors. In sum, the Lexit argument is excessively deterministic and underestimates the complexity of the EU in a variety of ways in order to make its case. Indeed, in its more journalistic incantations it can often be astonishingly glib in reducing the whole panoply of EU institutions and action to a one-dimensional, corporate-driven neoliberal conspiracy devoid of meaningful political contestation or social value (see, for example, Blakeley, 2019; Guinan & Hannah, 2017).

In fact, economically, the EU does relatively little to restrict a social democratic programme of state-led industrial development, as its critics often suggest: European Single Market rules only proscribe certain policy tools, like indiscriminate state-aid subsidies to declining sectors (Wren-Lewis, 2017, 2019). These have negligible use in a serious industrial strategy worthy of the name, and it reflects the paucity of Lexiteer thinking that 250 years of developmentalist theory and praxis is often reduced, again glibly, to little more than 'state aid' (Bishop, Payne et al., 2018). As Morris and Kibasi (2019) have argued, Brussels only 'restricts state aid where it wastes public money and exacerbates pan-European inequalities'. They also find that it does little to stop large-scale public investment or nationalization in strategic sectors. The limits placed on what states can do in terms of industrial policy have always been conditional rather than absolute, and often honoured in the breach (Davies, 2013). It has also seemingly, and somewhat ironically, passed almost unnoticed by many critics that, over the past few years, the EU has actually reformed, modernized and loosened its own rules in this area to permit much greater interventionism on the part of member-states, especially in emerging sectors and the 'green economy' (Pesaresi & Peduzzi, 2018).

Painting the Single Market as little more than a capitalist conspiracy (or protectionist racket) is simplistic and wrong: rather, it is an attempt to regulate, beyond the national level, global processes of production and consumption, and to do so to the advantage of workers and consumers as much as corporates. The balance between the two necessarily waxes and wanes, and the latter's interests frequently prevail over those of the former. But, because it is a site of ongoing political contestation, not a monolithic entity preserved in aspic, it is implausible to claim that this is an inherent feature. Opposing the Single Market *on principle* is also nonsensical: following this idea to its logical conclusion essentially implies that the regulation of *any* market over *any* geographical space irredeemably favours corporate power, which cannot possibly stand to reason. In the European context, it is *only* Single-Market regulation that can minimize the costs and secure the benefits of economic processes that are necessarily transnational in scope.

Socially speaking, Lexit also appears just as darkly regressive as its right-wing nationalist counterpart, especially when it comes to questions of migration and free movement (Parker, 2017). As soon as distinctions are drawn between those who are conditionally 'deserving' and 'undeserving' of access to welfare and other services, they too easily – some would say inevitably – slip into the racist territory favoured by nationalists and populists of all kinds (Shilliam, 2018). Such 'nativist socialism', as John Narayan (2019) calls it, largely equates the 'working class', on which Brexit supposedly depends, and for which it supposedly must be delivered, with the *white* working class. This xenophobia serves to elide the agency of non-white populations in their struggles against domestic legacies of colonialism and undermines collective anti-racist and anti-imperialist action by shattering national and global solidarity (Bhambra, 2017; Bhambra & Holmwood, 2018).

Nevertheless, our purpose here is not to adjudicate Brexit, but rather to expose the major question unanswered by Lexiteers: how does Britain leaving the EU help resolve the neoliberal pathologies that concern them and advance the interests of the left, either within Europe or globally? Immediately after 'exit' on 31 January 2020, Britain still had to negotiate with a genuine diplomatic and commercial superpower on the doorstep, from a position of distinct weakness. And it has to do so *in perpetuity*, as Brexit is an ongoing process, not an isolated event: it will never be 'done'. As it exited, it had already experienced a permanent reduction in the size of the economy of nearly 3 per cent (Hantzsche & Young, 2019) and will have suffered a cumulative loss of £200bn in output by the intended end of the 'transition period' in December 2020, due to its trend growth-rate 'untethering from its Group of Seven peers' (O'Brien, 2020). This astronomical sum equates to almost 8 per cent of GDP, or nearly a third of government spending, and largely represents expenses accrued *before* Brexit. Yet, unless this economic rupture is to become genuinely devastating, any substantive continuity trade and investment agreement will have to take on much of the EU's regulatory *acquis*, albeit with less meaningful control despite claims about greater sovereignty (Barnett, 2018). As David Adler (2019, p. 15) has sharply noted: 'national sovereignty is meaningless in the absence of international institutions that protect it, enable it, and insulate it from external coercive pressures'. This diminished country also has to find its niche within presently continuing neoliberal globalization. One commentator's disbelieving analysis captures the problem perfectly: the Lexiteers 'just know', says Aditya Chakrabortty (2019), that Brexit 'will bring the death of neoliberalism even though the neoliberals will still be in charge'.

As the shape of Boris Johnson's intended deregulatory revolution began to crystallize in the wake of the 2019 British election, left-wing dreams of 'disaster socialism' did seem excruciatingly misplaced. Ultimately, then, Lexit is a faulty diagnosis, to borrow Goldhammer's term, of the evolving global political economy of the 2020s. It runs away from the big challenge, which is how to tackle crisis-ridden neoliberal globalization at the global level. It is *even harder* now to conceive of 'socialism in one country' than in the 1980s, and it is remarkable just how *passé* – yet stubbornly resilient – such arguments are. For example, Amin spent part of his career advocating that developing countries 'delink' from the global economy as a solution to capitalist inequality (Amin, 1990). This unavoidably autarchic logic pervades much Lexiteer thinking, consequently appearing intrinsic, rather than incidental, to it. As Owen Worth (2018) asks: 'did Lexit ever have any serious pretensions in the first place capable of providing an internationalist alternative to the EU?' It seems that one of the great paradoxes of leftist thinking in general at the present moment is an almost-doctrinal commitment to internationalism whilst largely neglecting to offer a substantive internationalist analysis (Adler, 2019).

Another painful irony of Brexit is that the British parliament has been sidelined from having meaningful scrutiny of the second-stage trade negotiations: so much for 'taking back control' from the 'anti-democratic' EU. Members of the European Parliament (MEPs) will have greater oversight of the process than their British counterparts and the latter will even be dependent on the former for information about it. Since taking office, the Johnson administration has subverted normal democratic processes by refusing to respond to questions raised by the House of Lords European Union Committee (2020) in writing, thereby undermining its constitutionally-mandated legislative role. Advocacy of a rescaling of governance to the state level thus offers no guarantee that this will be any more responsive, legitimate or inclusive than the layers of EU governance within which such states have long been enmeshed. Indeed, it may be considerably less so. 'Much of the left still must learn', suggests Anthony Barnett (2017b), 'that the existing British state is the prison of their hopes'. So, while Lexiteers may be right that EU membership has been accompanied by a democratic deficit, arguably this reflects the excessive centralization and atrophying of the British state itself, its dysfunctional constitution, outdated electoral system, and lack of substantive regional devolution. Successive governments in London – not Brussels – have, over decades, failed to rectify these problems. Scapegoating the EU therefore appears to be just a little too convenient. Although we share the concern that states are insufficiently responsive to their polities, alleviating this seems even less likely in a Britain now gripped by Faragist tendencies and untethered from the currents of mainstream European politics.

States require a pragmatic, realistic account of the wider regional and global context, if they are to engage strategically with globalization. The extent of economic integration has come under scrutiny for its ecological footprint, impact on labour and the insecurity revealed by excessive dependence on international supply chains in times of crisis (Farrell & Newman, 2020a, 2020b). Yet global value chains (GVCs) and production networks (GPNs) are likely to endure to a significant extent (Chang & Andreoni, 2020; Yeung, 2016). Firms operating within them *want* transnational regulation, because there is no competitive logic in deviating from global standards, particularly when inordinately complex 'deterritorialized' production processes straddle multiple physical and virtual locations within the spaces over which the EU (for example) has governing competence. So, even if we are on the cusp of a new era of 'reshoring' and 'regionalizing' of production processes, this can only ever be partial: the sheer gamut of activities they encompass means that such regulation will remain vital. Britain's historical success in attracting foreign direct investment derives from its distinctive status as *both* a liberal market economy *and* member of the EU Single Market. The post-referendum haemorrhaging of investment (*Financial Times*, 2019) shows that cutting-edge firms will move to where regulation offers the most stable and extensive access to major markets. Accordingly, the game that states have to play involves sitting at the top table influencing the development of these rules and systems, ideally in socially beneficial ways. If they do not, and deglobalize alone, the game just continues without them. In sum, just like its rightist counterpart, 'deglobalization from the left' fails in its own terms. It offers elements of important critique, but no answer to the fundamental question of how to offer global citizens substantive solutions to the problems they face in an era of decaying neoliberalism.

Towards 'reglobalization'

Where, then, do we go from here? We have seen that neoliberal globalization, as we have known it in its various manifestations since the 1980s, has generated serious economic, social and political problems that increasingly outweigh its achievements. We have noted as well that the new models of both rightist and leftist deglobalization that have come to the fore in response to these emergent problems offer unsatisfactory solutions, precisely because, by proposing a negative retreat from globalization, they attack symptoms, not the condition itself. For many people, though, it seems as if we have run out of globalization road.

There is, however, no reason to despair, because the necessary initial moves forward have already been made in the preceding analysis. The *first* has been to recognise the growing contradictions of neoliberal globalization (and accordingly to re-intensify our critique of it). Governments of the centre and centre-left in the US, Britain and other parts of Europe have not only presided over much of the recent expansion of globalization, but have entrenched its legitimacy by seeking to render it a cross-party, almost universal, project of the West. The *second* has been to acknowledge that globalization could in theory have been done differently and could therefore be different again in the future. Yes, structures of political economy exercise powerful constraining influences on actors, but, as Mark Blyth (2003) reminded us a while ago now, they 'do not come with an instruction sheet'. Consequently, as we said earlier, we can – and must – retain the baby of globalization while jettisoning as much of the dirty neoliberal bathwater as possible.

The next moves we have to make are more contentious and take us to the heart of the argument that we want to address in this special issue. We suggest that globalization, of some sort, is almost certainly here to stay, whether we (or, for that matter, 'deglobalizers' of right and left) like it or not. All political economy now takes place unavoidably on a global stage. There can be no easy, or full-scale, retreat from that in a world in which so much economic activity and so many of the prospects of economic development are now shaped by the complex linkages formed by global value and production – and even global wealth and poverty – chains (Bair, 2017; Mayer & Phillips, 2017; Selwyn, 2019). The prospect, still held out by some, of there being available to us a return to a mythical world of autonomous national economies is simply delusionary. However, globalization does not have to be neoliberal in form and it is vital that, in future, it is not. As the British journalist Paul Mason (2016) starkly put it after the Brexit referendum: 'if we want to save globalization, we have to ditch neoliberalism'. His analysis focused on making the case for an alternative 'post-neoliberal' economic model and did not address in detail what needed to be done at the global level of politics. But the corollary of his argument is that globalization needs to be reformed, controlled, steered and, in effect, rebuilt around post-neoliberal values. This is definitely possible *theoretically*, but is it in the real world of political practice?

We suggest that there is actually a lot that 'our' states, acting on behalf of us as their citizens, can do collectively to reshape globalization for the future into a different, and more attractive set of economic, social and political processes. To quote one influential article in political economy: 'globalization makes of states what states make of it' (Hobson & Ramesh, 2002). They have acted previously to construct and adjust global orders, and they can do so again. This remains true, even during times when it seems as if little serious will is present amongst states to reconstruct the global order. Perhaps especially in such times: all eras are, by definition, temporary; the global context, ideas about it and possibilities for reshaping it can – particularly when crises hit – change rapidly (see Bishop & Payne, 2020). In any case, it is always important in politics to try to imagine what else might conceivably be done, especially in circumstances that appear difficult at first sight. Let us therefore be bold and begin to examine what an attempted reconfiguration of globalization by our states around a different set of post-neoliberal values might look like and how it might be achieved. We propose to describe this as a process of 'reglobalization', of re-doing globalization better.

In making this argument we build on insights from other analysts. A quarter of a century ago, the Harvard political economist Dani Rodrik (1997) famously asked in the title of a book *Has Globalization Gone Too Far?* A decade or so further on, he was calling in *The Globalization Paradox* (2012) for 'a sane globalization' grounded in the tighter regulation of trade and finance and the proper management of labour flows, so that 'we can and should tell a different story about globalization'. Instead of taking the 'hyper-globalization' line and 'viewing it as a system that requires a single set of institutions or one principal economic superpower', it makes more sense to consider it to be 'a collection of diverse nations whose interactions are regulated by a thin layer of simple, transparent, and commonsense traffic rules' (Rodrik, 2012, p. 280). He has continued to press these views right up to the present, but, crucially, he has never advocated rejecting globalization outright, rather just its neoliberal logics. In *Straight Talk on Trade* (Rodrik, 2017) his argument essentially runs that, in seeking to resist protectionist backsliding, neoliberals often oversold the merits of trade and services liberalization, downplaying the inevitable distributional dislocations. However, the solution is not to retreat from an open trading order – albeit one in which trade is a means to other developmental ends, rather than an end in itself – but to find ways to intervene more aggressively, in a collaborative way, to correct imbalances and assuage distributional costs within and between countries.

Eric Helleiner, in his account of *The Status Quo Crisis* (2014) – his take on the 2008 financial meltdown, understood as not changing as much about global governance as many, especially on the left, had initially anticipated and hoped – reinforced the same broad point by discerning in his assessment of what could come next a third scenario (between 'strengthened liberal multilateralism' and 'fragmentation and conflict') which he dubbed 'cooperative decentralization'. He was focusing on global financial governance specifically and suggested that in this sphere states could continue to develop certain minimum international standards through the Financial Stability Bureau. But he added a vital qualification: that, 'rather than detailed one-size-fits-all rules, those standards could be based around broad principles that allowed significant national or regional policy space' (Helleiner, 2014, p. 176). More recently, in *The Globalization Backlash*, Colin Crouch (2019, p. 10) called for 'for moderate forces of left and right to stand together for a regulated globalization against xenophobic forces'. He dismissed 'the illusion of economic sovereignty' and suggested that 'it is far more constructive' to work out how 'in some policy fields' this idea 'needs to give way to one of pooled sovereignty in pursuit of a better transnational regulation of the globalized economy' (Crouch, 2019, p. 48).

These are all invaluable glimpses of what reglobalization has to be like (that is, sane, cooperative, decentralized, regulated), but they do not specify with enough precision the political bargain that necessarily has to underpin such a process if it is to gain ground and take off. To frame this properly, we have to look back to look forward and recall the precise definition of the 'embedded liberalism' that John Ruggie (1982) defined as the key ingredient restored to the world economy at Bretton Woods in 1944. As Ruggie saw it, the task at Bretton Woods was to manoeuvre between the extremes of both nationalism and liberalism and craft a 'compromise' (his telling but oft-forgotten word) that would 'safeguard and even aid the quest for domestic stability without, at the same time, triggering the mutually destructive external consequences that had plagued the interwar period'. In a key passage he went on to say this of his celebrated 'embedded liberalism compromise':

> Unlike the economic nationalism of the thirties, it would be multilateral in character; unlike the liberalism of the gold standard and free trade, its multilateralism would be predicated upon domestic interventionism. (Ruggie, 1982, p. 393)

This analysis contains the vital clue that opens up the politics of reglobalization. It shows how we can begin to create a new normative framework within which to reshape globalization. We choose to describe this as 're-embedded post-neoliberalism', recognizing that this is a formulation that needs some further elaboration despite its manifest reference back to, and adjustment of, Ruggie's original and well-known formulation.

Of course, one crucial element of his analysis was that the compromise between different social forces was historically specific and derived from prevailing social conditions. Memories of the Great Depression, the devastation of the two world wars and fears regarding the communist 'threat' encouraged Western capitalist elites to accept significant restrictions on their power in return for greater social peace and equality. Moreover, the US was both able and willing to underwrite the liberal order, at least until it began to break down in the 1970s, specifically because globalization meant that the capacity to exercise genuine hegemony – i.e. to be able to ensure widespread acquiescence and recast the regime when necessary – had passed beyond a single state, even one as powerful as the US (see Payne, 2005). Consequently, the enlightened leadership that we are calling for here was only one half – the agential half – of an equation that has a crucial structural component. We focus primarily on the former here, but reflect on the prospects for the latter emerging in the article that bookends the special issue (Bishop & Payne, 2020).

Firstly, then, what do we mean by deploying the apparently open-ended notion of 'post-neoliberalism'? Like all critical political economists, we acknowledge the power of path-dependency, but contend nevertheless that we are entering an era beyond the neoliberalism of the recent past, even if we are not quite there yet and cannot, as such, be sure of its precise ideological shape. Indeed, while some have sought to envision theoretical and practical forms of post-neoliberalism – most notably in Latin America during the 'Pink Tide' (Grugel & Riggirozzi, 2019) – these have not been developed or expressed fully, have remained regional rather than becoming global in scope, and have experienced a sustained backlash from reactionary populist forces (Grugel & Riggirozzi, 2018). The lesson is clear: if progressives do not envision an ordered and socially-beneficial form of globalization to fill this emerging space, reactionaries will quickly chart an illiberal and regressive one, built around a destructive, authoritarian form of intensified neoliberalism (Bruff, 2014; Bruff & Tansel, 2019). It is therefore incumbent on progressive thinkers and reformers to frame more convincingly what 'post-neoliberalism' could mean and to do so in a politically realistic way.

We consider that globalization as a political project can only be expressed as *a form of* liberalism, albeit one that is 'post-' (meaning distinct to) the kind of neoliberalism that has prevailed in recent times. Globalization is, after all, fundamentally grounded in notions of openness and freedom. If the challenges we face as a society regarding the rules we set about the environment, tax, finance, migration and so on in a context of disorientating upheaval are to be managed in a way that is remotely equitable, this can only happen at the global level according to some kind of post-neoliberal ideological settlement. It is vital to note here that liberalism as an intellectual tradition in political economy has long contained within it a tension between a 'pure' and a 'compensatory' variant, with each ascendant at different times. Although 'pure' *neo*liberalism crashed and burned in the global financial crisis, the 'compensatory' strand – which first emerged in the English 'new liberalism' of T.H. Green and L.T. Hobhouse from 1880 to the First World War (see Vincent, 1990) and was rejuvenated in the writings of John Maynard Keynes – remains available to us when faced with the challenge of rethinking post-neoliberal reglobalization. It was undoubtedly repressed, but never fully eliminated, during neoliberalism's long ascendancy from the 1980s onwards. Indeed, it can even be argued that many subtly different 'neoliberal*isms*' made their appearance during these decades. As Andrew Gamble (2009:, p. 4) once put it: 'neoliberalism has many faces'. This included a recognizable – if mild in retrospect – form of 'compensatory *neo*liberalism' associated for a period with the 'Third Way' philosophy of Bill Clinton, Tony Blair and Gerhard Schröder in the mid-1990s and early 2000s (Giddens, 1994).

Much could be said to elucidate the body of 'compensatory liberal' thought fully, but for present purposes the summary provided by McKinlay and Little (1986) will suffice: 'the major divergence of the compensatory from the pure liberal is the contention by the former that the pure liberal devotes insufficient attention to the issue of the equality of the distribution of choice and opportunity'. We suggest that 'post-neoliberalism' can most plausibly be built around a renewed 'compensatory' liberalism that is substantially 'dialled down' from, and thus markedly different to, the prevailing characteristics of the hyper-neoliberal era. This might not sound very ambitious and it is certainly not utopian. But it does have the great merit of being politically credible and plausible, of itself still quite radical, and, in our view, genuinely 'post-neoliberal'. Anthony Arblaster (1984:, p. 348) argued some years ago that what is 'best about liberalism' – i.e. a belief in freedom and equality – 'is too good to be left to the liberals'. Possessed of that concern about the equality of the distribution of choice, opportunity, and, crucially in our view, outcomes, highly compensatory forms of liberalism – and, to be clear, we mean significantly more compensatory than those offered during a 'Third Way' era that embodied different political, economic, ideological, institutional and ecological constraints – can effectively build a meaningful social democracy.

Secondly, what is the significance in this context of the concept of embeddedness and why do we need to attach it to this vision of 'post-neoliberalism'? The term derives from the economic history of Karl Polanyi (2001 [1944]), makes a strong appearance in sociology via the work of Mark Granovetter (1995) and, as we have seen, was picked up in political economy by Ruggie. It refers to the endowment within public agencies of the authority and capacity to manage domestic and international economic affairs actively. As Fioretos and Heldt (2019, p. 1097) have recently put it: 'A highly embedded system is one in which public agencies have the authority to intervene in capital, labour, product and other markets. In highly *dis*embedded systems, by contrast, public agencies lack effective means to structure the behaviour of market participants.'

Such agencies come in many forms, but at the global level we are talking essentially of the ability and willingness of 'our' states, acting on behalf of us as their citizens, to respond with a 'compensatory' instinct to intervene energetically in economic and social matters in order to enlarge, and equalize to some degree, the range of choice available to their peoples. In this conception of global governance, states would be able to pursue legitimate social purposes and enjoy the necessary national policy spaces to manage their economic development successfully, without fear of retreat into a regressive nationalism. They would in fact be encouraged to work together in a collective, cooperative way, acknowledging the multilateral imperative to ensure the fairest distribution of gains over time (Buzdugan & Payne, 2016). We have done our best here to elaborate what is unquestionably a contentious notion. We see 're-embedded post-neoliberalism' as distinctive in its normative ethos, but also flexible and malleable in its practice, providing a framework for different positive futures. It needs to be fleshed out in many areas of global public policy, and to be put into action, if we are to begin to deliver on the prospect and promise of reglobalization.

Conclusion: reglobalization in action

This special issue has been designed with that endeavour in mind. We do not propose here to spend time explaining each article within it in detail, save to say that, in the pieces that follow, our authors collectively offer detailed explorations of some of the gains, as well as the limits of the possible, in reforming the global political economy in the spirit of reglobalization in their own particular areas of policy expertise. The first article, authored by Andrew Baker and Richard Murphy, addresses reform of global taxation via 'public shaming' associated with tax transparency initiatives. In the second, Ben Clift and Te-Anne Robles consider recent attempted reforms within the International Monetary Fund (IMF) to embed more deeply intellectual shifts that take concerns with inequality more seriously. The next two articles address questions of trade: James Scott and Rorden Wilkinson examine how the WTO, currently facing the biggest crisis in its short history, might become a more development-focused body; whilst Erin Hannah, Adrienne Roberts and Silke Trommer provide a gendered account of how global trade politics might become even more responsive to the deep-seated inequalities that shape globalization.

After this, Hayley Stevenson examines climate politics, in particular the ways in which questionable ideas that can be described as 'bullshit' proliferate too easily in this policy domain, inhibiting attempts at creating genuine global action. The penultimate article, by Antoine Pécoud, addresses global migration: an increasingly crucial issue-area, yet one where reglobalization has probably the furthest to travel given the massive underdevelopment of international action currently in this field. In the concluding contribution, we revisit, summarize and reflect as editors on the collective significance of these articles, discuss some of the areas that have not been covered in them and offer our own account of what, exactly, needs to be done to steer in the direction of reglobalized governance. In this connection we set out an agenda for a retooled, repurposed and reinvigorated Group of 20 (G20) and ask if this much-maligned body could yet still underpin a progressive internationalist, re-embedded, post-neoliberal reglobalization, in an era of pronounced crisis.

Acknowledgements

A number of people gave their time to review and, in many cases, re-review articles for this special issue. Some people read more than one, and, indeed, one person reviewed the entire issue. For this, we are hugely indebted to them and our authors, and we offer our sincerest gratitude to all of them for helping us make, we hope, an important collective intervention of which the whole is substantially greater than the sum of its excellent individual parts.

Disclosure statement

No potential conflict of interest was reported by the author(s).

ORCID

Matthew Louis Bishop http://orcid.org/0000-0001-6981-6241
Anthony Payne http://orcid.org/0000-0002-8151-9722

References

Adler, D. (2019). The international institutional turn: The missing ingredient in Labour's new political economy. *Renewal: A Journal of Social Democracy*, *27*(4), 11–22.

Amin, S. (1990). *Delinking: Towards a polycentric world*. Zed Books.

Amin, S. (2016, August 8). Brexit and the EU implosion: National sovereignty — for what purpose? *Monthly Review Online*. https://mronline.org/2016/08/08/amin080816-html

Arblaster, A. (1984). *The rise and decline of Western Liberalism*. Basil Blackwell.

Bair, J. (2017). Contextualising compliance: Hybrid governance in global value chains. *New Political Economy*, *22*(2), 169–185. https://doi.org/10.1080/13563467.2016.1273340

Barnett, A. (2017a). *The lure of greatness*. Unbound.

Barnett, A. (2017b, September. 21). The lure of Lexit must be resisted – socialism in one country is a fantasy. *New Statesman*. https://www.newstatesman.com/politics/uk/2017/09/lure-lexit-must-be-resisted-socialism-one-country-fantasy

Barnett, A. (2018, June 25). Why Brexit won't work: The EU is about regulation not sovereignty. *Open Democracy*. https://www.opendemocracy.net/en/opendemocracyuk/why-brexit-won-t-work-eu-is-about-regulation-not-sovereignty/

Bhambra, G. K. (2017). Brexit, Trump, and 'methodological whiteness': On the misrecognition of race and class. *The British Journal of Sociology*, *68*(S1), S214–S232. https://doi.org/10.1111/1468-4446.12317

Bhambra, G. K., & Holmwood, J. (2018). Colonialism, postcolonialism and the liberal welfare state. *New Political Economy*, *23*(5), 574–587. https://doi.org/10.1080/13563467.2017.1417369

Bhattacharyya, G. (2018). *Rethinking racial capitalism: Questions of reproduction and survival*. Rowman & Littlefield.

Bickerton, C., & Tuck, R. (2017). A Brexit proposal. https://thecurrentmoment.files.wordpress.com/2017/11/brexit-proposal-20-nov-final1.pdf

Bishop, M. L. (2016). Rethinking the political economy of development beyond "The Rise of the BRICS". *Sheffield Political Economy Research Institute Paper* No. 30. http://speri.dept.shef.ac.uk/wp-content/uploads/2016/07/Beyond-the-Rise-of-the-BRICS.pdf

Bishop, M. L. (2018). Trade war: What is it good for? https://www.globalpolicyjournal.com/sites/default/files/G7%20%27Trade%20War%27%20Brief%20-%20Matthew%20Louis%20Bishop.pdf

Bishop, M. L., & Murray-Evans, P. (2020). Five little B(R)ICS: Huffing and puffing, but not blowing your house in. *New Political Economy*, *25*(5). https://doi.org/10.1080/13563467.2019.1584166

Bishop, M. L., & Payne, A. (2020). Steering towards reglobalization: Can a reformed G20 rise to the occasion? *Globalizations*. https://doi.org/10.1080/14747731.2020.1779964

Bishop, M. L., Payne, A., Sen, K., Breslin, S., Öniş, Z., Muzaka, V., Booth, D., Lindsay, C., & Yeung, H. W. (2018). Revisiting the developmental state. http://speri.dept.shef.ac.uk/wp-content/uploads/2018/02/SPERI-Paper-No.-43-Revisiting-the-developmental-state.pdf

Bishop, M. L., & Zhang, X. (2020). Why is China a reluctant leader of the World Trade Organization? *New Political Economy*, *25*(5). https://doi.org/10.1080/13563467.2019.1584170

Blair, T. (2005). Labour leader's speech. Brighton. http://www.britishpoliticalspeech.org/speech-archive.htm?speech=182

Blakeley, G. (2019, January 16). Why the left should champion Brexit. *New Statesman*. https://www.newstatesman.com/politics/economy/2019/01/why-left-should-champion-brexit

Blyth, M. (2003). Structures do not come with an instruction sheet: Interests, ideas, and progress in political science. *Perspectives on Politics*, *1*(4), 695–706. https://doi.org/10.1017/S1537592703000471

Blyth, M. (2016, November 15). Global Trumpism. *Foreign Affairs*. https://www.foreignaffairs.com/articles/2016-11-15/global-trumpism

Borger, J. (2018, September 26). Trump urges world to reject globalism in UN speech that draws mocking laughter. *The Guardian*. https://www.theguardian.com/us-news/2018/sep/25/trump-united-nations-general-assembly-speech-globalism-america

Bourguignon, F. (2015). *The globalization of inequality*. Princeton University Press.

Breslin, S. (2017, October 9). Revisiting the developmental state 3: Fitting China into the debate. *SPERI Comment*. http://speri.dept.shef.ac.uk/2017/10/09/revisiting-the-developmental-state-3-fitting-china-into-the-debate/

Bruff, I. (2014). The rise of authoritarian neoliberalism. *Rethinking Marxism*, *26*(1), 113–129. https://doi.org/10.1080/08935696.2013.843250

Bruff, I., & Tansel, C. B. (2019). Authoritarian neoliberalism: Trajectories of knowledge production and praxis. *Globalizations*, *16*(3), 233–244. https://doi.org/10.1080/14747731.2018.1502497

Buzdugan, S., & Payne, A. (2016). *The long battle for global governance*. Routledge.

Chakrabortty, A. (2019, February 25). If Labour aids a Tory Brexit it will be destroyed by what follows. *The Guardian*. https://www.theguardian.com/commentisfree/2019/feb/25/labour-aids-tory-brexit-destroyed

Chang, H., & Andreoni, A. (2020). Industrial policy in the 21st century. *Development and Change*, *51*(2), 324–351. https://doi.org/10.1111/dech.12570

Chin, G., & Thakur, R. (2010). Will China change the rules of global order? *The Washington Quarterly*, *33*(4), 119–138. https://doi.org/10.1080/0163660X.2010.516145

Crouch, C. (2019). *The globalization backlash*. Polity.

Davies, W. (2013). When is a market not a market?: 'exemption', 'externality' and 'exception' in the case of European state aid rules. *Theory, Culture & Society*, *30*(2), 32–59. https://doi.org/10.1177/0263276412456567

Enloe, C. (2016). *Globalization and militarism: Feminists make the link*. Rowman & Littlefield.

Farrell, H., & Newman, A. (2020a). Chained to globalization: Why it's too late to decouple. *Foreign Affairs*, *99* (1), 70–80.

Farrell, H., & Newman, A. (2020b, March 16). Will the coronavirus end globalization as we know it? *Foreign Affairs*. https://www.foreignaffairs.com/articles/2020-03-16/will-coronavirus-end-globalization-we-know-it

Financial Times. (2019, August 19). Brexit has chilling effect on UK inward investment. https://www.ft.com/content/bdc9f940-bb92-11e9-b350-db00d509634e

Fioretos, O., & Heldt, E. C. (2019). Legacies and innovations in global economic governance since Bretton Woods. *Review of International Political Economy*, *26*(6), 1089–1111. https://doi.org/10.1080/09692290.2019.1635513

Gamble, A. (2009). The *Western Ideology*. *Government and Opposition*, *44*(1), 1–19. https://doi.org/10.1111/j.1477-7053.2008.01273.x

Gamble, A. (2014). *Crisis without end? The unravelling of Western prosperity*. Palgrave.

Gamble, A. (2016). *Can the welfare state survive?* Polity.

Giddens, A. (1994). *Beyond left and right*. Polity.

Goldhammer, A. (2016, September 9). How French socialism built — and destroyed — the European Union. *Foreign Policy*. https://foreignpolicy.com/2016/09/09/how-french-socialism-built-and-destroyed-the-european-union/

de Graaff, N. (2020). China Inc. goes global: Transnational and national networks of China's globalizing business elite. *Review of International Political Economy*, *27*(2), 208–233. https://doi.org/10.1080/09692290.2019.1675741

Granovetter, M. (1995). *Getting a job: A study of contacts and careers*. University of Chicago Press.

Grugel, J., & Riggirozzi, P. (2018). Neoliberal disruption and neoliberalism's afterlife in Latin America: What is left of post-neoliberalism? *Critical Social Policy*, *38*(3), 547–566. https://doi.org/10.1177/0261018318765857

Grugel, J., & Riggirozzi, P. (2019). Facing the future: The legacies of post-neoliberalism. *Development and Change*, *38*(3), 547–566. https://doi.org/10.1111/dech.12508

Guinan, J., & Hannah, T. (2017, July 20). Lexit: The EU is a neoliberal project, so let's do something different when we leave it. *New Statesman*. https://www.newstatesman.com/politics/brexit/2017/07/lexit-eu-neoliberal-project-so-lets-do-something-different-when-we-leave-it

Hantzsche, A., & Young, G. (2019). Prospects for the UK economy. *National Institute Economic Review, 250*, F4–F33. https://doi.org/10.1177/002795011925000103

Harvey, D. (2005). *A brief history of neoliberalism*. Oxford University Press.

Hay, C. (2001). What place for ideas in the structure-agency debate? Globalisation as a "Process without a subject"'. http://www.raggedclaws.com/criticalrealism/archive/cshay_wpisad.html

Hay, C., & Wincott, D. (2012). *The political economy of European welfare capitalism*. Palgrave.

Held, D., McGrew, A., Goldblatt, D., & Perraton, J. (1999). *Global transformations: Politics, economics and culture*. Polity Press.

Helleiner, E. (2014). *The status quo crisis: Global financial governance after the 2008 meltdown*. Oxford University Press.

Hobson, J. M., & Ramesh, M. (2002). Globalisation makes of states what states make of it: Between agency and structure in the state/globalisation debate. *New Political Economy*, *7*(1), 5–22. https://doi.org/10.1080/13563460120115499

Hopewell, K. (2016). *Breaking the WTO: How emerging powers disrupted the neoliberal project*. Stanford University Press.

Hopewell, K. (2017). When market fundamentalism and industrial policy collide: The tea party and the US export–import bank. *Review of International Political Economy*, *24*(4), 569–598. https://doi.org/10.1080/09692290.2017.1316297

Hopewell, K. (2019). US-China conflict in global trade governance: The new politics of agricultural subsidies at the WTO. *Review of International Political Economy*, *26*(2), 207–231. https://doi.org/10.1080/09692290.2018.1560352

Höpner, M. (2018, November 5). Social Europe is a myth. *Social Europe*. https://www.socialeurope.eu/social-europe-is-a-myth

House of Lords European Union Committee. (2020). *Brexit: The revised withdrawal agreement and political declaration*, 1st Report of Session 2019-20. http://www.parliament.uk/hleu

Hunt, T., & Stanley, L. (2019). From 'there is no alternative' to 'maybe there are alternatives': Five challenges to economic orthodoxy after the Crash. *The Political Quarterly*, *90*(3), 479–487. https://doi.org/10.1111/1467-923X.12707

Hutton, W. (2017, November 12). As Trump fawns over Xi, global politics is now a "strong man" game. *The Guardian*. https://www.theguardian.com/commentisfree/2017/nov/12/doanld-trump-fawns-over-xi-global-power-strong-man-game

James, P., & Steger, M. B. (2014). A genealogy of "globalization": The career of a concept. *Globalizations, 11*(4), 417–434. https://doi.org/10.1080/14747731.2014.951186

Jinping, X. (2017). Keynote at the World Economic Forum. https://america.cgtn.com/2017/01/17/full-text-of-xi-jinping-keynote-at-the-world-economic-forum

Jones, L. (2016, May 24). The EU referendum: Brexit, the politics of scale and state transformation. *The Disorder of Things*. https://thedisorderofthings.com/2016/05/24/the-eu-referendum-brexit-the-politics-of-scale-and-state-transformation/

Klein, N. (2014). *This changes everything: Capitalism vs. The climate*. Simon & Schuster.

Koram, K., & Nisancioglu, K. (2017, October 31). Britain: The empire that never was. *Critical Legal Thinking*. http://criticallegalthinking.com/2017/10/31/britain-empire-never/

Lanchester, J. (2010). *Whoops!: Why everyone owes everyone and no one can pay*. Penguin.

Lanchester, J. (2013, February 7). Recognising success in the war on poverty. *SPERI Comment*. http://speri.dept.shef.ac.uk/2013/02/07/recognising-success-war-poverty/

Lapavitsas, C. (2019). *The left case against the EU*. Polity.

Lidington, D. (2018, April 10). Building a Global Britain'. Speech given in Beijing, China. https://www.gov.uk/government/speeches/building-a-global-britain

Lin, J. Y. (2014). *The quest for prosperity: How developing economies can take off*. Princeton University Press.

Lin, J. Y., Cai, F., & Li, Z. (2003). *The China miracle: Development strategy and economic reform*. Chinese University Press.

Lowrey, A. (2018, December). The "Madman" behind Trump's trade theory. *The Atlantic*. https://www.theatlantic.com/magazine/archive/2018/12/peter-navarro-trump-trade/573913/
Mason, P. (2016, June 27). The global order is dying. But it's an illusion to think Britain can survive without the EU. *The Guardian*.
Mayer, F. W., & Phillips, N. (2017). Outsourcing governance: States and the politics of a "global value chain world". *New Political Economy*, *22*(2), 134–152. https://doi.org/10.1080/13563467.2016.1273341
McKinlay, R. D., & Little, R. (1986). *Global problems and world order*. Frances Pinter.
Morris, M., & Kibasi, T. (2019). *State aid rules and Brexit*. Institute for Public Policy Research. https://www.ippr.org/files/2019-01/1548088552_brexit-state-aid-jan19.pdf
Muzaka, V., & Serrano, O. R. (2020). Teaming up? China, India and Brazil and the issue of benefit-sharing from genetic resource use. *New Political Economy*, *25*(5). https://doi.org/10.1080/13563467.2019.1584169
Narayan, J. (2019). British black power: The anti-imperialism of political blackness and the problem of nativist socialism. *The Sociological Review*, *67*(5), 945–967. https://doi.org/10.1177%2F0038026119845550 10.1111/eulj.12232.
Navarro, P. (2008). *The coming China wars: Where they will be fought and how they can be won*. Pearson.
Navarro, P. (2015). *Crouching tiger: What China's militarism means for the world*. Prometheus.
Navarro, P., & Autry, G. (2011). *Death by China: Confronting the dragon – A global call to action*. Pearson.
O'Brien, F. (2020, January 10). $170 billion and counting: The cost of Brexit for the U.K. *Bloomberg Economics*. https://www.bloomberg.com/news/articles/2020-01-10/-170-billion-and-counting-the-cost-of-brexit-for-the-u-k
Ohmae, K. (1990). *The borderless world: Power and strategy in the interlinked economy*. Collins.
Ohmae, K. (1995). *The end of the nation state*. Free Press.
Parker, O. (2017). Critical political economy, free movement and Brexit: Beyond the progressive's dilemma. *The British Journal of Politics and International Relations*, *19*(3), 479–496. 10.1177/1369148117711082
Payne, A. (2005). *The global politics of unequal development*. Palgrave.
Payne, A. (2016, July 26). "Who Dun Brexit": "Globalisation" or "Global neoliberalism"? *SPERI Comment*. http://speri.dept.shef.ac.uk/2016/07/26/who-dun-brexit-globalisation-or-global-neoliberalism/
Peck, J. (2011). *Constructions of neoliberal reason*. Oxford University Press.
Pesaresi, N., & Peduzzi, R. (2018). The modernisation of state aid for economic and social development. In B. Nascimbene, & A. Di Pascale (Eds.), *The modernisation of state aid for economic and social development* (pp. 17–42). Springer.
Phillips, T. (2017, November 9). Trump praises China and Blames US for trade deficit. *The Guardian*. https://www.theguardian.com/world/2017/nov/09/donald-trump-china-act-faster-north-korea-threat
Pieterse, J. N. (2020). *Globalization and culture: Global mélange* (4th ed.). Rowman & Littlefield.
Piketty, T. (2014). *Capital in the twenty first century*. Harvard University Press.
Piketty, T. (2020). *Capital and ideology*. Harvard University Press.
Polanyi, K. (2001). *The great transformation: The political and economic origins of our time*. Beacon Press.
Rodrik, D. (1997). *Has globalization gone too far?* Columbia University Press.
Rodrik, D. (2012). *The globalization paradox: Democracy and the future of the world economy*. W. W. Norton.
Rodrik, D. (2017). *Straight talk on trade: Ideas for a sane world economy*. Princeton University Press.
Ruggie, J. G. (1982). International regimes, transactions, and change: Embedded liberalism in the postwar economic order. *International Organization*, *36*(2), 379–415. https://doi.org/10.1017/S0020818300018993
Sachs, J., & Wyplosz, C. (1986). The economic consequences of President Mitterrand. *Economic Policy*, *1*(2), 261–306. https://doi.org/10.2307/1344559
Saunders, R. (2019, January 7). The myth of Brexit as imperial nostalgia. *Prospect*. https://www.prospectmagazine.co.uk/world/the-myth-of-brexit-as-imperial-nostalgia
Scharpf, F. W. (2017). De-constitutionalisation and majority rule: A democratic vision for Europe. *European Law Journal*, *23*(5), 315–334. https://doi.org/10.1111/eulj.12232
Selwyn, B. (2017). *The struggle for development*. Polity.
Selwyn, B. (2019). Poverty chains and global capitalism. *Competition & Change*, *23*(1), 71–97. https://doi.org/10.1177/1024529418809067
Seymour, R. (2016, June 22). Brexit and the Left. *Jacobin*. https://www.jacobinmag.com/2016/06/brexit-yanis-varoufakis-boris-johnson-farage-ukip-corbyn-eu/

Sharma, R. (2016, July 28). Globalisation as we know it is over – and Brexit is the biggest sign yet. *The Guardian*. https://www.theguardian.com/commentisfree/2016/jul/28/era-globalisation-brexit-eu-britain-economic-frustration

Shilliam, R. (2018). *Race and the undeserving poor: From abolition to Brexit*. Agenda.

Siles-Brügge, G. (2014). Explaining the resilience of free trade: The Smoot–Hawley myth and the crisis. *Review of International Political Economy*, *21*(3), 535–574. https://doi.org/10.1080/09692290.2013.830979

Siles-Brügge, G. (2019). Bound by gravity or living in a "post geography trading world"? Expert knowledge and affective spatial imaginaries in the construction of the UK's post-Brexit trade policy. *New Political Economy*, *24*(3), 422–439. https://doi.org/10.1080/13563467.2018.1484722

Stetler, H. (2017, April 18). The rise of Jean-Luc Mélenchon and France's "post-democracy". *The New Republic*. https://newrepublic.com/article/142110/rise-jean-luc-melenchon-frances-post-democracy

Streeck, W. (2016, November 7). Why Europe can't function as it stands. *Verso Blog*. https://www.versobooks.com/blogs/2926-wolfgang-streeck-why-europe-can-t-function-as-it-stands

Streeck, W. (2017). *How will capitalism end?* Verso.

Tansel, C. B. (2017). Authoritarian neoliberalism: Towards a new research agenda. In C. B. Tansel (Ed.), *States of discipline: Authoritarian neoliberalism and the contested reproduction of capitalist order* (pp. 1–28). Rowman & Littlefield.

Tooze, J. A. (2018). *Crashed: How a decade of financial crises changed the world*. Penguin.

Trump, D. J. (2017a, November 10). Remarks by President Trump at APEC CEO Summit, Da Nang, Vietnam. https://www.whitehouse.gov/briefings-statements/remarks-president-trump-apec-ceo-summit-da-nang-vietnam

Trump, D. J. (2017b, January 17). The inaugural address. Washington, DC https://www.whitehouse.gov/briefings-statements/the-inaugural-address/

Trump, D. J. (2018, September 25). Speech to the UN General Assembly. https://www.vox.com/2018/9/25/17901082/trump-un-2018-speech-full-text

Vincent, A. (1990). The new liberalism in Britain 1880–1914. *Australian Journal of Politics & History*, *36*(3), 388–405. https://doi.org/10.1111/j.1467-8497.1990.tb00664.x

Von Tunzelmann, A. (2019, August 12). The imperial myths behind Brexit in Britain. *The Atlantic*. https://www.theatlantic.com/international/archive/2019/08/imperial-myths-behind-brexit/595813/

Wade, R. H. (2017). Is Trump wrong on trade? A partial defense based on production and employment. *Real-World Economics Review*, *2*(79), 43–63.

Watson, M., & Hay, C. (2003). The discourse of globalisation and the logic of no alternative: Rendering the contingent necessary in the political economy of new labour. *Policy and Politics*, *31*(3), 289–305. https://doi.org/10.1332/030557303322034956

Weinhardt, C., & Ten Brink, T. (2020). Varieties of contestation: China's rise and the liberal trade order. *Review of International Political Economy*, *27*(2), 258–280. https://doi.org/10.1080/09692290.2019.1699145

Weisskircher, M. (2018, August 30). Will Germans rise up for a new left-wing movement? What to know about Aufstehen. *LSE EUROPP Blog*. https://blogs.lse.ac.uk/europpblog/2018/08/30/will-germans-rise-up-for-a-new-left-wing-movement-what-to-know-about-aufstehen/

White, J. (2015). Emergency Europe. *Political Studies*, *63*(2), 300–318. https://doi.org/10.1111/1467-9248.12072

Worth, O. (2017). Whither Lexit? *Capital & Class*, *41*(2), 351–357. https://doi.org/10.1177/0309816817711558c

Worth, O. (2018, December 5). Lexit: Did it ever really exist? *Marxist Sociology Blog*. https://bit.ly/2PpPaDW

Wren-Lewis, S. (2017, July 24). Lexit. *Mainly Macro*. https://mainlymacro.blogspot.com/2017/07/lexit.html

Wren-Lewis, S. (2019, January 6). Lexit misdirection. *Mainly Macro*. https://mainlymacro.blogspot.com/2019/01/lexit-misdirection.html

Yeung, H. W.-C. (2016). *Strategic coupling: East Asian industrial transformation in the new global economy history*. Cornell University Press.

Younge, G. (2018, February 3). Britain's imperial fantasies have given us Brexit. *The Guardian*. https://www.theguardian.com/commentisfree/2018/feb/03/imperial-fantasies-brexit-theresa-may

Zhang, X., & Keith, J. (2017). From wealth to power: China's new economic statecraft. *The Washington Quarterly*, *40*(1), 185–203. https://doi.org/10.1080/0163660X.2017.1302746

Creating a race to the top in global tax governance: the political case for tax spillover assessments

Andrew Baker and Richard Murphy

ABSTRACT

'Reglobalization' requires global governance mechanisms that can promote norm and normative change constitutive of a 'post-neoliberal order'. Mitigating the race to the bottom in taxation, which can harm public provision and social mobility, is a specific challenge requiring the creation of new tools. This requires going beyond the current reporting tools of global tax governance to focus more systematically on government policies. We develop a political case for conducting assessments of a phenomenon known as 'tax spillovers'. These are harmful impacts one country's tax policies have on other countries, that can also undermine the redistributive capacity of the home tax system. We identify five enabling conditions that give tax spillover assessments political salience, traction and feasibility. Devising and theorizing policy tools that are politically feasible is a pressing task for the reglobalization project that is deserving of scholarly, as well as practitioner, attention.

The 'race to the bottom' in taxation is a well-known proposition in an era of globalization (Plümper et al., 2009). It refers to countries, states and cities competing with one another by offering tax cuts, reliefs, loopholes or subsidies to encourage the relocation of economic activity and mobile capital to their domain. In the process, however, states can find their own tax base and revenues are eroded, squeezing their 'fiscal self-determination' (Dietsch & Rixen, 2014; Van Apeldoorn, 2018). Governmental capacity to deliver public goods can deteriorate (IMF, 2014; Swank & Steinmo, 2002), while the rising relative tax burden on lower-income groups and less mobile factors of production can increase inequality (Baker & Murphy, 2020). The international impact of this is not spread evenly. Across Africa, for example, corporate tax revenues have shown an average decline of over 20 per cent since the 1990s (Keen, 2013). Even if it does not lead to the extreme scenario of zero tax rates on mobile capital as outlined in the zero-capital-tax-equilibrium hypothesis (Frey, 1990), the 'race to the bottom' involves a progressive downward movement that threatens public provision and social mobility. In this article, we emphasize that a primary challenge for any 'reglobalization' project is to mitigate this race by devising and theorizing effective policy tools and frameworks that are politically feasible.

The dangers of tax-base erosion as a symptom of the 'race to the bottom' were acknowledged and prioritized by both the Group of 20(G20) and the Organisation for Economic Cooperation and Development (OECD) through the launching of the Base Erosion and Profit Shifting (BEPS) initiative in 2013. The major objective of BEPS has been to ensure that multinational enterprises (MNEs) are taxed where 'economic activities take place and value is created'. Neither BEPS, nor the so-called BEPS II modification of rules on taxation rights responding to digitalization announced in 2019, have entirely neglected government policy. However, the focus has been on increasing the accountability of private actors (Lips, 2019).[1] Changing underlying conceptions of appropriate governmental behaviours and incentives has been much less of a priority. Yet the 'race to the bottom' involves government policy responses that can undermine the capacity of domestic tax systems to engage in redistribution (distributive integrity), while aggravating inequality between developed and developing countries (Rixen, 2011). Because this can be unintentional and is not always fully recognized, efforts to combat the 'race to the bottom' also need to focus on governmental policies through the creation of tools that can more fully illuminate such processes and their consequences.

One of the primary challenges posed by Bishop and Payne's (2020) concept of reglobalization is the need to create feasible global governance mechanisms that can promote norm and normative change constitutive of a 'post-neoliberal order'. Consequently, we consider how to encourage a 'race to the top' as a new overarching norm in global tax governance. We develop the normative and political case for conducting assessments of the harmful effects of a phenomenon known as 'tax spillovers.' These are the impacts of one country's tax policies, rules and practices on other countries, or on other aspects of the tax system within the same country, which undermine capacity to raise revenue or use the tax system for redistributive purposes.

We identify five enabling conditions or rationales that combine to give tax spillover assessments some degree of political salience, traction and feasibility.[2] Combined, these conditions make tax spillover assessments a plausible candidate for being an achievable frontier in global tax governance. These are: an empirical data rationale; a minimal normative rationale; a multiple constituency demand rationale; an institutional incentives rationale; and a reputational purpose rationale. Any intellectual project with the aspiration of re-engineering global governance to prioritize alternative values and norms also needs to give serious consideration to the sets of conditions that make change plausible and achievable. In this contribution, we move beyond our recent work, which outlined the soft-law dynamics of a new spillover evaluation framework (Baker & Murphy, 2019a), to establish more fully the political case for spillover assessments. We use literature on NGO benchmarking of revolutionary and reformist types to suggest that hybrid modes of working are often essential to increase political appeal and traction (Broome & Quirk, 2015a; Seabrooke & Wigan, 2015). We show how such hybrid modes of working have informed the development of spillover assessment proposals to date. Prior field and agenda presence are important in building broad cross-cutting coalitions of support and developing political momentum for proposals. Ultimately, reconfiguring global economic governance requires the creation of practical tools that can populate the reglobalization agenda, while responding to the demands, concerns and priorities of multiple stakeholders. This is a challenge requiring the attention of scholars of global governance as well as policy makers.

Norm change in tax governance: the nature of the problem

Changing dominant international norms is a long and arduous process. Scholars reflecting on the enduring quality of economic ideas after the financial crisis of 2008 identified their 'path dependent' and 'sticky' characteristics (Blyth, 2013; Underhill, 2015). Norms are widely shared notions of appropriate, acceptable actor behaviours, informed by normative principles of good conduct that are in turn embedded in and promoted by particular sets of governance arrangements and practices (Finnemore, 1996; Florini, 1996; Ruggie, 1982; Thomson, 1993). Consequently, norms are even more likely to display qualities of stickiness and path dependence, precisely because ideas are often merely one ingredient feeding into highly contingent cycles of norm change. Norm change can therefore be viewed as a protracted multi-step process.

Such a multi-step process has been present in the emergence of the new tax policy tools, when the G20 called for Automatic Information Exchange (AIE) and Country by Country Reporting (CBCR) in 2013. Early evidence suggests that the operation of these new reporting and information requirements are inducing a partial norm shift, with AIE reducing the use of tax havens by multinationals and high-net-worth individuals (Ahrens & Bothner, 2019). The introduction of these tools involved several steps. First, following the financial crisis of 2008, with fiscal retrenchment widespread across the G20 from 2010 onwards, a series of public leaks about the tax-avoidance activities of large well-known MNEs, such as Starbucks, Amazon, Apple and Google, stoked public anger and media outcry (Birks, 2017). At the same time, analytical work established that tax avoidance and profit shifting was widespread, depriving exchequers of revenue and depleting public services (Crivelli et al., 2015; Henry, 2012; OECD, 2013; Zucman, 2014). Second, demands for these companies to pay fair amounts of tax became commonplace in political and public debate around the world (Campbell & Helleloid, 2016; Dallyn, 2017; Seabrooke & Wigan, 2016). Third, politicians at the Group of 8 (G8) and G20 summits in 2013 provided political momentum by calling on the OECD to begin administering and developing the new reporting mechanisms, with both AIE and CBCR featuring in communiqués (G8, 2013; G20, 2013). Fourth, the specifics of AIE and CBCR reporting standards were further developed by OECD staff in conjunction with the G20. Both mechanisms increased available information and transparency for tax authorities by giving more detailed breakdowns on MNE activity in the case of CBCR and creating greater access to income recorded in other jurisdictions for tax authorities in the case of AIE. Crucially, the cases of AIE and CBCR illustrate the importance of having practical reporting tools and instruments that combine claims to moral authority with technical credibility (Seabrooke & Wigan, 2016). Fifth, initial evidence on the operation of AIE suggests that it is reducing willingness to use tax havens because this information can now be more easily accessed and publicized (Ahrens & Bothner, 2019). New reporting standards can therefore encourage behavioural changes, but, as with any reporting standard or evaluation framework, implementation and detail can always be questioned. This partial norm change's five step process is illustrated below in Figure 1.

We can see that, even in this truncated account, partial norm change represented by growing opprobrium for tax avoidance and use of tax havens required a complex chain of interdependent events and conditions. In reality, the sequence was not a neat linear one. Part four of the cycle, for example, began to take form initially prior to phase one, continuing through phases two and three, before being finalized in phase four. One of the reporting tools that became a mainstay of the OECD's BEPS framework began to be developed in civil society from 2003 onwards.[3] The above account nevertheless provides useful insights into the types of conditions required for norm change in global tax governance and the kinds of proposals that are politically achievable.

Thinking in terms of contingent multi-step processes also increases awareness of the scale of obstacles likely to be encountered by more ambitious proposals, such as unitary taxation favoured by some tax-justice campaigners (Picciotto, 2012). Unitary taxation seeks to calculate a single global profit for a corporate group based on a consolidated set of accounts. A formulary apportionment would then be applied to determine the correct share of tax owing to each individual country (Avi-Yonah & Clausing, 2007), with each country having the right to set whatever rate it determined appropriate (Rixen, 2011). From a tax-justice perspective such a proposal would potentially be very effective in ensuring a fairer revenue distribution for countries and reducing the potential for tax avoidance. However, the scale of institutional transformation and political will required to make

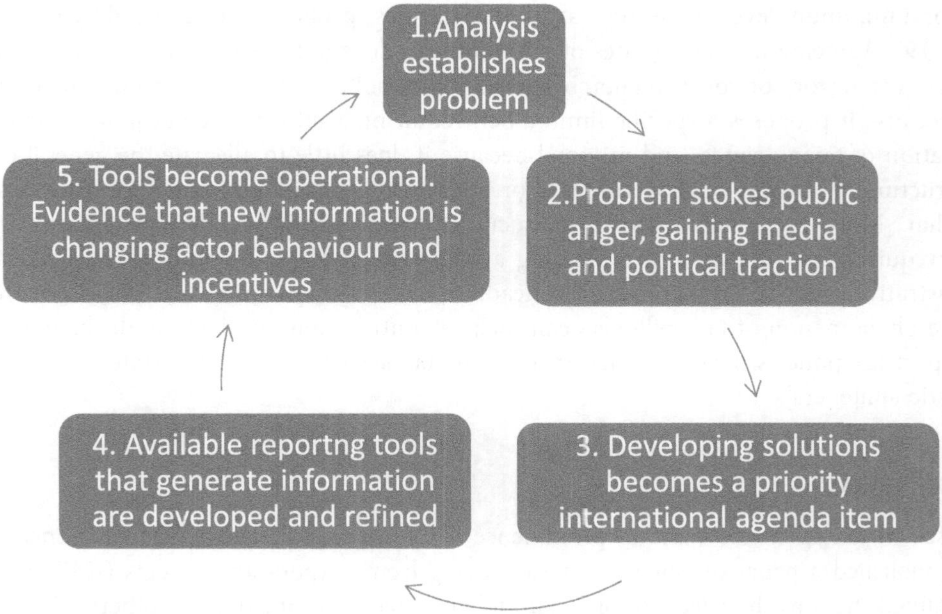

Figure 1. A cycle of partial norm change in global tax governance.

such a proposal work is problematic. States would need to agree common accounting bases, which do not presently exist (Sikka & Murphy, 2015). The definition of the corporate tax base would also need to be overseen by some kind of international tax organization (ITO) with sanction powers. Aside from difficulties creating and agreeing on the design of such an international organization, likely protracted disputes between government winners and losers in revenue terms would be a further political obstacle. The proposal would revolutionize global tax governance, but the scale of shift and degree of international cooperation and agreement required to bring it to fruition make it a distant prospect.

Political plausibility and the often painfully slow pace of international cooperation is also why building on and extending the logics of BEPS, AIE and other reporting requirements, such as the European Union's (EU) directives on administrative cooperation relating to various forms of information exchange, may provide a more feasible direction of travel for international tax reform in the medium term. One criticism of BEPS is that it falls short of protecting states from threats to their 'fiscal self-determination' brought about by tax competition between states, where fiscal self-determination is understood as the ability to achieve policy goals through legislative programmes (Van Apeldoorn, 2018, p. 484). Following this logic, an adequate protection of fiscal self-determination would need to consider, and at least include, some oversight of the tax rates set by states (Van Apeldoorn, 2018). Most existing reporting and information exchange requirements, although involving public authorities, are about improving available information on the tax-related activities of private actors. There is very little systematic consideration in existing reporting tools of how tax-competition strategies pursued by states can pose levels of risk to other states' revenue-collection capacity or how they might undermine the way the tax system as a whole coheres (Rixen, 2011). Tax spillover assessments are designed to increase available information on such risks.

Following a meeting at Chantilly in France in July 2019, Group of 7 (G7) finance ministers tasked the OECD with preparing a 'comprehensive agreement' on 'the general architecture' of rules for a minimum level of effective taxation of business profits, to be prepared by January 2020 (G7, 2019). Agreeing minimum rates of tax, however, does not necessarily challenge, or change, the overall trajectory of governmental behaviour. As a policy measure it is simultaneously ambitious because it proposes a specific limit, albeit requiring a difficult technical agreement on the reallocation of taxing rights, and minimal because it does little to alleviate the general competitive structural pressures on governments or address the behaviours and incentives associated with that. More meaningful efforts to document and discourage the 'race to the bottom' would require reporting on and evaluating a wider range of tax loopholes, breaks, reliefs and administrative practices, rather than just headline rates of corporation tax. This is where assessing the phenomenon of tax spillovers can make a contribution, particularly through a focus on the impact tax policies have on other areas of the tax system in the same state, or what we call 'domestic spillovers'.

Tax spillovers

The issue of tax spillovers came to prominence in 2014 when the International Monetary Fund (IMF) published a paper on spillover effects arising from corporation tax cuts (IMF, 2014). The IMF defined them as the effects of one country's tax rules and practices on others (IMF, 2014, p. 2). The paper distinguished between base spillovers, or losses in inward investment, and strategic ones that result from policy decisions to further cut corporation tax rates. On this basis, the Fund developed econometric equations to generate estimates of both. These were found to have a 'significant and sizable' impact in reducing corporate tax bases and rates in developing countries, with the impact two or three times higher than in OECD members (IMF, 2014, p. 7). A one-point reduction in corporation tax in all countries would reduce a typical state's corporate tax base by 3.7 per cent, implying a sizable effect, given that average corporate tax rates had fallen by 5 per cent over the previous decade (IMF, 2014, p. 19). Revenue loss due to spillovers was estimated to be 13 per cent in non-OECD countries (IMF, 2014, p. 20).

The IMF's work also acknowledged methodological difficulties, with accurate country-level estimates being especially difficult using econometric equations (IMF, 2014, p. 15). In an effort to provide a foundation for assessing tax spillovers on a country-by-country basis we created a new spillover assessment tool kit (Baker & Murphy, 2019a). Our framework moved beyond the IMF's work in five ways. First, we showed that the initial legislative intent behind the introduction of corporation tax in jurisdictions like the United States (US) and United Kingdom (UK) was not solely to raise revenue. Rather, corporate taxes served a defensive purpose, reinforcing or buttressing other parts of the tax system, such as income tax, by reducing incentives to hide income in corporate structures. Second, based on this definition we broadened the conception of spillovers beyond the effects of headline rates of corporation tax to ask whether tax and administrative practices undermine other parts of tax systems, both domestically and internationally. We asked, for example, whether a country's corporation tax policies and practices undermine and pose risks to its income-tax base, or that of other countries. Thirdly, qualitatively evaluating and documenting spillovers provides a more, comprehensive and wide-ranging reading of the scale and extent of potential spillover risks that comprise the 'race to the bottom'. Fourthly, we gave these assessments a minimally normative purpose of discouraging and reducing the harm states do to their own and other countries' tax system as a consequence of their policies. Fifthly, the qualitative scoring system enabled areas of greatest weakness and risk in a tax system to be identified, allowing targeted reform agendas to be formulated and proposed.

In simple terms, spillovers are the often unseen and largely unmeasured externalities and risks that arise from the pursuit of tax competition (most commonly for mobile paper profits). The framework we advance is informed by the observation that such competition can change the structures of tax systems, domestically as well as internationally (Rixen, 2011). In developed countries a common pattern is to cut nominal rates of corporation tax, with average corporation tax falling from 32 per cent in 2000 to 25 per cent in 2015 across the OECD, but simultaneously to expand the number of entities liable for corporation tax (broadening). This shifts the burden from highly profitable and mobile MNEs to smaller and medium-sized companies. When nominal corporate taxes on retained profits fall below income tax, there is also an incentive to classify income as corporate. Authorities then face incentives to address that by reducing the top rates of income tax or reducing taxes on financial investments to avoid appearing to flatten the income-tax structure. All are examples of 'domestic spillovers' caused by tax competition that weaken the overall redistributive integrity of a tax system and push relative tax burdens towards lower-income groups and less mobile factors of production such as labour (Baker & Murphy, 2020). In developing countries, tax competition and the resulting relocation of paper profits – or other special deals – often simply reduce the overall tax base, because of limited administrative capacity to collect more income tax or broaden tax bases. These are international spillovers, and as the IMF analysis showed, they harm developing countries most. Our framework uses three systematic scoring grids (domestic spillovers, international risks generated and vulnerability to international risks) to assess the risk levels posed by the practices characteristic of specific parts of tax systems, both domestically and internationally.

In applying this in a UK spillover assessment, we found the biggest domestic spillover risks posed to the UK's income tax base were from limited 'close company' provisions that encouraged the shift of income into corporate structures at lower rates, and from the weak administration of capital gains (at lower rates) that allowed income to be disguised as capital gains. The most prominent international spillover risk that the UK generated for other jurisdictions was the ease of creating a company and of allocating income earned elsewhere to that company (Baker & Murphy, 2019c). In this way, spillover assessments can identify policies that undermine other parts of the tax system and harm its redistributive capacity, and those policies most likely to harm other tax systems, undermining developing countries' capacity to pay for public goods.

Assessing national policies

Moving beyond current global governance tax initiatives, which mostly increase information on the activities of private actors, requires assessing and reporting on national tax policies and their spillover risks. Such reporting exercises on national policies have become increasingly common (Cooley & Snyder, 2015). Peer review and multilateral surveillance exercises function through a mix of formal recommendations and informal dialogue, public scrutiny, comparisons and even rankings of countries. This is followed by public reactions to the publication of results by electorates, interest groups, public officials and politicians (Broome & Quirk, 2015a; Pagani, 2002, pp. 5–6; Schäfer, 2006). Such review and grading processes create the basis for 'symbolic judgements' on countries' relative performances that function through unfavourable comparisons with peers (Broome & Quirk, 2015b, p. 828; Sharman, 2007). These symbolic judgements can in turn unleash a 'politics of bad performance', sparking a review of existing practices, while providing ammunition for critics of the status quo. More subtly, such evaluations and reviews can gradually reframe policy dialogue and debates, as well as notions of appropriate behaviour.

So-called benchmarks are essentially evaluation frameworks that collate and report information on particular government policies. One of the major insights to emerge from the benchmark literature is that measurement systems and forms of evaluation are difficult to separate meaningfully from their underpinning political values and preferences (Broome et al., 2018; Broome & Quirk, 2015a, 2015b). Normative criteria are often projected into many existing evaluation exercises by specifying appropriate conducts, behaviours and good practices (Broome & Quirk, 2015b, p. 826). Most existing benchmarks, rather than offering watertight scientific measurement, effectively engage in a form of 'norm evaluation', with the consequence that they most commonly reinforce pre-existing norms (Broome et al., 2018, p. 3). In other words, benchmarks have to date largely been conservative governance tools concerned with maintaining existing established norms. According to such logic, however, and given the fundamental underlying normative quality of many existing ones, they could also be designed to challenge and change existing normative logics.

The finding in the benchmark literature that choice of norm is usually prior in the construction of multilateral evaluation frameworks is pivotal (Broome et al., 2018; Broome & Quirk, 2015a, 2015b). A first step in designing a benchmark or evaluation framework is the choice of norm (or behaviours to be encouraged/ discouraged). Creating new benchmarks that reflect and promote different values and priorities is a practical contribution scholars of global governance can make to the reglobalization project. Those with experience, understanding and knowledge of how many existing ones function can usefully apply that expertise in designing new prototype benchmarks and evaluation frameworks. We see this activity as a significant part of the reglobalization agenda, as both an intellectual and practical undertaking.

One important contribution to the benchmark literature distinguishes between reformist and revolutionary benchmarks as ideal types (Seabrooke & Wigan, 2015). The former seek to create change within a dominant system, flowing in the same direction as '*established normative trends*' (Seabrooke & Wigan, 2015, p. 889). They are also expected to have prior issue-salience and are generally advocated by large-scale established NGOs. These organizations then outsource benchmark creation, or refinement tasks, to outside experts, before seeking buy-in from a range of stakeholders. By contrast, the latter seek to change both how the basic units of the system are seen and the logics of the system itself. Expert activists – usually connected to smaller, less established NGOs – then attempt to persuade larger NGOs, stakeholders and authorities of their case, and to contest, dispute and overturn dominant methodologies by presenting alternatives that shine a different light on a particular problem or issue. This ideal-type distinction is indeed a neat heuristic device. In practice, as active participants in the field, we found that practical realties necessitated a pragmatic, hybrid, flexible mode of operation, involving a combination of reformist and revolutionary logics.

In the rest of the article we document and reflect on our experiences of designing a spillover assessment framework and the sets of politics and progress that has entailed to date. In particular, we identify five enabling conditions that have been present in the spillover case that have given the issue, field and agenda presence, and were similarly present when AIE and CBCR were introduced. These elements can be considered necessary, but not sufficient, conditions. Veto points and the absence of political will from large states remain the biggest obstacle in any case of global governance reform and the most significant factor hampering extensive meaningful take-up of spillover assessment.

Political enabling conditions present in the spillover case

The framework for conducting national spillover assessments that we created (Baker & Murphy, 2019a) has several conscious design features that are intended to deepen and broaden its appeal for a range of actors. In presenting these features we are not claiming that they are a scientific threshold, but rather a guide to the kind of strategic thinking required to position proposals to give them the best chance of political acceptance. Our more limited claim is that populating the reglobalization agenda with specific politically viable tools requires attention to the conditions that give proposals field and agenda presence and enables cross-cutting constituencies to be built.

An empirical data rationale

As with AIE and CBCR, tax spillovers became an issue with salience and traction due to empirical analysis that quantified the phenomenon. Using econometric techniques to highlight that harmful spillovers were most pronounced in developing countries, estimating a 13 per cent revenue loss, the IMF research established them as a real-word problem (IMF, 2014). Within a year, two European governments implicated in the notorious 'Double Irish with a Dutch sandwich' profit-shifting scheme – The Netherlands and Ireland – commissioned their own analyses of the spillovers produced by their jurisdictions (IBFD, 2015; Kosters, 2015). Rather than mute potential criticism, however, these assessments gave further momentum to calls for country-level spillover analysis. For development NGOs, these reports became a focus of criticism and a point of reference for how not to conduct spillover assessments, sparking a search for alternative methodologies. Oxfam, ActionAid and Christian Aid all began to call for governments to enter willingly into spillover assessments, while highlighting the inadequacies of the Dutch and Irish assessments (ActionAid, 2018; Oxfam, 2015; Christian Aid, 2017a, 2017b). Oxfam instigated events in the UK parliament to discuss and promote spillover assessments (APPG Inclusive Growth, 2017), while ActionAid and Christian Aid began to commit budget to the issue by commissioning their own analyses (ActionAid, 2018; Christian Aid, 2017a, 2017b).

In keeping with reformist benchmarking, therefore, the IMF analysis established issue salience with large established NGOs which began to pursue questions of how national, or country-level, assessments might be conducted in a dialogue with outside experts. In this way 'tax spillovers' became an accepted, if contested, part of the discourse of international tax governance and a credible way of analysing and identifying 'race to the bottom' dynamics. In 2018 the platform for collaboration on tax (PCT), involving the IMF, OECD, the United Nations (UN), the World Bank Group (WBG) and stakeholder groups, issued a statement declaring a broad aspiration to 'analyze and report on the spillovers and opportunities from changes in the international tax environment on and for developing countries' (PCT, 2018). A call for the UK government to conduct a regular spillover assessment was made in the UK parliament in 2016 (APPG RT, 2016). Likewise, tax spillovers remain part of the ongoing research programme of staff in the Fiscal Affairs Department in the IMF, with further papers and books planned (Discussions with IMF Staff, December 2018). The European Commission's Directorate General for Customs and Taxation is also involved in discussions on how spillovers might be assessed, including considering qualitative approaches (Correspondence with European Commission officials, February 2019).[4] In short, the IMF analysis of 2014 has given spillovers field and agenda presence. In keeping with previous scholarship in international political economy on the importance of viable policy proposals in technical areas like finance and tax having prior presence, spillover assessments now have both institutional access and a body of established prior work to draw on (Baker, 2013; Porter, 2003).

A normative rationale

In the area of tax, existing literature has established the potency of fusing expertise with moral authority (Seabrooke & Wigan, 2016). Tools like CBCR fed off public anger at the palpable sense of injustice at the limited tax payed by many leading multinationals. To penetrate public consciousness and develop political support, technical proposals are most effective when harnessed to claims about morality, justice and fairness. Technical instruments, with a clear message about the rightness of their objectives, stand the best chance of building political and public support. The benchmarking literature has also established how choice of normative objective informs the design of evaluation frameworks (Broome & Quirk, 2015a).

Cognisant of both these observations, we designed our spillover assessment framework, with a minimally normative objective that would appeal widely and resonate morally with a range of actors. Recognizing the merits of building on established prior empirical rationales, we used the IMF's finding in 2014 that spillovers were resulting in significant harms for developing countries by reducing tax bases. In our formulation, spillover assessment was given the purpose of identifying (and discouraging) harms caused by tax competition, both domestic and international, in terms of lost revenue and the undermining of the overall 'distributional integrity' of a tax system. Rather than seeking to advance a complex argument about the unjust and morally problematic nature of 'luring' capital through 'strategic intent' (Dietsch, 2015; Dietsch & Rixen, 2014), we made a more straightforwardly intuitive claim that governments should seek to minimize the harms caused by their tax policies. Demonstrating 'strategic intent' is difficult and can be contested, while unintentional but avoidable harms remain part of the problem of the 'race to the bottom'.

Preventing unintentional harms becomes a challenge in an era of globalization because global competitive forces can have unintended distant consequences, creating a need to protect governments and individuals from avoidable harms (Linklater, 2002, p. 329). Negligence, or failure to take due care to prevent the risk of harm to others, is ethically problematic, because harms that could have been avoided still occur, even if they are largely unintentional (Linklater, 2002, p. 330). Enabling unintentional harms caused by tax competition to be better identified and understood by governments, international organizations and civil society actors alike is something to which spillover assessment can contribute, paving the way for remedial action.

Reducing inequality is now widely accepted as a priority agenda item for the G7 and established organizations such as the OECD, the IMF and the World Bank, while tax is increasingly recognized as the primary means of effacing inequality (Piketty, 2014; Saez and Zucman, 2019; Baker & Murphy, 2020). Normatively, our framework works with the grain of this aspiration, while recognizing the practical difficulties of making progress because of the structural pressures governments face. Ultimately, a gap exists between such rhetoric and much tax practice. The stark reality is that many tax systems are structured in ways that exacerbate domestic and international inequality. A variety of partly concealed reliefs and preferential arrangements can undermine other parts of a tax system and its functioning as a whole, while luring capital from other jurisdictions, both intentionally and unintentionally. For example, in other research we estimate that 81 per cent of UK personal wealth is held in heavily tax-incentivized assets at a cost of £86 billion a year to the tax base through what are effectively social tax expenditures (Baker and Murphy, 2020; Morel et al., 2018). By evaluating such practices and their consequences, while publishing information on them, spillover assessments can stimulate reform debates.

Rather than contributing to the 'race to the bottom' in taxation, our spillover framework takes a position that advanced states have a moral and ethical imperative to lead a new global 'race to the top' by demonstrating good behaviours and generating negligible international (and domestic) spillover risks. The spillover framework has the purpose of encouraging and promoting such behaviours. Achieving such norm change, even gradually, would be transformatory. It would challenge the dominant competitive logic of the existing system, 'reversing existing normative trends' (Seabrooke & Wigan, 2015). Spillover assessments with the kind of normative purpose and methodological design we propose are usually characteristic of revolutionary benchmarks. Yet, at the same time, by working with a concept that is already accepted by major international organizations and NGOs, with the aspiration of gradually encouraging domestic policy changes, the proposal is also strategically reformist. Combining reformist and revolutionary elements in this way increases the likely acceptance of and support for spillover from a number of parties, while retaining a clear objective for change that guides the design of the assessment framework and its overall purpose.

A multiple constituency demand rationale

In designing a spillover assessment framework we sought to give the assessment exercise multiple uses for multiple actors and to create incentives for a range of domestic actors to support entering into such assessments. Most importantly, spillover assessment has to appeal to governments by offering sources of information they might find useful. We set out several potential uses for governments in the tool kit (Baker & Murphy, 2019b, p. 2). Spillover assessments can assist governments to identify how loopholes, reliefs and or administrative shortcomings pose risks to the tax base and the tax system as a whole, as well as revealing how their targeted removal might raise additional revenue without increasing rates or extending the tax base. Spillover assessments can also document whether incentives and other arrangements to encourage particular behaviours built into the tax system are working to best effect, or are maybe having unintended consequences that undermine other parts of the tax system or tax base with detrimental social consequences. They also provide an enhanced view of how the tax burden is distributed and whether specific groups and sectors are paying appropriate shares. A range of business and industry groups may also find such information useful. Governments may also want to know about the effectiveness of their tax administration and whether the funds they invest in these agencies are being used to best effect. Finally, spillover assessments can give governments a sense of their own vulnerability to aggressive tax competition practices abroad, as well as how such vulnerabilities could be reduced. Consequently, spillover assessment has been strategically framed as a device and source of information for promoting informed, constructive policy dialogue about how tax systems cohere as a whole and weaknesses that could be addressed.

In civil society, spillover is already on the agenda of the largest best-resourced development NGOs. Such a group of NGOs focused on taxation and inequality issues, including Oxfam, ActionAid, Eurodad and the Tax Justice Network, recently called in the *London Declaration* for spillover assessments to take a qualitative form and to go beyond corporation tax in order to evaluate a wider range of potential domestic spillovers (GIFT, 2019; Tax Justice UK, 2019). The World Bank-sponsored platform for promoting civil society dialogue on fiscal matters, the Global Initiative for Fiscal Transparency (GIFT), increasingly views spillover assessments as a way of increasing transparency, information and deepening and enriching civil society dialogue on tax revenue cycles, particularly in developing countries where information and data can be scarce and administrative capacity limited. GIFT is developing proposals for spillover assessment in some of its latest commissioned research (dialogue between authors and GIFT, December 2019). Spillover assessments in this reading are seen as a means of increasing information on the functioning of tax systems and their practices for a range of stakeholders, including civil servants and tax administrators, industry professionals, trade unions, political parties, campaign groups and business lobbies from different sectors.

Multiple appeal and the cooperation of numerous parties is seen as essential to the plausibility of spillover, not least because surveying multiple parties with experience of the operation of a tax system in order to build up assessors' impressions of how widespread certain practices are, is integral to the spillover methodology we propose. In this regard, a process of building coalitions to support the introduction of spillover assessments is already underway in a number of developing countries, especially in Latin America, through the GIFT initiatives. In the European Parliament, the Socialist and Democrat party groups have been urging the European Commission to start undertaking spillover assessments of European states (SDG, 2019), with the Commission itself engaging in a discussion about the forms a spillover methodology might take. In short, the spillover framework we created was a response to a prior demand from a range of organizations, interest groups and bureaucracies which were already thinking in terms of how to evaluate them. Spillover assessment is not a distant abstract proposal. Rather, it involves the creation of a specific toolkit that already has political traction and presence in a variety of settings.

The biggest obstacles to spillover assessment becoming an established feature of global tax governance are the reservations of large advanced states. For example, a recent IMF paper on the negative spillover effects of cuts in US corporation tax (Beer et al., 2018) is unlikely to improve the Trump administration's negative attitude towards multilateral governance more generally. As one OECD official conceded, the problem with any form of multilateral peer review, especially when large states are involved, is that assessments can only cover what that a government wants or consents to (Confidential discussions with the authors, September 2019). The current US government has strongly defended US-owned digital companies in recent G7 debates about taxing digital companies, while European governments were muted in their criticisms. Likewise, when the European Union released a blacklist of non-cooperative tax jurisdictions in 2017, it identified smaller jurisdictions but, as with previous declarations, left out six EU member-states that met the criteria: Malta, Luxembourg, Ireland, Cyprus, Netherlands and the United Kingdom. The United States also managed to avoid the blacklist, despite providing very little cooperation (Lips & Cobham, 2017). This is part of a more general pattern in which tax 'blacklists' tend to identify the usual suspects amongst smaller states (Sharman, 2010), with larger states reluctant to be critical of one another.

For these reasons, we have avoided framing spillover assessment as a form of 'blacklisting', because this is likely to strike too adversarial a tone and run into opposition from larger states. In this respect, the spillover proposal is different from proposals such as the financial secrecy index (FSI), which is essentially a tool for exposing the tax secrecy provisions of larger states (Cobham et al., 2015; Seabrooke & Wigan, 2015). How to extend global tax governance to persuade states to engage in more systematic evaluations of their own tax policies is a key and difficult challenge, but at least new forms of effective cooperation on taxation matters have emerged in recent times (Christensen & Hearson, 2019). Notably, buy-in from governments and stakeholders, deciding voluntarily to enter into policy dialogue in order to obtain useful information from the exercise, rather than simply being on the receiving end of criticism, has been present in the case of other assessments of government policies and practices. Such an element was, for example, an important factor in building stakeholder consent for corporate governance assessments, which have informed the design of this framework (Baker, 2012).

Ultimately, the nature of the current political leadership in the United States and the United Kingdom, with their relative embrace of tax competition, means the multiple constituency demand rationale, despite being present in the spillover case, is also the weakest of the enabling conditions.

Nevertheless, parliamentarians in both the EU and the UK have made noises supportive of spillover assessment, indicating that it not only has issue presence, but some political support in both jurisdictions.

An institutional incentives rationale

To be feasible, spillover assessments will require traction with established international organizations, fitting with their working methods and conceptions of bureaucratic turf. The fact that both the European Commission and the IMF have for some time talked about the existence of tax spillovers as a significant problem means that the first test is largely passed. The second test is more problematic. The IMF, for example, obtains much of its authority as a reputational intermediary (Broome, 2008) from an epistemological commitment to rigorous econometrics as a foundation for powerful evidence-based policy prescriptions. The 2014 IMF paper thus used econometrics to establish spillovers as an agenda item in international tax governance. However, at the same time, that paper expressed reservations about using such methods to arrive at accurate country-level estimates. The Fund has not sought to position itself as the institution to conduct country-level spillover assessments. Moreover, if, as we contend, spillover assessment should be deployed to seek to improve policy dialogue and identify targeted reforms, more qualitative forms of assessment, such as the one we propose, do have a prior track record (Baker, 2012).

In this respect, our tool-kit consciously draws on the working methods of previous World Bank assessment exercises, notably the corporate governance Reports on the Observance of Standards and Codes (ROSCs). We purposely sought to reproduce aspects of that methodology and logic. These World Bank reports were qualitative and remedial, as well as diagnostic, and involved collating assessors' impressions of how widespread particular practices were based on widespread stakeholder consultation, interviews and questionnaires, as well as analysis of legal statutes and regulations (Baker, 2012). Moreover, these assessments were intended to publish information for a range of stakeholders, resulting in and catalysing an enhanced stakeholder policy dialogue that would help identify reform paths, empowering certain regulatory authorities. Because of their function in catalysing policy dialogue, the assessment process was voluntary and involved a reciprocal exchange between regulatory authorities and assessors. We recognize that such a voluntary opt-in approach is likely to be necessary if spillover assessments are actually to take place and have domestic resonance, even if that reduces the critical tone of reports. In other words, qualitative tax spillover assessments are informed by a precedent of previous qualitative evaluations of country-governance practices, as a prior from of multilateral assessment that fits with the logic and skills profile of an existing institution and its working methods. The proposal for an alternative methodology for assessing spillovers contained in our assessment framework, although characteristic of revolutionary benchmarking, also has a reformist aspiration. It is perhaps unsurprising, therefore, that the World Bank-funded GIFT programme has shown most interest in piloting domestic spillover assessments in selected developing countries as a tool for increasing fiscal-revenue-cycle transparency, precisely because they resonate with working methods with which key personnel are familiar (GIFT, 2019).

A reputational purpose rationale

Finally, as already documented, existing forms of multilateral assessment and benchmarking are usually informed by a clear sense of purpose and engage in norm evaluation (Broome et al., 2018). Our spillover framework has the very clear intent of identifying and discouraging forms of tax competition and policies that pose the biggest threats to other countries' tax bases, while potentially undermining the coherence of a tax system as a whole. The framework contains a systematic method for grading these risks. Likely to be more prominent, however, are the policy dialogue and recommendations that suggest ways for governments to ameliorate these risks and enhance the security of their own tax revenues. Spillover assessments are designed to contribute to changing the reputational incentive structures around what is acceptable and appropriate behaviour (Sharman, 2007). However, for the time being, we have left open the question of attaching sanctions to bad performance. Existing research suggests reputation on taxation matters works most effectively when accompanied by legally enforceable sanctions (Eggenberger, 2018; Hakelberg, 2016), although that has usually involved large states targeting small states. The problem is that spillovers arising from states pursuing tax-competition strategies can characterize all states in different forms, without states necessarily crossing the threshold to carry the stigma of being a tax haven, which is what 'blacklists' and sanctions have usually been aimed at. Peer pressure and policy dialogue to reduce harmful spillovers may not be an ideal best-fit solution, but they remain preferable to a world where they are simply ignored or accepted.

Conclusions

Reglobalization is a useful and interesting concept because of its compelling call to imagine alternative futures and to consider how global governance might be refashioned. But it should also be seen as a practical call to action for scholars of global governance, within which they can become active participants in re-designing global governance mechanisms and processes. In this contribution, we have presented a new governance tool that already has some political traction and field presence with a range of actors. As a practical project of governance with aspirations of normative change, reglobalization requires that such tools are strategically framed and positioned. Our experience as actors in the field to date suggests such tools will need to: be grounded in solid robust empirical research that establishes that a particular set of processes constitute a problem requiring a solution; have a clear sense of defensible, moral, normative purpose; be capable of appealing to and fulfilling the demands of multiple constituencies, creating coalitions of support amongst governments and civil society; fit with existing institutional incentives, priorities and methodologies; and, finally, have a clear sense of how reputational incentives can be used to promote changes in behaviours and norms.

In designing a form of tax-spillover analysis we have been mindful of these considerations and have used them to inform the design of the proposed framework, with a view to enhancing its political appeal and plausibility. We acknowledge that the support of powerful states, given their previous reluctance to expose their own tax policies to much in the way of outside scrutiny, remains a significant likely obstacle. For this reason, we have avoided framing the assessment exercise as a form of 'blacklisting'. Instead, we have emphasized the intent of promoting enhanced policy dialogue to identify and suggest reform pathways to reduce harmful spillovers, rather than merely to 'name and shame', although this does not rule out that possibility. The tool-kit we have created is merely one step on the road to reforming global tax governance. It has the advantage of a prior institutional footing and organizational backers in current policy debates. Drawing on the literature on benchmarking, we have shown how the proposal has involved a pragmatic combination of reformist and revolutionary elements. AIE and BEPS have been important developments in global tax governance, but the appropriate norms for framing and informing national government tax policies have not received sufficient attention to date. Tax spillover assessments are one means of addressing that.

The conditions and rationales we present help to give us a picture of how a cycle of norm change might emerge in global tax governance without, of course, guaranteeing such an outcome.

Notes

1. BEPS action 5, for example, specifies 6 categories of taxpayer-related rulings on which authorities should exchange information. See https://www.oecd.org/tax/beps/beps-action-5-harmful-tax-practices-peer-review-transparency-framework.pdf. The purpose behind this exchange of information is to increase the set of information that authorities have on the treatment of taxpayers in other jurisdictions, so as to reduce the risk of profit-shifting activity. It is quite limited in scope and intent and is not about assessing the levels of tax competition pursued by a jurisdiction or the consequences of that competition.
2. Much of the evidence presented in this article is a function of the authors being direct and active participants in this new emerging policy field, working closely and engaging in a dialogue with various non-governmental organizations (NGOs) and international organizations (IOs) to produce a new framework for assessing tax spillovers. Our experience in that exercise has informed the political enabling conditions we identity in this contribution.
3. See Murphy (2003). Accounting literatures had been proposing a similar idea since the 1970s.
4. As authors, we were invited to participate in these in March 2019.

Acknowledgements

The authors would like thank two anonymous reviewers and the editors for comments on an earlier version of this article. Any remaining shortcomings are the authors' responsibility alone.

Disclosure statement

No potential conflict of interest was reported by the author(s).

ORCID

Andrew Baker http://orcid.org/0000-0001-6677-930X
Richard Murphy http://orcid.org/0000-0003-4103-9369

References

ActionAid. (2018). Stemming the spills: Guiding framework for undertaking national tax spillover analyses. http://www.actionaid.org/sites/files/actionaid/stemming_the_spills_online.pdf

Ahrens, L., & Bothner, F. (2019). The Big Bang: Tax Evasion after Automatic exchange of information Under FATCA and CRS. *New Political Economy*. https://doi.org/10.1080/13563467.2019.1639651

APPG Inclusive Growth. (2017). Tax spillover: A new framework. https://www.inclusivegrowth.co.uk/appg_publications/tax-spillover-new-framework/

APPG Responsible Tax. (2016). A more responsible global tax system or a sticking plaster? An examination of the OECD's Base Erosion and Profit Shifting (BEPS) process and recommendations. file:///C:/Users/admin/Downloads/Sticking-Plaster-APPG-Responsible-Tax-Report%20(1).pdf.

Avi-Yonah, R. S., & Clausing, K. A. (2007). A proposal to adopt formulary apportionment for corporate income taxation: The Hamilton Project. U of Michigan Law & Economics, *Olin Working Paper* (07-009).
Baker, A. (2012). The 'public interest' agency of international organizations? The case of the OECD principles of corporate governance. *Review of International Political Economy*, *19*(3), 389–414. https://doi.org/10.1080/09692290.2011.552789
Baker, A. (2013). The new political economy of the macroprudential ideational shift. *New Political Economy*, *18*(1), 112–139.
Baker, A., & Murphy, R. (2019a). The political economy of 'Tax Spillover': A new multilateral framework. *Global Policy*, *10*(2), 178–192. https://doi.org/10.1111/1758-5899.12655
Baker, A., & Murphy, R. (2019b). A tax spillover assessment for the United Kingdom. https://doi.org/10.1111/1758-5899.12655
Baker, A., & Murphy, R. (2019c). Tax spillovers: The assessment procedure. https://doi.org/10.1111/1758-5899.12655
Baker, A., & Murphy, R. (2020). Modern monetary theory and the changing role of tax in society. *Social Policy & Society*, *19*(3), 454–469. https://doi.org/10.1017/S1474746420000056
Beer, S., Klemm, M. A. D., & Matheson, M. T. (2018). *Tax spillovers from US corporate income tax reform*. International Monetary Fund.
Birks, J. (2017). Tax avoidance as an anti-austerity issue: The progress of a protest issue through the public sphere. *European Journal of Communication*, *32*(4), 296–311. https://doi.org/10.1177/0267323117710898
Bishop, M. L., & Payne, A. (2020). The political economies of different globalizations: Theorizing reglobalization. *Globalizations*. doi:10.1080/14747731.2020.1779963
Blyth, M. (2013). Paradigms and paradox: The politics of economic ideas in two moments of crisis. *Governance*, *26*(2), 197–215. https://doi.org/10.1111/gove.12010
Broome, A. (2008). The importance of being earnest: The IMF as a reputational intermediary. *New Political Economy*, *13*(2), 125–151. https://doi.org/10.1080/13563460802018216
Broome, A., Homolar, A., & Kranke, M. (2018). Bad science: International organizations and the indirect power of global benchmarking. *European Journal of International Relations*, *24*(3), 514–539. https://doi.org/10.1177/1354066117719320
Broome, A., & Quirk, J. (2015a). The politics of numbers: The normative agendas of global benchmarking. *Review of International Studies*, *41*(5), 813–818. https://doi.org/10.1017/S0260210515000339
Broome, A., & Quirk, J. (2015b). Governing the world at a distance: The practice of global benchmarking. *Review of International Studies*, *41*(5), 819–841. https://doi.org/10.1017/S0260210515000340
Campbell, K., & Helleloid, D. (2016). Starbucks: Social responsibility and tax avoidance. *Journal of Accounting Education*, *37*, 38–60. https://doi.org/10.1016/j.jaccedu.2016.09.001
Christensen, R., & Hearson, M. (2019). The new politics of global tax governance: Taking stock a decade after the financial crisis. *Review of International Political Economy*, *26*(5), 1068–1088. https://doi.org/10.1080/09692290.2019.1625802
Christian Aid. (2017a). Global linkages: Re-examining the empirical basis of the 2015 Tax spillover analysis. https://www.christianaid.ie/sites/default/files/2018-02/global-linkages-tax-report.pdf
Christian Aid. (2017b). 'Impossible' structures: tax outcomes overlooked by the 2015 tax spillover analysis. https://www.christianaid.ie/sites/default/files/2018-02/impossible-structures-tax-report.pdf
Cobham, A., Janský, P., & Meinzer, M. (2015). The financial secrecy index: Shedding new light on the geography of secrecy. *Economic Geography*, *91*(3), 281–303. https://doi.org/10.1111/ecge.12094
Cooley, A., & Snyder, J. (2015). *Ranking the world*. Cambridge University Press.
Crivelli, E., De Mooij, R. A., & Keen, M. M. (2015). *Base erosion, profit shifting and developing countries (No. 15-118)*. International Monetary Fund.
Dallyn, S. (2017). An examination of the political salience of corporate tax avoidance: A case study of the tax justice network. *Accounting Forum*, *41*(4), 336–352. https://doi.org/10.1016/j.accfor.2016.12.002
Dietsch, P. (2015). *Catching capital: The ethics of tax competition*. Oxford University Press.
Dietsch, P., & Rixen, T. (2014). Tax competition and global background justice. *Journal of Political Philosophy*, *22*(2), 150–177. https://doi.org/10.1111/j.1467-9760.2012.00419.x
Eggenberger, K. (2018). When is blacklisting effective? Stigma, sanctions and legitimacy: The reputational and financial costs of being blacklisted. *Review of International Political Economy*, *25*(4), 483–504. https://doi.org/10.1080/09692290.2018.1469529

Finnemore, M. (1996). Norms, culture, and world politics: Insights from sociology's institutionalism. *International Organization*, *50*(2), 325–347. https://doi.org/10.1017/S0020818300028587

Florini, A. (1996). The evolution of international norms. *International Studies Quarterly*, *40*(3), 363–389. https://doi.org/10.2307/2600716

Frey, B. S. (1990). *Intergovernmental tax competition. Influence of tax differentials on international competitiveness.* Kluwer Academic, 89–114.

G20. (2013). G20 leaders' declaration. St Petersburg, 6 September. http://www.g20.utoronto.ca/2013/2013-0906-declaration.html

G7. (2019). G7 finance ministers meeting: What are the outcomes? https://www.elysee.fr/en/g7/2019/07/20/g7-finance-ministers-meeting-what-are-the-outcomes

G8. (2013). Lough Erne G8 Leaders Communiqué. https://www.gov.uk/government/publications/2013-lough-erne-g8-leaders-communique

GIFT. (2019). Global Initiative for Fiscal Transparency (GIFT) Newsletter, September. http://fiscaltransparency.net/newsletters/GIFT_newsletter_SEP_19.html

Hakelberg, L. (2016). Coercion in international tax cooperation: Identifying the prerequisites for sanction threats by a great power. *Review of International Political Economy*, *23*(3), 511–541. https://doi.org/10.1080/09692290.2015.1127269

Henry, J. S. (2012). The price of offshore revisited. *Tax Justice Network*, *22*, 57–168.

IBFD. (2015). *Spillover analysis: Possible effects of the Irish tax system on developing economies.* Irish Department of Finance. http://www.budget.gov.ie/Budgets/2016/Documents/IBFD_Irish_Spillover_Analysis_Report_pub.pdf

IMF. (2014). Spillovers in international corporate taxation. IMF Policy Paper, 9 May. https://www.imf.org/external/np/pp/eng/2014/050914.pdf

Keen, M. (2013). Taxation and development—again. In C. Fuest & R. Zodrow (Eds.), *Critical issues in taxation and development* (pp. 13–44). MIT Press.

Kosters, B. (2015). *Spillover analysis: Research for Dutch MoFA.* http://www.finance.gov.ie/sites/default/files/8%20-%20Bart%20Kosters.pdf

Linklater, A. (2002). The problem of harm in world politics: Implications for the sociology of states-systems. *International Affairs*, *78*(2), 319–338. https://doi.org/10.1111/1468-2346.00253

Lips, W. (2019). Great powers in global tax governance: A comparison of the US role in the CRS and BEPS. *Globalizations*, *16*(1), 104–119. https://doi.org/10.1080/14747731.2018.1496558

Lips, W., & Cobham, A. (2017). Paradise lost-who will feature on the common EU blacklist of non-cooperative tax jurisdictions? *Open Data for Tax Justice*. https://biblio.ugent.be/publication/8539538/file/8539545

Morel, N., Touzet, C., & Zemmour, M. (2018). Fiscal welfare in Europe: Why should we care and what do we know so far? *Journal of European Social Policy*, *28*(5), 549–560. https://doi.org/10.1177/0958928718802553

Murphy, R. (2003). A proposed international accounting standard, on behalf of the Association for Accountancy and Business Affairs. http://visar.csustan.edu/aaba/ProposedAccstd.pdf

OECD. (2013). Action on base erosion and profit shifting. https://www.oecd.org/ctp/BEPSActionPlan.pdf

Oxfam. (2015). What's the UK's role in fixing the broken international tax system?, *Oxfam blog* by Luke Gibson. https://www.oxfam.org.uk/blogs/2015/10/uk-role-in-fixing-broken-international-tax-system

Pagani, F. (2002). Peer review as a tool for co-operation and change-an analysis of an OECD working method: Feature. *African Security Review*, *11*(4), 15–24. https://doi.org/10.1080/10246029.2002.9628141

PCT. (2018). Platform for collaboration on tax first global conference on taxation and SDGs platform partners' statement at the closing of the conference, 16 February. http://www.un.org/esa/ffd/wp-content/uploads/2018/02/platform-for-collaboration-on-tax-2018_conference-statement.pdf

Picciotto, S. (2012). *Towards unitary taxation of transnational corporations.* Tax Justice Network, pp.1–17.

Piketty, T. (2014). *Capital in the twenty first century.* London: Harvard University Press.

Plümper, T., Troeger, V. E., & Winner, H. (2009). Why is there no race to the bottom in capital taxation? *International Studies Quarterly*, *53*(3), 761–786. https://doi.org/10.1111/j.1468-2478.2009.00555.x

Porter, T. (2003). Technical collaboration and political conflict in the emerging regime for international financial regulation. *Review of International Political Economy*, *10*(3), 520–551.

Rixen, T. (2011). Tax competition and inequality: The case for global tax governance. *Global Governance*, *17*(4), 447–467. https://doi.org/10.1163/19426720-01704004

Ruggie, J. G. (1982). International regimes, transactions, and change: Embedded liberalism in the postwar economic order. *International Organization*, *36*(2), 379–415. https://doi.org/10.1017/S0020818300018993

Saez, E., & Zucman, G. (2019). How would a progressive wealth tax work? Evidence from the economics literature. Unpublished paper. February, 5. https://static1.squarespace.com/static/5a0c602bf43b5594845abb81/t/5d07e45cdac3c8000122fefe/1560798300955/FEBRUARY+2019+How+woulda+progressive+wealth+tax+work.pdf

Schäfer, A. (2006). A new form of governance? Comparing the open method of co-ordination to multilateral surveillance by the IMF and the OECD. *Journal of European Public Policy*, *13*(1), 70–88. https://doi.org/10.1080/13501760500380742

SDG. (2019). Fair tax report by the socialists and democrats group. European Parliament. https://www.socialistsanddemocrats.eu/sites/default/files/2019-01/Fair%20tax%20Brochure%20Final%20EN.pdf

Seabrooke, L., & Wigan, D. (2015). How activists use benchmarks: Reformist and revolutionary benchmarks for global economic justice. *Review of International Studies*, *41*(5), 887–904. https://doi.org/10.1017/S0260210515000376

Seabrooke, L., & Wigan, D. (2016). Powering ideas through expertise: Professionals in global tax battles. *Journal of European Public Policy*, *23*(3), 357–374. https://doi.org/10.1080/13501763.2015.1115536

Sharman, J. C. (2007). Rationalist and constructivist perspectives on reputation. *Political Studies*, *55*(1), 20–37. https://doi.org/10.1111/j.1467-9248.2007.00643.x

Sharman, J. C. (2010). Dysfunctional policy transfer in national tax blacklists. *Governance*, *23*(4), 623–639. https://doi.org/10.1111/j.1468-0491.2010.01501.x

Sikka, P., & Murphy, R. (2015). Unitary taxation: Tax base and the role of accounting. SSRN 2633997.

Swank, D., & Steinmo, S. (2002). The new political economy of taxation in advanced capitalist democracies. *American Journal of Political Science*, *46*, 642–655. https://doi.org/10.2307/3088405

Tax Justice UK. (2019). Understanding how tax systems undermine themselves. http://www.taxjustice.uk/blog/understanding-how-tax-systems-undermine-themselves

Thomson, J. E. (1993). Norms in international relations: A conceptual analysis. *International Journal of Group Tensions*, *23*(1), 67–83.

Underhill, G. R. (2015). The emerging post-crisis financial architecture: The path-dependency of ideational adverse selection. *The British Journal of Politics and International Relations*, *17*(3), 461–493. https://doi.org/10.1111/1467-856X.12056

Van Apeldoorn, L. (2018). BEPS, tax sovereignty and global justice. *Critical Review of International Social and Political Philosophy*, *21*(4), 478–499. https://doi.org/10.1080/13698230.2016.1220149

Zucman, G. (2014). Taxing across borders: Tracking personal wealth and corporate profits. *Journal of Economic Perspectives*, *28*(4), 121–148. doi:10.1257/jep.28.4.121

The IMF, tackling inequality, and post-neoliberal 'reglobalization': the paradoxes of political legitimation within economistic parameters

Ben Clift and Te-Anne Robles

ABSTRACT

In a quest for political legitimacy and traction since the global financial crisis and the Arab Spring, the International Monetary Fund (IMF) has become much more engaged in tackling inequality through its surveillance and other operations. This article analyses the depth and strength of this egalitarian commitment to reorient Fund actions. Notwithstanding shifts in high-level IMF rhetoric, we find that rigidity in the IMF's mind-set and priorities is a major roadblock to substantive transformation. In a fine-grained analysis of Fund surveillance we investigate the conceptualization and operationalization of inequality and social protection as 'macro-critical' issues (essential for growth and stability). We argue that the IMF's political legitimation operates within restrictive economistic parameters that flow from its technocratic compulsions. This paradoxically exacerbates the Fund's legitimacy problems. We explore the Fund's efforts to address the rhetoric-practice gap, but find that the kinds of economists they hire, and the mind-set their models reflect, limit its capacity for tackling inequality.

Introduction

Rising income inequality, a pervasive feature of twenty-first century capitalism, has become increasingly politically salient. One might expect the Bretton Woods institutions to be more part of the problem than part of the solution; yet, in the last decade, the leadership of the International Monetary Fund (IMF) has sought to increase Fund engagement in tackling inequality. The financial crisis raised anew concerns about whether global finance threatens economic and social stability. The Fund, as custodian of the stability of the international monetary system, has sought to enhance its involvement in social protection and inequality questions. Key IMF figures have noted how the merits of neoliberalism had been 'oversold' by the Fund and others. Deputy Director of the IMF Research Department, Jonathan Ostry, and colleagues brought together a range of IMF research and other work to highlight the adverse effects of austerity on inequality, and through that on growth (Ostry et al., 2016). The effects of both fiscal consolidation and capital-account liberalization, they noted, had contributed to rising inequality and jeopardized a durable expansion. The Fund prescriptive discourse consistently links widening inequalities (which, political economy scholars have noted, are often driven by advancing financialization) to the IMF's core mandate of sustaining economic growth and stability. Could the IMF be an agent of reframing actually existing neoliberal globalization? We ask that question here in relation to one aspect of the IMF's engagement surrounding global finance, economic stability and social outcomes more broadly.

The Fund has long sought to reduce poverty. For example, this was central to the discourse on 'high-quality growth' of the former managing director Michel Camdessus in the 1990s (Camdessus, 1998). Many have criticized the IMF's earlier poverty-alleviation remedies as little more than 'Washington Consensus' fare – let free markets reign and a rising tide will (eventually) float all boats. The shift from poverty reduction to a more thoroughgoing and encompassing approach to tackling inequality through a wider array of policy responses was a significant departure. Today's IMF addresses the macroeconomic implications of relative deprivation and sees tackling inequality (including through progressive income tax) as a key macroeconomic component of securing the durable growth and stability at the core of its mandate. In Fund parlance, inequality is now deemed a 'macro-critical social indicator'. This is important because the interpretive framework through which the IMF assesses and evaluates economic policy crucially shapes its views on 'sound' policy which, in turn, informs all its interactions with national authorities.

In this article we explore the scale and strength of this commitment to revisit IMF thinking on inequality and social protection, and consider impediments to Fund reform. Questions have been raised about the disjuncture between a new prescriptive discourse on tackling inequality, on the one hand, and continuity in programme and other IMF practices, on the other. We focus on the somewhat neglected sphere of IMF surveillance, chosen because it is what the Fund spends most of its time doing and is where it dedicates the majority of its resources. Through its multilateral and bilateral surveillance mandate, the Fund works to shape emergent inter-subjective understandings of appropriate economic policy and fiscal and welfare regimes for both borrowing and non-borrowing member countries. Moreover, Fund surveillance shapes other aspects of its operations, including lending programmes. We ask how far, within surveillance activities, the Fund can deliver on its egalitarian commitments. This feeds on debates about change at the IMF (Grabel, 2017) and accusations of 'organised hypocrisy' – the supposed gap between the Fund's words and deeds (Kentikelenis et al., 2016). The Fund, in becoming a vocal champion of tackling inequality, risks opening up new legitimacy gaps analogous to those exposed by mission creep following the East Asian financial crisis (Best, 2007). Focusing on IMF surveillance, the new analytical insights and fresh empirical evidence presented here offer a pragmatic prognosis of the scope for the IMF to augur a less inequality-riven, perhaps 'post-neoliberal', form of 'reglobalization'.

We explore the Fund's efforts to address the rhetoric-practice gap that it has itself recognized by analysing key IMF and Independent Evaluation Office (IEO)[1] documents, released over the period 2017–2019, on operationalizing social protection in surveillance. Our argument is that the IMF's quest for political legitimation in part explains efforts to reorient its prescriptive discourse towards more progressive, egalitarian territory. Yet efforts to operationalize IMF concerns for inequality and social protection are crucially mediated by the Fund's organizational culture and intellectual parameters. Furthermore, the Fund is not a monolithic organization: some key IMF actors and certain operational divisions are more attuned to, and find it easier to adopt, the inequality agenda than others. The Fund finds articulating a 'tackling inequality' vision at the level of broad prescriptive discourse straightforward. However, at desk level and in operational terms, the IMF's mind-set, intellectual culture and organizational characteristics mean it is harder to give life to these insights. We question how 'organised' any hypocrisy is, finding varied dynamics and voices in play within a differentiated institution (Chwieroth, 2010; Clift, 2018; Kaya & Reay, 2019). For all this internal diversity, some overarching institutional characteristics curtail the IMF's egalitarian inclinations. The IMF's technocratic compulsions operate in ways that paradoxically exacerbate the IMF's legitimacy problems. Its reorientation operates within restrictive economistic parameters that undermine policy efficacy, reflecting orthodox economic ideas deeply imbued in the Fund's mind-set. The Fund would need to pursue its auto-critique of neoliberalism much further, alter its core conception of technical authority and significantly change the way this is used in the conduct of global economic governance, *if* it ever sought to deliver fully on the 'post-neoliberal reglobalization' envisaged in this Special Issue.

Context and back story – inequality's march to macro-criticality

When the Arab Spring erupted, the IMF felt wrong-footed by events because its bilateral surveillance had failed to detect the turmoil brewing within the affected political economies. Its overriding focus on inflation and the balance of payments had overlooked simmering tensions linked to inequalities of wealth and power within these societies. Amidst the surge to prominence of groups like 'Occupy Wall Street', Dominique Strauss-Kahn (hereafter DSK), then Managing Director, wanted to end the IMF's marginalization from debates about globalization and inequality. When the conversation turned to how the IMF could become more engaged, Jonathan Ostry, who was by chance deputizing for the then IMF Chief Economist Olivier Blanchard at a meeting with DSK, introduced his recent work on inequality and the duration of growth spells. Ostry 'made the point [to DSK] that a core objective of the Fund is to come up with policy advice that underpins macro-financial stability. So if we can show that avoiding excessive inequality is in fact essential for strong, healthy and sustainable growth (which I believe the research I have been engaged in does show), then indeed there is a direct link between issues of inequality and distribution and issues that lie at the core of the IMF's mandate' (Interview with Ostry, Washington DC, June 2013).

This new emphasis was part of a wider concern about the distributive effects of macroeconomic policies. As Ostry noted in this interview, 'the period of great moderation was only great for a small portion of the population, and so it was not delivering broad-based benefits (as seen for example in the stagnation of median wages in a number of countries)'. Fiscal policies can be an important spur to growth, 'because avoiding excessive levels of inequality can actually help economies grow more strongly and more sustainability'. Therefore, 'fiscal redistribution, unless you do it in an extreme fashion, can bring about both greater equality and stronger, healthier growth. The efficiency losses from redistributive fiscal policies, moreover, appear to be small, unless redistribution is extreme' (Interview with Ostry, Washington DC, June 2013). Interest in the growth/inequality linkage blossomed, then, in the early 2010s as a way to harness intervention in debates about inequality to the Fund's core mandate.

Soon after, the notion of limiting inequality as macro-critical (that is, essential to economic stability and growth) was born. This was an important turning point for the Fund. But to what extent was the change embraced throughout such a large and complex organization? What about the obstacle potentially posed by an economics profession historically disinclined to focus on such questions? As Ostry (Interview with Ostry, Washington DC, June 2013) himself observed of his efforts to explore the macroeconomics of inequality, 'it has been much harder to get that into the mainstream'.

The IMF on inequality – 'organised hypocrisy'?

Assessments of the IMF's rhetoric-practice gap identify varying degrees of continuity and change. For instance, a focus on the inclusion of social-spending targets in Fund lending arrangements in 2009 gives the impression of quick operational change. In this instance, tracing specific processes, such as the legislative mandate passed by the United States Congress, alignment with the Fund leadership's preferences and staff compliance, suggests that the IMF's hierarchical structure actually served to hasten top-down reform (Clegg, 2014). However, the mere inclusion of hard-to-implement and mostly non-binding social spending targets is a problematic indicator of substantive Fund operational reform. Such a narrow focus on social-spending targets neglects the broader discursive shift presented by IMF management. Kentikelenis et al. (2016) cast a wider net, analysing understandings of policy space contained in Fund loan agreements between 1985 and 2014. They find that IMF programmes failed to incorporate the changes advocated in institutional rhetoric. Instead, the authors note a continuing practice of layering cosmetic rhetorical and operational reforms, a process they term 'organised hypocrisy'.

In their analysis of paradigmatic shifts in the IMF's operationalization of the 'Washington Consensus', Kaya and Reay identify 'fragmented change', whereby shifts occur 'at different speeds, at the same and/or different times, via different organisational dynamics' (Kaya & Reay, 2019, p. 391). These insights into differentiated organizational dynamics helpfully move beyond binary change vs. continuity debates, admitting the necessary complexity to analysing the IMF's unique yet contentious role in global economic governance.

For their part, Nunn and White emphasize the Fund's strategic direction, exploring the emergence of a 'new global politics of inequality' (Nunn & White, forthcoming) and a turn to 'progressive neoliberalism' (Fraser, 2017) in IMF operations. Key drivers are seen to be increasing anxieties about risk management and defending global market integration against various destabilizing threats. From this perspective, therefore, growing IMF concern about narrowing inequalities and gender gaps (Nunn & Price, 2019) may be less about abandoning neoliberalism and more about containing negative effects on the growth and stability of global markets.

The rhetoric-practice gap is also exacerbated by the IMF's strategic goal of bolstering its legitimacy and technical authority to act as the custodian of global stability. This conditions how the Fund thinks about policy issues, accentuating the appeal to supposedly apolitical and 'scientific' economic expertise and models that pervades the IMF's internal culture (Clift, 2018, 2019). This reflects the IMF's longstanding technocratic tendency towards depoliticization and economization (Boas & McNeill, 2004). Others have highlighted the effects of such economization. Kranke and Yarrow note the watering-down of a potentially radical agenda (on macroprudential policy and systemic risk) through the kind of economistic analysis used in its take-up by the Fund (Kranke & Yarrow, 2019). Similarly, Farnsworth and Irving note the IMF's 'relegation of social policy to its economic uses' (Farnsworth & Irving, 2018, p. 135). The desire to remain camped on familiar economistic ground so as to enhance its technical authority helps explain why the IMF's operationalization of inequality as macro-critical takes the form it does.

The challenges of the widening breadth and limited depth of IMF operational involvement in inequality and social spending reveals anew the tensions between technocratic compulsions and legitimacy pressures, similar to those identified with respect to the Fund's Poverty Reduction Strategy Papers (Momani, 2008). The claims mentioned earlier of Kentikelenis, Stubbs and King about the institutionalization of 'organised hypocrisy' unavoidably impart a coherence and consistency to the Fund as an organization. Yet this jars with other studies that emphasize incoherence (Grabel, 2017), inconsistency (Momani & Hibben, 2018) or fragmentation (Kaya & Reay, 2019). Grabel notes that 'the rhetoric-research-practice gap reflects something more than public relations imperatives', revealing 'increasing contestation and even confusion within the Fund' (Grabel, 2017, p. 20). Nunn and White (2017) echo this, referring to the Fund's struggle to navigate external legitimation strategies in the face of internal institutional barriers. Tracing the operationalization of social spending's macro-criticality offers fresh insight into the sources of these inconsistencies. Key among them is lack of clarity amongst IMF staff about what treating inequality as macro-critical actually entails in practice.

All these studies, in their different ways, highlight internal tensions that are both intellectual and institutional and show how these compounded external pressures facing the Fund, particularly following the 2008 crash. Our account adds to Kaya and Reay's nuanced picture of different organizational dynamics at work in the IMF. We foreground the particular problem of seeking political legitimation within economistic parameters and highlight the legitimacy gaps it promotes. This offers a new twist on what Best calls the 'paradigm dilemma' (Best, 2007, p. 481) when the IMF moves outside its neoclassical economics home range to justify its actions. The technocratic, economistic approach delivers a form of scientific legitimacy, but limits the efficacy of policy initiatives. The Fund perceives macroeconomic models as a source of objectivity and even-handedness that depoliticize IMF actions (Clift 2019). Yet the IMF is continually surprised by events outside the parameters of its models, such as the East Asian financial crisis and the Arab Spring. Furthermore, in realms (like tackling inequality) that are underexplored in mainstream economics, the IMF lacks the requisite models and analytical tools to underpin its surveillance.

Prioritizing social spending and social protection within IMF surveillance

Central to previous IMF Managing Director Christine Lagarde's push for 'a new multilateralism' (Lagarde, 2019b) was her clarion call to make social spending 'a core component of the social contract needed to fulfil the missions [of the IMF]' (Lagarde, 2019a). Yet such declarations have still to make a substantial difference in IMF operations. The Fund sought to address this rhetoric-practice gap through a series of guidance notes and strategic frameworks. These reveal a more circumspect tone. Lagarde's statement that, 'in all our programmes, protecting the poor and vulnerable is now, and will continue to be, a core objective' was qualified significantly: 'in the real world, the best of intentions run up against the firmest budget constraints' (Lagarde, 2019a).

The IMF's 'real world' after the global financial crisis was characterized by reduced fiscal space and increased risks and spillovers. Following post-crisis criticisms, the IMF sharpened its analysis of spillovers and macro-financial linkages. The 2012 Integrated Surveillance Decision expanded the coverage of Article IV consultations to all potential and actual spillovers from a member country's domestic policies to the effective operation of the international monetary system (IMF, 2013b). Having underscored the need for policymakers to be mindful of the external implications of their domestic policy choices, Fund surveillance gradually specified the scope for Article IV consultations: 'issues of growth, job creation, and income distribution need to be considered to the extent that they have a bearing on domestic and balance of payments stability' (IMF, 2013a, p. 6). Its definition of macro-criticality remained vague: 'if it affects, or has the potential to affect, domestic or external stability, or global stability' (IMF, 2015, p. 36).

Mindful, perhaps, of well-versed concerns about IMF mission creep, the IMF emphasized that *selectivity is critical* (IMF, 2015, p. 5, emphasis in original) in this broader approach to surveillance. Staff 'should exercise judgment in selecting issues for in depth coverage, and take a risk-based approach, leveraging the expertise of functional departments and other institutions' (IMF, 2015, p. 7). Together with Fund expertise and membership buy-in, the principle of macro-criticality became the main criterion for identifying operational priorities. This potentially opens the door to focus more on inequality and social protection, since the Fund deems these 'macro-critical'. Yet the limits of Fund expertise in these realms suggested otherwise. Furthermore, the shadow of more traditional Fund concerns for external and fiscal sustainability always looms large. Fund operational discussion foregrounds the costs of social protection and notes 'a guiding principle' of 'efficient redistributive policies that do not compromise macroeconomic stability and growth' (IMF, 2018c, p. 12). Thus *how* Fund surveillance missions are selective in the realms of inequality means that social protection is seen narrowly as a cost, rather than a public good.

The paper *How to Operationalise Gender Issues in Country Work* (IMF, 2018b) makes equality 'macro-critical' by linking macroeconomic stability and gender equality. Assessed primarily through female labour force participation, this can be macro-critical through three channels, namely: (i) income inequality; (ii) output and productivity; and (iii) economic resilience. Hence, widening the IMF's operational agenda is justified in an overtly social tenor; yet applying the principle of macro-criticality is still done in a restrictive, fiscal sustainability-centred manner. The case of social protection illustrates how treating inequality as macro-critical creates more confusion than clarity in setting the boundaries of IMF operations. Expanding the scope of Fund surveillance to encompass social protection and tackling inequality is hamstrung by the (relative lack of) availability of internal expertise. Indeed, uncertainty amongst Fund staff about how to operationalize commitments to social protection crucially limits progress.

How the IMF understands social protection

In *The IMF and Social Protection,* social protection is considered central to macroeconomic stability, 'since maintaining social and political support for sustainable macroeconomic policies can depend crucially on avoiding excessive stress on vulnerable groups' (IEO, 2017, p. 3). The policy paper *A Strategy for IMF Engagement in Social Spending* (IMF, 2019a) (which was a response to the IEO report's recommendations) adopts for operational purposes a somewhat constricted view of social protection. The IMF's narrow interpretation comprises education and health spending, as well as social insurance and social assistance programmes, but excludes policies related to long-term poverty reduction, development, job creation and labour-force participation. IMF work specifies the channels through which social spending can be macro-critical, namely, fiscal sustainability, spending adequacy and spending efficiency. Of these, the criterion of spending adequacy is potentially contentious since 'spending adequacy in a specific country context may depend on a wide range of historical, political, and social factors' (IMF, 2019a, p. 24). Given the Fund's limited basis for building in-house expertise, staff economists and their existing analytical frameworks will likely still be ill-equipped, even with a narrower framework for social-spending macro-criticality.

The Fund notes that 'macro-criticality is a necessary but not sufficient condition' (IMF, 2019a, p. 22) for inclusion in IMF surveillance, as certain issues fall outside its domain of expertise. The scarcity of prior Fund expertise on inequality affects how the institution approaches the selectivity necessitated by perennial limits on resources. Building up fresh in-house expertise will only be considered if 'a critical mass of members finds a particular structural issue to be of macro-critical importance' (IMF, 2019a, p. 22). Guidance on breadth and depth of engagement also tasks staff with identifying analytical and data gaps and approaching external development partners for inputs. Yet relying on internal cognitive filters (e.g. a shared predilection for prioritizing fiscal sustainability) before seeking external expertise risks a narrow reading of what constitute the IMF's social protection 'analytical and data gaps'. Furthermore, the Fiscal Affairs Department is tasked with leading the internal coordination and collaboration with external experts, once again favouring a particular fiscal sustainability lens. These tensions and dissonances, which include the contested boundaries of what constitutes social protection, affect the depth and scope of IMF social and egalitarian involvement.

Social spending in the surveillance agenda

Despite increased IMF involvement in social spending, social protection is largely absent from discussions of the Fund's future surveillance priorities. Addressing the application of the principle of macro-criticality and the widening scope of surveillance, the IMF launched a number of macrostructural pilot initiatives to strengthen its analytical work on inequality, gender and climate change. While these facilitated better integration of emerging macro-critical issues within macroeconomic analysis, they unearthed blind spots and knowledge gaps, with the Fund arguing at one point that 'the analytical basis for assessing key structural gaps, reform pay-offs and costs, as well as sequencing and packaging need to be further developed' (IMF, 2018d, p. 20). This was especially true for low-income developing countries and small emerging economies. The familiar refrain emphasized selectivity and prioritization based on the IMF's technical comparative advantage and existing expertise.

The 2019 Financial Surveillance Report paid little attention to social protection, but underlined the 'difficult trade-offs' that have emerged with the massive expansion in the Fund's surveillance operations (IEO, 2019, p. 1). Given its limited resources and expertise, 'the IMF cannot be expected to be at the cutting edge on all issues'. Clear priority is afforded to 'macrofinancial linkages and cross-border spillovers', along with enhancing 'financial expertise among its staff' to 'strengthen financial and macrofinancial surveillance' (IEO, 2019, p. 3). Future Fund social-protection surveillance 'will likely be anchored in a mindset of risk management' (Lagarde, 2019b, p. 7), rather than one driven by Lagarde's 'social contract' to ensure that social spending protects the poor and vulnerable. Reflecting these limited ambitions, the Fund envisages only minor resource implications resulting from its social protection strategy (IMF, 2019a).

The politics of and impediments to reform

There are, as Grabel points out, limits to how much coherence and consistency, as well as how much substantive change, we should expect from a large, complex, bureaucratic, international institution like the Fund (Grabel, 2017, ch. 5). Nevertheless, the Fund is a deeply hierarchical organization and it is surprising that, with so much political capital invested in tackling inequality from on high, progress has been modest. This raises the spectre of fresh 'legitimacy gaps' (Best, 2007; Seabrooke, 2007). Our explanation centres on the structure of the organization, but also on the mind-set of the foot soldiers, as well as the Fund's senior figures.

As proponents of what Grabel (2017) has termed the 'continuity thesis' have highlighted, as a large, bureaucratic, international institution with well-entrenched standard operating procedures, as well as low and slow staff turnover, the Fund finds it difficult to effect rapid change. Its bureaucratic culture is one important source of stasis (Lütz et al., 2019). Olivier Blanchard, when reflecting on attempting to alter the centre of gravity of Fund thinking [albeit not specifically on inequality] during his time as Chief Economist, made reference to the familiar 'supertanker analogy', adding 'I think of myself as a tugboat … if it tries to pull a supertanker with too much angle the chain will break', 'so you have to choose your angle and you have to admit that it is going to take a long time' (Interview with Blanchard, Washington, DC, June 2013).

The multilateral nature of the institution and its internal power relations create further impediments to thoroughgoing reform of its approach to inequality. The Fund's norm of 'even-handed' treatment of its very diverse membership, being seen to treat each in a uniform manner, adds to the difficulties of changing how the Fund 'gets done'. Procedurally, in order to sustain 'throughput legitimacy' of Fund evaluation processes (Scharpf, 1999; Schmidt, 2013), the IMF favours economic modelling as the mechanism for uniformity of treatment of different members (Clift 2019). By and large, however, Fund models have not been altered or adapted to incorporate the newfound inequality concerns. Therefore the Fund lacks some of the mechanisms it would normally deploy to address inequality issues in an even-handed manner.

Similarly, the Fund attaches importance to policy templates, operational guidance notes and strategic frameworks that it can apply in a consistent manner. Yet in their construction these often have differing policy implications for different kinds of countries. Granted, consideration of specific country circumstances will lead to variations in policy recommendations; however, the issue here concerns blanket approaches towards policy capacity. For example, the Fund's standard approach favours allowing the free play of 'automatic stabilizers' (e.g. unemployment insurance) to deliver social protection and economic stabilization during a downturn. That presumes the existence of a social policy infrastructure characteristic of advanced welfare states in the global North, notably in Europe. In many other countries, these automatic stabilizers are much less developed or non-existent. The Fund's views on automatic stabilizers are not readily applicable in the global South. Such biases built into IMF policy frameworks can mean that adopting a 'consistent' position (as here on automatic stabilizers) has widely divergent policy and equity implications across the Fund's diverse membership.

Another impediment to even-handed treatment relates to the Fund's innate and congenital concern for fiscal sustainability. One of its primary functions is to promote stability and secure repayment of its loans. As a consequence, a concern for member-states' fiscal sustainability is hard-wired into the IMF's *modus operandi*. Social and other spending commitments have always raised questions about how affordable, well-directed and temporary they are. What the Fund calls 'political economy' concerns (about rent-seeking behaviour) are also never far away. The bottom line is that the Fund approaches differently the policy capacities (for efficient spending and effective policy implementation) of advanced economies compared to emerging economies. New policy commitments in costly areas of social policy swiftly raise questions about fiscal sustainability, and these questions are historically somewhat more starkly posed for emerging market economies. One Fund insider likened the uncertainty surrounding a country coming up against its borrowing limits as comparable to walking in the fog close to the water's edge. In such a scenario, it is crucial whether one is on a beach or at the top of a cliff! The IMF's deficit-bias concerns mean that, especially for lower-income countries, the Fund always presumes this takes place on top of a cliff, such that that country's fiscal credibility could fall off at any moment with disastrous consequences. The Fund's staff are ever mindful that governments can apparently enjoy fiscal credibility right up until the point when it evaporates in an instant and the government finds itself cut off from market finance.

A further significant impediment is the nature of the IMF staff's educational background and their similar training, combined with the Fund's recruitment practices. The mind-set of Fund economists operating at desk level in approaching questions of social protection and tackling inequality is crucially important. Momani identifies the Fund's 'selective recruitment of conservative macroeconomists' (Momani, 2010, p. 31; see also Momani, 2005, 2007, and Chwieroth, 2007). As an institution staffed by economics PhDs trained at a modest number of leading mainstream economics departments, primarily in the United States and (to a lesser extent) Europe, Momani denotes 'the Fund's economic paradigm' as a singular intellectual edifice (Momani, 2005, p. 183). Similarly, Nelson underlines the training of most IMF economists at 'a handful of highly ranked American economics departments that serve as incubators for neoliberal ideas' (Nelson, 2014, p. 309). Other studies unearth somewhat greater variety in IMF economic thinking (Ban, 2015; Chwieroth, 2010), whilst reaffirming the tendency to recruit exclusively mainstream economists.

This prior training in important respects sets the intellectual parameters of the Fund's thinking. The disciplinary norms, pre-dispositions and pre-suppositions of mainstream macroeconomics shape the interpretive framework through which the IMF assesses and evaluates 'sound' policy. There have been numerous critiques that Fund recruitment delivers a lack of diversity in terms of gender, region and academic background (Momani, 2005, 2010; Momani & Hibben, 2018; Vetterlein, 2010). Limited staff diversity in educational background and disciplinary training was identified as an important cause of Fund failings in the response to earlier crises (Crow et al., 1999, pp. 71–72; IEO, 2003). The need to broaden the IMF staff's educational background and skill-mix to tackle 'groupthink' was re-emphasized following the 2008–2009 crash (IEO, 2011, pp. 1, 17, 21, 42, 45). After belt-tightening, including staff layoffs in 2006–2007, the Fund's revival and re-injection of Funds in 2009 saw increased hiring. This heralded a new wave of recruits, some more open to the new thinking being championed within the post-crash Fund. As Clift (2018, p. 9) puts it, 'Strauss-Kahn and Blanchard, along with other like-minded individuals recruited or promoted to senior positions, strengthened the market-sceptical, Keynesian "subculture" within the Fund' (see also Ban, 2015; Clift, 2019; Momani & Hibben, 2018). As a result, there has been some limited broadening of the 'gene pool', with Fund economists drawn from a slightly wider range of North American and European universities, including some not-so-conservative economics departments.

However, given the slow pace of change and low staff-turnover, these newer recruits co-exist with what Momani and Hibben term a 'more conservative ideological and organizational residue of three decades of the Washington Consensus paradigm' (Momani & Hibben, 2018, p. 24). Even with a slightly more diverse group of (still mainstream) macroeconomists, disciplinary strictures were not really escaped. The Fund still overwhelmingly hires macroeconomists, who bring a particular mind-set to engaging with social and equality issues. The IEO notes that 'social protection issues', when addressed by the Fund, 'generally had a macroeconomic rather than a social focus' (IEO, 2017, p. 18). Scholars also bemoan the Fund's ongoing narrowly economistic conception of social policy, notwithstanding its 'greater mention of concerns for social justice' (Farnsworth & Irving, 2018, pp. 124–127, 135). Understanding 'stability' through the lens of the Fund's mind-set and its extant expertise means 'macro-critical' issues, such as inequality, will necessarily be reflected in IMF operations as a matter of fiscal sustainability. Failure to break free from this analytical straitjacket significantly limits the depth and effectiveness of Fund social-protection and tackling-inequality operations.

Tackling inequality within economistic parameters

This sedimentation of institutional practices and intellectual orientation has hindered substantive Fund reform on social protection. In its review of operational guidelines, the IMF invoked the centrality of technical expertise and resource limitations to delimit what it can and cannot do on social protection. Mistakenly dismissing this as 'organised hypocrisy' minimizes the genuine uncertainty among Fund economists about what exactly the macro-critical dimensions of inequality and social protection entail in operational terms. Furthermore, viewing the Fund's travails in operationalizing its inequality concerns as a manifestation of ongoing 'productive incoherence' (Grabel, 2017) underplays the strategic rationale driving the IMF's choice to foreground its technocratic authority. The IMF's narrow economistic approach is how the Fund resolves (albeit problematically) the dilemma of simultaneously highlighting its commitment to social protection and retreating from dedicating the necessary resources to support this commitment effectively in the operational sphere.

To understand this legitimacy dilemma, we need to consider key characteristics of the academic macroeconomics from which the IMF reproduces itself and draws its genetic material. The extremely limited displacement of work on inequality within mainstream economics presents problems. Fund claims to technical and scientific expertise are integral to its intellectual authority and scientific culture. They rest on corroborating its economic policy analysis with reference to eminent, highly respected economists and state-of-the-art macroeconomics. Yet questions about inequality and unequal relationships of power and wealth are not ones macroeconomists are in the habit of asking. Mainstream economists absolve themselves from normative comment on distributional concerns via the convenient fiction that distributional questions are best 'left to the market'. James Galbraith has colourfully bemoaned the complete absence of inequality research, 'ghettoized' and excluded from mainstream macroeconomics and leading journals. He writes: 'if your interest is in the global macroeconomics of inequality – in the personal or household distribution or pay structures considered over time and across continents and countries, you are what is known in the technical literature as shit-out-of-luck' (Galbraith, 2019, p. 1).

It follows, firstly, that PhDs from leading institutions (the gene pool from which the IMF routinely recruits) will not have focused on these issues; and, secondly, that the leading macroeconomics journals will not offer models or insights to help the Fund in tackling inequality through macroeconomic policy. This in turn limits the intellectual and 'scientific' authority behind its policy propositions. On what evidential basis within macroeconomics can Fund missions advance the case for any particular per cent additional spending on social protection, or specific taxation changes aimed at tackling inequality? The IMF can readily exalt tackling inequality in its broad prescriptive discourse, but finds it much more challenging operationally to advise on specific minimum thresholds (for example) for social spending. This relates to both the constitutional niceties of its relations with member-states (respecting their sovereignty) and the marginality of inequality issues within mainstream economics. This creates difficulties in making the economic case in favour of specific policies that the IMF would normally deem necessary. The inequality agenda thus raises to new levels tensions between the Fund's technocratic compulsions and its legitimacy pressures. In substance, the IMF remains centred on its rigid technocratic orientation which thereby bolsters its authority to act as an arbiter of sound policy and custodian of economic stability. This also allows it to maintain only a narrow and shallow engagement in areas (such as inequality) beyond its established areas of expertise. However, the Fund has thus far failed to recognize fully the difficulties underlying the paradox of seeking political legitimation within these economistic parameters.

A survey of mid-level IMF economists supports the view that their training does not equip them to tackle social issues. While there is a strong consensus on the importance of staff involvement in social protection, only roughly 50 per cent felt that they were given clear guidance on how exactly this should be carried out. This problem is amplified by the lack of staff expertise: less than half of the staff surveyed felt that their mission-team's level of expertise was fair (i.e. at least one team member had some expertise) and over a quarter indicated that no one in their team had any expertise (Wojnilower & Monasteski, 2017, p. 2). The IMF acknowledges this and relies to a large extent on external development partners, especially the World Bank (Kranke, 2019; Park & Vetterlein, 2010; Vetterlein, 2010). Yet collaboration with the World Bank runs the risk of exacerbating groupthink, as the Fund recognizes that working with the Bank is easier due to their similar approaches towards targeted social protection (IEO, 2019). On the other hand, collaboration with other major development partners, such as the United Nations and the International Labour Organisation, is patchy; only 13 per cent of staff surveyed indicated that their engagement with these institutions was highly effective (Wojnilower & Monasteski, 2017, p. 13).

This survey also underscores how the boundaries of Fund engagement in social protection are contested, including within the Fund. There is striking polarization amongst Fund staff on involvement beyond analysing the fiscal cost of social protection. For instance, regarding improving social protection policies, one fifth of staff feels that either that the IMF should always (21 per cent) or never (20 per cent) be involved (Wojnilower & Monasteski, 2017, p. 21). Outside the Fund, external stakeholders have critiqued the IMF's analytical frameworks and its operationalization of inequality and social protection as macro-critical. A specific concern is how it is used to justify the Fund's preference for targeted social benefits and, more broadly, the failure to account for long-term growth effects and social and distributional costs (Wojnilower, 2017). On the ground, the reality of how the Fund's staff routinely operate jars with the IMF management view of social protection not as a cost but rather as an investment for public well-being (Lagarde, 2019a).

With regard to how social protection raises questions about even-handedness, views on the adequacy of social protection's integration into IMF analysis differ depending on the respondent's department area. The assessment was most positive among those working on advanced economies (56 per cent) and lowest among those covering low-income countries (34 per cent) and African countries (35 per cent), arguably the areas where social protection is more pressing as a problem (Wojnilower & Monasteski, 2017, p. 19). These limits to operational guidance and technical expertise affect staff perceptions of what the IMF's role in social protection should be.

These findings reveal the footprints of the paradox of legitimacy that the Fund faces in tackling inequality and social-protection policy issues. The kind of expert legitimacy to which the Fund normally has recourse is limited in this sphere because mainstream economics does not address inequality issues either extensively or effectively. This 'narrowness of the economic paradigm', as identified by Best (2007, p. 484), raises an important question: on what intellectual authority can the Fund rest its actions in this new sphere of activity?

Given these characteristics of the economics profession, the Fund would need to recruit from a wider range of more heterodox economists – and indeed non-economists – to develop greater scientific expertise in these policy areas. Momani and Hibben call for a 'shift in staff make-up that would diversify its expertise and conceptions of successful economic policy' (Momani & Hibben, 2018, p. 29) in order to bolster IMF legitimacy (see also Momani, 2010; Park & Vetterlein, 2010). Recruitment diversity was also taken up by Christine Lagarde during her bid to become Managing Director (Lagarde, 2011). Yet diversity of Fund hiring practices remains within confined limits – with some progress on gender, race and region. In terms of academic background, however, the Fund largely remains an economic monoculture. The Fund does not hire non-mainstream economists, be they post-Keynesian, feminist, Austrian, or other genres within the field. Its staff remains largely cut from the same cloth, and IMF thinking and actions on tackling inequality and social protection suffer as a result.

Conclusion

The IMF has acquired a reputation as an archetypal 'Washington Consensus' institution, almost the last place wherein one might expect to find critique of the neoliberal order. Yet, as we have shown in relation to inequality, the IMF has demonstrated scope to shift the boundaries of what constitutes 'legitimate' policy and to amend how it interprets and enacts its mandate. The Fund now sees tackling inequality as an appropriate goal for macroeconomic policy. This matters because those who can make authoritative knowledge claims, such as the Fund, enjoy a privileged position within the intersubjective process of constructing economic rectitude.

Much progress was made under Lagarde's leadership. New Managing Director Kristalina Georgieva's curtain-raiser speech espoused the idea of 'inclusive growth' and underlined the link between reducing inequality and securing durable growth. She made mention of 'reducing excessive inequality', but it was not centre-stage, nor top-priority (Georgieva, 2019). Extant economistic approaches to technical authority remain, with no indication that the IMF's auto-critique of neoliberalism will be pursued far enough to resolve the paradox at the heart of its approach to tackling inequality. Economization is a handy tool that the IMF can deploy to avoid politicization and bolster technocratic authority. In this sense, the incoherence produced by the paradox of political legitimation within economistic parameters is neither decentralized nor evolutionary (Grabel, 2017) and reflects no more than short-sighted strategic priorities.

Drilling down into how the Fund operationalizes tackling inequality and social protection in its surveillance work highlights the tensions and contested boundaries of its new-found view of inequality as macro-critical. The confusion and lack of consensus at the Fund on the coverage and effectiveness of its social-protection work has fuelled unmet expectations, further aggravated by the high-level rhetoric generally deployed (IEO, 2017). The kind of organization the Fund is, the kinds of economists it hires and the kind of mind-set their models reflect all limit the IMF's capacity for tackling inequality. The Fund's preoccupation with asserting its legitimacy by foregrounding its particular brand of technocratic economic expertise strips the IMF's inequality agenda of its transformative potential.

In navigating this multitude of conflicting internal and external tensions, the Fund leverages limited staff expertise and the consequent uncertainty surrounding macro-criticality to justify both widening institutional involvement and limited operational reform. In short, for mainstream economists and many Fund staff, and in contrast to Lagarde's vision for making social spending a 'core component' of the 'social contract needed to fulfil' IMF missions (Lagarde, 2019a), social spending is viewed straightforwardly as a cost, not an investment. Concerns about deficit bias and the efficacy of fiscal institutions limit Fund enthusiasm for redistribution or raised social spending. A narrow focus on targeted and means-tested social protection crowds out concern for the broader societal and public goods that a generous welfare settlement can provide.

The lens of existing Fund expertise means 'macro-critical' issues such as inequality will necessarily be reflected in IMF operations as a matter of fiscal sustainability, rather than part of a 'social contract' to deliver inclusive growth. Despite recognized analytical and knowledge gaps, Fund discussions of future surveillance priorities indicate that resources and internal expertise will be shifted *away* from social protection. More importantly, the analytical framework remains embedded in the IMF's traditional areas of technical expertise and thus falls short of addressing the shortcomings identified by both Fund staff and external stakeholders. The blinkers imposed by seeking political legitimation within these economistic parameters impose significant limits on the depth and effectiveness of Fund operations in tackling inequality and social protection.

Taking the foregrounding of technical expertise as operationally non-negotiable for the IMF, there is room to build expertise in ways that better support concerns with macro-critical inequality. The risk-management mind-set needs to be broadened, not overturned. Resource constraints will obviously impose limitations, but dedicating more IMF resources to building non-macroeconomic financial expertise could secure greater political legitimacy and reduce the persistent rhetoric-practice gap.

More fundamentally, perhaps it is time to reconsider the grounds on which technical authority is built in the conduct of global economic governance. IMF operationalization of social protection reveals three problematic premises:

(1) That technical expertise on its current narrow basis should be a primary criterion for asserting authority in global governance;
(2) That the intellectual cohesion and technical sophistication valued by proponents of mainstream macroeconomics serve as the best basis for productive policy dialogue;
(3) That the goals of objectivity and even-handedness can only be realized through rigid economization.

None of these assumptions constitute a secure basis on which to addresses the tensions, paradoxes and legitimacy shortfalls arising from the Fund's foray into tackling inequality. None escapes the pathology of political legitimation within economistic parameters outlined in this article.

The political conditions for such a reconsideration are not propitious. Deeper Fund involvement in social protection will only be considered if deemed necessary by 'a critical mass' (IEO, 2017, p. 7) of member countries. Given significant variations in country authorities' views on the effectiveness of IMF programmes on social spending (IEO, 2017), and given the regressive taxation agenda of the Trump administration in the United States amongst others, arriving at a consensus will be extremely difficult. With Trump and other populists cutting taxes on the rich whilst pushing back against 'globalism', these are inauspicious conditions for more egalitarian activism from the Fund. To be fair, the IMF has not held back in its critique of US social spending and fiscal policy (IMF, 2016, 2018a). The Trump administration's combative response contrasts with the more accommodating tone formerly adopted under President Obama. US Executive Directors stressed their strong disagreement with the Fund's assessment of US fiscal policies (Claver-Carone & Vivitsky, 2018).

Yet, even if global political conditions were more conducive and even if the kinds of internal IMF recruitment and practice changes outlined here were implemented, it is still not clear that the IMF could be an effective agent of greater equality. There remain real questions as to whether an institution like the Fund can tackle inherently political issues, such as tackling equality, without instrumentalizing them into something that can be addressed through an economic lens (Best, 2014). Indeed, even amongst those who have been most vocal in their criticisms, the demand for more substantive internal reform is relatively muted. Instead, feedback from academics, civil society organizations and other international development institutions indicates a preference that the Fund returns to the backseat on social-spending issues (Mombrial & Feher, 2019, p. 13). If the Fund wants to maintain and build further its legitimacy as a key actor in global economic governance, then arguably it cannot afford to continue to seek political legitimation within economistic parameters.

Note

1. The IEO provides independent assessments of various aspects of IMF operations. While it reports to the Executive Board, the IEO is independent of the IMF management.

Acknowledgements

Te-Anne Robles would like to thank the University of Edinburgh's Institute for Advanced Studies in the Humanities for the financial support provided during the writing of this article. The authors would particularly like to thank Jack Copley for helpful comments.

Disclosure statement

No potential conflict of interest was reported by the author(s).

Funding

This work was supported by Leverhulme Trust: [grant number MRF-2017-063].

ORCID

Ben Clift http://orcid.org/0000-0001-6983-5768

References

Ban, C. (2015). Austerity versus stimulus? Understanding fiscal policy change at the International Monetary Fund since the great recession. *Governance*, *28*(2), 167–183. https://doi.org/10.1111/gove.12099

Best, J. (2007). Legitimacy dilemmas: The IMF's pursuit of country ownership. *Third World Quarterly*, *28*(3), 469–488. https://doi.org/10.1080/01436590701192231

Best, J. (2014). *Governing failure: Provisional expertise and the transformation of global development finance*. Cambridge University Press.

Boas, M., & McNeill, D. (Eds.). (2004). *Global institutions and development: Framing the world?* Routledge.

Camdessus, M. (1998). *Income distribution and sustainable growth: The perspective from the IMF at fifty*. MIT Press.

Chwieroth, J. M. (2007). Neoliberal economists and capital account liberalization in emerging markets. *International Organization*, *61*(2), 443–463. https://doi.org/10.1017/S0020818307070154

Chwieroth, J. M. (2010). *Capital ideas: The IMF and the rise of financial liberalization*. Princeton University Press.

Claver-Carone, M., & Vivitsky, S. (2018). *Statement by the Executive Director for United States – 2018 Article IV consultation* (IMF Country Report No. 18/207). International Monetary Fund. https://www.imf.org/~/media/Files/Publications/CR/2018/cr18207.ashx

Clegg, L. (2014). Social spending targets in IMF concessional lending: US domestic politics and the institutional foundations of rapid operational change. *Review of International Political Economy*, *21*(3), 735–763. https://doi.org/10.1080/09692290.2013.833958

Clift, B. (2018). *The IMF and the politics of austerity in the wake of the global financial crisis*. Oxford University Press.

Clift, B. (2019). Contingent Keynesianism: The IMF's model answer to the post-crash fiscal policy efficacy question in advanced economies. *Review of International Political Economy*, *26*(6), 1211–1237. https://doi.org/10.1080/09692290.2019.1640126

Crow, J., Arriazu, R., & Thygesen, N. (1999). *External evaluation of IMF surveillance*. International Monetary Fund.

Farnsworth, K., & Irving, Z. (2018). Deciphering the International Monetary Fund's (IMF) position on austerity: Incapacity, incoherence, and instrumentality. *Global Social Policy*, *18*(2), 119–142. https://doi.org/10.1177/1468018117729821

Fraser, N. (2017). The end of progressive neoliberalism. *Dissent*, *2*(1). https://www.dissentmagazine.org/online_articles/progressive-neoliberalism-reactionary-populism-nancy-fraser

Galbraith, J. K. (2019). A global macroeconomics–yes, macroeconomics, dammit–of inequality and income distribution. *Review of Keynesian Economics*, *7*(1), 1–5. https://doi.org/10.4337/roke.2019.01.01

Georgieva, K. (2019). *Decelerating growth calls for accelerating action*. Speech by the IMF Managing Director. https://www.imf.org/en/News/Articles/2019/10/03/sp100819-AMs2019-Curtain-Raiser

Grabel, I. (2017). *When things don't fall apart: Global financial governance and developmental finance in an age of productive incoherence*. MIT Press.

Independent Evaluation Office of the IMF (IEO). (2003). *IMF and recent capital account crises. Indonesia, Korea, Brazil.*

Independent Evaluation Office of the IMF (IEO). (2011). *IMF performance in the run-up to the financial and economic crisis: IMF surveillance in 2004–07*. https://www.ieo-imf.org/ieo/files/issuespapers/Crisis_Final_Issues_Paper_Web.pdf

Independent Evaluation Office of the IMF (IEO). (2017). *The IMF and social protection*. https://ieo.imf.org/~/media/IEO/Files/evaluations/completed/07-24-2017-the-imf-and-social-protection/sp-2017evalreport.ashx

Independent Evaluation Office of the IMF (IEO). (2019). *IMF financial surveillance*. https://ieo.imf.org/~/media/IEO/Files/evaluations/completed/01-15-2019-financial-surveillance/typeset-report/fis-report-glossy-version.ashx

International Monetary Fund (IMF). (2013a). *2013 spillover report – analytical underpinnings and other background* (IMF Multilateral Policy Issues Report). https://www.imf.org/external/np/pp/eng/2013/070313a.pdf

International Monetary Fund (IMF). (2013b). *Integrated surveillance decision factsheet*. www.imf.org/external/np/exr/facts/pdf/isd.pdf

International Monetary Fund (IMF). (2015). *Guidance note for surveillance under Article IV consultation* (IMF Policy Papers). https://www.imf.org/~/media/Websites/IMF/imported-full-text-pdf/external/np/pp/eng/2015/_031915.ashx

International Monetary Fund (IMF). (2016). *United States: Staff report for the 2016 Article IV consultation* (IMF Country Report No. 16/226). https://www.imf.org/external/pubs/ft/scr/2016/cr16226.pdf

International Monetary Fund (IMF). (2018a). *United States: Staff report for the 2018 Article IV consultation* (IMF Country Report No. 18/207). https://www.imf.org/~/media/Files/Publications/CR/2018/cr18207.ashx

International Monetary Fund (IMF). (2018b). *How to operationalize gender issues in country work* (IMF Policy Papers). https://www.imf.org/~/media/Files/Publications/PP/2018/pp060118howto-note-on-gender.ashx

International Monetary Fund (IMF). (2018c). *How to operationalize inequality issues in country work* (IMF Policy Papers). https://www.imf.org/~/media/Files/Publications/PP/2018/pp060118howto-note-on-inequality.ashx

International Monetary Fund (IMF). (2018d). *2018 interim surveillance review* (IMF Policy Papers). https://www.imf.org/~/media/Files/Publications/PP/2018/pp030718-2018-interim-surveillance-review.ashx

International Monetary Fund (IMF). (2019a). *A strategy for IMF engagement in social spending* (IMF Policy Papers). https://www.imf.org/~/media/Files/Publications/PP/2019/PPEA2019016.ashx

Kaya, A., & Reay, M. (2019). How did the Washington Consensus move within the IMF? Fragmented change from the 1980s to the aftermath of the 2008 crisis. *Review of International Political Economy*, *26*(3), 384–409. https://doi.org/10.1080/09692290.2018.1511447

Kentikelenis, A. E., Stubbs, T. H., & King, L. P. (2016). IMF conditionality and development policy space, 1985–2014. *Review of International Political Economy*, *23*(4), 543–582. https://doi.org/10.1080/09692290.2016.1174953

Kranke, M. (2019). IMF-World Bank cooperation before and after the global financial crisis. *Global Policy*, https://doi.org/10.1111/1758-5899.12743

Kranke, M., & Yarrow, D. (2019). The global governance of systemic risk: How measurement practices tame macroprudential politics. *New Political Economy*, *24*(6), 816–832. https://doi.org/10.1080/13563467.2018.1545754

Lagarde, C. (2011, June 23). *Statement by Christine Lagarde to the IMF Executive Board* (Press Release No. 11/253). https://www.imf.org/en/News/Articles/2015/09/14/01/49/pr11253

Lagarde, C. (2019a, June 14). Forging a stronger social contract—the IMF's approach to social spending. *Speech delivered at the International Labour Organisation*. https://www.imf.org/en/News/Articles/2019/06/14/sp061419-md-social-spending

Lagarde, C. (2019b). *Joint responsibility, shared rewards: The Managing Director's Global Policy Agenda* (IMF Policy Paper). IMF. https://www.imf.org/~/media/Files/Publications/PP/GPA/2019/sm2019-gpa-041119.ashx

Lütz, S., Hilgers, S., & Schneider, S. (2019). Accountants, Europeanists, and monetary guardians: Bureaucratic cultures and conflicts in IMF-EU lending programs. *Review of International Political Economy, 26*(6), 1187–1210. https://doi.org/10.1080/09692290.2019.1632916

Momani, B. (2005). Recruiting and diversifying IMF technocrats. *Global Society, 19*(2), 167–187. https://doi.org/10.1080/1360082050004 4878

Momani, B. (2007). IMF staff: Missing link in Fund reform proposals. *The Review of International Organizations, 2*(1), 39–57. https://doi.org/10.1007/s11558-006-9002-x

Momani, B. (2008, June 6–8). *IMF rhetoric on reducing poverty and inequality*. Paper presented at the Brooks World Poverty Institute and CIGI Workshop on Global Governance, Poverty, and Inequality.

Momani, B. (2010). 'Internal or external norm champions: The IMF and multilateral debt relief'. In S. Park & A. Vetterlein (Eds.), *Owning development: Creating policy norms in the IMF and the World Bank* (pp. 29–47). Cambridge University Press.

Momani, B., & Hibben, M. R. (2018). *What's wrong with the IMF and how to fix it*. Polity Press.

Mombrial, N., & Feher, C. (2019). *Consultation with third parties: Overview of results* (IMF Engagement on Social Spending Background Paper 1). IMF.

Nelson, S. C. (2014). 'Playing favorites: How shared beliefs shape the IMF's lending decisions'. *International Organization, 68*(2), 297–328. https://doi.org/10.1017/S0020818313000477

Nunn, A., & Price, S. (2019, March 27–30). *Gender, the smart economics of progressive neoliberalism, and IMF policy advice*. Paper presented at the international studies Annual Conference, Toronto.

Nunn, A., & White, P. (2017). The IMF and a new global politics of inequality? *Journal of Australian Political Economy, 78*, 186–231.

Nunn, A., & White, P. (forthcoming). Limitations in the "new global politics of inequality": The rhetoric-practice gap in IMF soft policy advice to its "inequality pilots". *Globalizations*.

Ostry, J. D., Loungani, P., & Furceri, D. (2016). Neoliberalism: Oversold. *Finance & Development, 53*(2), 38–41. https://www.imf.org/external/pubs/ft/fandd/2016/06/ostry.htm

Park, S., & Vetterlein, A. (2010). Owning development: Creating global policy norms in the World Bank and the IMF. In S. Park & A. Vetterlein (Eds.), *Owning development: Creating policy norms in the IMF and the World Bank* (pp. 3–26). Cambridge University Press.

Scharpf, F. (1999). *Governing Europe: Effective and democratic?* Oxford University Press.

Schmidt, V. (2013). 'Democracy and legitimacy in the European Union revisited: Input, output and 'throughput'. *Political Studies, 61*(1), 2–22. https://doi.org/10.1111/j.1467-9248.2012.00962.x

Seabrooke, L. (2007). 'Legitimacy gaps in the world economy: Explaining the sources of the IMF's legitimacy crisis'. *International Politics, 44*(2-3), 250–268. https://doi.org/10.1057/palgrave.ip.8800187

Vetterlein, A. (2010). Lacking ownership: The IMF and its engagement with social development as a policy norm. In S. Park & A. Vetterlein (Eds.), *Owning development: Creating policy norms in the IMF and the World Bank* (pp. 93–112). Cambridge University Press.

Wojnilower, J. (2017). *External perspectives of the IMF and social protection* (IEO Background Document BD/17-01/02). IEO. https://ieo.imf.org/~/media/IEO/Files/evaluations/completed/07-24-2017-the-imf-and-social-protection/sp-bd2-external-perspectives-of-the-imf-and-social-protection-web.ashx?la=en

Wojnilower, J., & Monasteski, C. (2017). *The IMF and social protection: IEO survey of IMF staff* (IEO Background Document BD/17-01/03). IEO. https://ieo.imf.org/~/media/IEO/Files/evaluations/completed/07-24-2017-the-imf-and-social-protection/sp-bd3-ieo-survey-of-imf-staff-web.ashx?la=en

Reglobalizing trade: progressive global governance in an age of uncertainty

James Scott and Rorden Wilkinson

ABSTRACT

In this article we explore what a programme of 'reglobalization' could look like for the governance of global trade. Our focus is on the centrepiece of the current commercial order, the World Trade Organization (WTO). Our aim is to illustrate the potential value of a reformulated WTO not just for commercial relations globally but also for other areas of social concern. We seek to be both practical and challenging. We seek to be practical by establishing what a programme of WTO reform might look like in the near-to-medium term, including changes to the negotiating process and opening up the WTO to non-state actors. We seek to be challenging by setting the transformation of global trade governance within the context of a thorough process of reglobalization wherein the primary public mechanisms of global governance are reoriented towards the delivery of progressive social and environmental outcomes.

Trade has been at the forefront of the globalization project, both in its first major instance in the nineteenth century and also in the reconstruction and deepening of an integrated global economy seen in the second half of the twentieth century and continuing through to the present day. Increased cross-border movements of goods and services were not only a key constituent element of globalization but also underpinned other aspects of global integration, such as driving the growth of foreign direct investment. More recently, these processes have intensified with the rise of so-called value-chain production, splitting the production process of goods across multiple countries and intensifying trade in unfinished products (Horner & Nadvi, 2018; Selwyn, 2019).

However, processes of trade-based globalization have not been smooth and have elicited political contestation both between and within states. At the international level, trade integration and the associated formulation of agreements governing and advancing that project have led to political cleavages, primarily but not always neatly (a point to which we return below) along the axis of developed versus developing countries – a feature of the General Agreement on Tariffs and Trade (GATT) from its inception (Wilkinson & Scott, 2008). At the domestic level, both developed and developing countries have seen repeated, if at times incoherent, backlashes against the new supremacy of trade integration in response to, among other things, deindustrialization, land and pension reform, and the ensuing loss of economic securities.

It is perhaps not surprising that trade-based globalization has come to be contested in this way. Key elements of the economic justification for pursuing greater liberalization are violated by the realities of the contemporary economic system, but this has not translated into a deep official questioning of that agenda. For instance, the redistribution from winners to losers that is necessary if all are to benefit from liberalization has all too often become both politically impossible, since there is no political support for such tax and spend policies, and economically problematic, because the winners are increasingly un-taxable (Driskill, 2012; Rodrik, 2017). Furthermore, the latest research has rekindled interest in the effect on wages and living standards of increased trade from low-wage economies into the developed countries, finding that these concerns were too readily dismissed by flawed economic analysis when they first emerged in the 1980s (Wood, 2018). New studies are finding lasting detrimental impacts on wages and unemployment within areas facing increased import-based competition, particularly following the re-emergence of China (Autor et al., 2016).

In short, the model of globalization that has previously been pursued, of which the World Trade Organization (WTO) has been a core element, has led to contradictions and tensions. This period has been forensically analysed by Branko Milanovic (2016), who finds that two groups have benefited and two suffered in the latest phase of globalization. The winners are the rich everywhere and the middle classes in the emerging countries, while the losers are the economically marginalized in the developed countries, the post-Soviet states and much of the poorest in the world, particularly in sub-Saharan Africa. In other words, globalization has unquestionably helped to generate significant economic wealth, but the distribution of those gains has not been sufficiently equitable and the resulting tensions are increasingly unsustainable politically. Too much has gone to giant corporations and wealthy individuals in the rich world without 'trickling down' to more disadvantaged groups. Meanwhile the gains in the developing world have been concentrated among too few countries, while others have faced deindustrialization, a constriction of development opportunities and further economic marginalization.

While it is certainly not the case that all of these effects are the result of trade, the intensification of trade flows has been a core, and highly visible, element of globalization. Consequently, it is reasonable to conclude that the trade system is ripe for the kind of 'reglobalization' called for in this special issue (Bishop & Payne, 2020a, 2020b). Trade has always been at the heart of economic transformation and development. Its wealth-creating opportunities must continue to be nurtured ('deglobalization' is not the answer), but simultaneously reform is needed to address the contradictions and tensions within commercial governance which now threaten to deal lasting damage to rules-based multilateral trade and have indeed already been expressed in the current clarion call for WTO reform (Azevêdo, 2019). Global growth is no longer being stoked by rising commercial flows, with a decline in the rate at which trade is expanding from an average yearly growth of 10.4% for 1998–2008 to 3.9% for 2008–2018. While some of this may be the result of rising non-tariff barriers during the long global downturn following the 2007–2008 financial crisis, multiple other factors are contributing. Wages have risen considerably in emerging markets, diminishing the incentives for businesses to off-shore production and even driving a degree of 'on-shoring' (Johnson, 2019), with, for example, the 'Made in China 2025' initiative leading to China manufacturing goods domestically that were previously imported and so contributing to the decline in trade growth.

Our aim in this article is to respond to the call to think about how a project of reglobalization might unfold by focusing on a re-articulation of the current system of trade governance, mindful that a consensus currently prevails on the need for WTO reform (Baliño, 2019). Our purpose is to show how small and large adjustments can be made that will result in meaningful changes in the outcomes produced. Our intention is not to call for a redesign of the system such that trade flows are restricted or reduced. Rather, our objective is a refashioning, such that the outcomes of commercial flows are more equitably distributed and the capacity to trade, particularly among the world's poorest populations, is enhanced. Accordingly, our focus is on the governance of global trade and our concern is with the current complex of rules, ideas, institutions and power relations as they are manifest in and around the regulatory centrepiece of contemporary global commerce: the WTO.

The article unfolds as follows. In section one we set out how the current political context and contemporary trade tensions make it a difficult moment for comprehensive WTO reform, even if a notable appetite exists among member-states for system adjustments. Section two turns to exploring some relatively simple proposals for incremental reform which, though not comprehensive in themselves, would begin to move the dial in a more progressive direction and could plausibly be the focus of a coalition of states and other actors motivated to effect system change. The penultimate section takes our argument further and advances several possibilities for more thorough-going, fundamental reforms of global trade governance. In section four we offer our conclusion.

The political context of reform

Multiple political tensions make this perhaps an unpropitious moment to engage in redesigning the rules and underpinning norms of global trade governance, though paradoxically it is precisely those same tensions that make clear the need for such a change in direction. We mention three here. The first is the Trump administration's departure from, and visceral repudiation of, the previous contours of United States (US) post-war trade policy. Although the administration's actions can be seen as returning to what has been a deep and recurrent thread of economic nationalism within US commercial policy (Helleiner, 2019), the effect has been to plunge the WTO into crisis. President Trump's Twitter claim that 'Trade wars are good and easy to win' (Trump, 2018), coming a day after announcing tariffs of up to 25% on all steel and aluminium imports, was a prologue to launching a more protracted battle specifically against China and its purportedly unfair trade policies. While US concerns about China's policies, particularly relating to its enforcement of intellectual property rights in key high-tech areas, stretch back many years, the Trump administration eschewed the previous policy of challenging these policies primarily through carefully prepared cases taken to the WTO's dispute settlement mechanism in favour of unilateral, WTO-inconsistent retaliation. This has formed one part of a broader rejection of multilateralism and WTO processes. Indeed, opposition to the WTO has stretched as far as President Trump musing on the possibility of US withdrawal from the organization (Donnan & Baschuk, 2018).

Beyond the actions and proclamations of the Trump administration, the multilateral trade system faces further difficulties, not least from the continued rise of regionalism as the primary focus of trade policy. 'Brexit' is partially unravelling the world's most comprehensive free trade area, the European Union (EU), and distracting its members from wider trade agendas. Some concerns have arisen that the loss of the United Kingdom, traditionally one of the champions of liberalism, from the EU may diminish the EU's commitment to trade opening (Beattie, 2019a), That said, others have noted that the future trade policies of the EU are unclear. At present, the reaction of the European Commission to Brexit has been to portray itself as a champion of free trade in the face of rising protectionism elsewhere (de Ville & Siles-Brügge, 2019). Nonetheless, even without the tortuous process of Brexit, the EU is facing significant challenges from the rise of populism which will draw more of its attention inward to address these political tensions that have lately been bubbling up to the surface. Despite the Trump administration withdrawing the US from the Trans-Pacific Partnership, it was completed by the remaining parties, forming the Comprehensive and Progressive Trans-Pacific Partnership, which came into force on 30 December 2018. Such regional processes risk the fragmentation of the global trade system to the detriment of multilateral processes within the WTO (Winters, 2017).

The continued shift toward regionalism is partly a consequence of the problems of the WTO's negotiating function, which is the third source of political tension we highlight here. Although the WTO was able to celebrate the signing in 2017 of its first ever fully multilateral agreement, the Trade Facilitation Agreement (TFA) (see Hannah et al., 2018), this belies an enduring seizure within the organization's negotiation process. Most notably, there is a continued lack of consensus on the position of the Doha round. While many members consider the round to have been set aside at the 2015 Nairobi Ministerial Conference, thereby clearing the agenda for new areas of negotiation primarily on a plurilateral basis (Froman, 2015), this view has not been accepted by all. A significant minority has argued that because there was no consensus on this interpretation no formal decision has been taken (since the WTO operates on the principle of consensus) and the Doha work programme therefore remains the primary area of negotiation (Prabhu, 2017; Wilkinson et al., 2016).

The difficulties in the negotiating function reflect more deep-seated divisions among members over the very purpose of the WTO. As with many areas, this division maps loosely onto a developed/developing country split, often making this a suitable first-order-of-approximation analytical lens. Broadly speaking, much of the developing world feels that the WTO should be a mechanism for tackling obstacles to development and overcoming its adverse incorporation into the global trade system, and a forum in which the power disadvantages it faces in bilateral negotiations can be mitigated. Meanwhile, for much of the developed world the purpose of the WTO is to provide a rules-based system of governance that progressively brings trade relations ever further under the rule of international law and opens up trade opportunities through liberalization.

However, as in all cases such a short-hand must be understood to contain considerable implicit caveats. Developed countries are not homogeneous in outlook and developing countries are even more heterogeneous. To suggest that India, Brazil, South Africa and China are strictly developing countries ignores the leading-edge sectors that each country's economy comprises. Equally, their elevation up the international pecking order as 'rising' powers obscures the structural problems that each faces, notably the existence of large tracts of enduring poverty and destitution not to mention – with perhaps the exception of Brazil – growing inequalities. Moreover, parts of the developed world harbour populations that inhabit conditions that are little different from their counterparts in developing countries. Consequently, most metrics and serious intellectual interrogations render the stratifications into developed/developing, North/South, rich/poor deeply problematic (Payne, 2005), as do understandings of the extent to which global economic geography is changing (Dicken, 2011).

The current crisis within the WTO's Dispute Settlement Body (DSB) is a prime example of the divisions between the rich countries. For the EU and many others, trade governance does not have clearly defined limits but spills over into trade-related areas, making WTO law inevitably incomplete. Where disputes arise for which there are no clearly defined existing legal rules, the EU (and others) are willing to accept the DSB ruling based on broader principles. The US, on the other hand, has a sharply differing view on the role of the DSB. For the US, the WTO should be little more than a narrow technical machinery for overseeing the application of rules and obligations. In this conception, where clear rules do not yet exist it is not the role of the DSB to fill in those legal gaps from general principles and thereby set about constructing a body of jurisprudence that will underpin future decisions. According to the US, this is judicial overreach and in response the Trump administration has blocked the appointment of new Appellate Body members, bringing the DSB to crisis point. Without a functional Appellate Body, trade disputes will be increasingly resolved through bilateral negotiation, rather than the rule of law – something that has been suggested was the aim of the Trump administration all along (Beattie, 2019b).

These differences of opinion between member-states are nothing new. They are nonetheless important because of the way they act as lenses within WTO reform debates. Each conflicting perception of the purpose and function of the WTO generates its own focus for what needs to be reformed and in what ways. All members agree that the WTO needs reform and regularly call for such, but moving toward a substantive and meaningful package of reform is impossible while there are such divergent opinions on the direction reform should take. The focus for many developing countries is on achieving better and more effective participation, improved trade outcomes and the resources to build capacity. For the EU, reform tends to focus on deepening existing commitments and harmonizing trade practices globally. For the United States, particularly under the Trump administration, reform of the WTO has become opening up new areas of economic interest and protecting particular strategic interests, while also rolling back provisions seen as restricting or disadvantaging US economic activity and its capacity to act as a sovereign entity.

Altogether, these factors make it a difficult moment to contemplate significant reform of the global trade system and its normative underpinnings. Arguably, there has never been less unity on the desired direction of the multilateral system. On the other hand, almost all of the issues noted above can trace their roots, at least partially, to the current model of trade governance, meaning that they are a consequence of the *type* of globalization that has been pursued. As such, it would be fruitless to wait for an alternative moment to begin the process of WTO reform. The next section begins to sketch out some of the ways the multilateral trade system might be remodelled in the spirit of reglobalization.

Light and realizable reform

The WTO's negotiating function has become mired in difficulty and a source of political tension. Reflecting the club-like nature of the GATT, negotiations were based around a process of competitive bargaining, in which each contracting party fought for the potential commercial advantages that it could extract from others while simultaneously seeking to protect areas of special interest. An inevitable consequence of such a process was that the interests of the most powerful states, with the greatest number of bargaining chips, best resources and greatest coercive tools, prevailed, while those of the less powerful were marginalized. This problem was recognized in the GATT's early years, notably in what became known as the Haberler Report of 1958, commissioned to examine the failure of developing countries' trade to expand as rapidly as that of industrialized countries (GATT, 1958). As we pass the 60th anniversary of the Report's publication, that crucial problem of the inequities generated by creating new commercial opportunities through competitive bargaining remains at the heart of the WTO's negotiating stalemate (Wilkinson, 2014).

Related to this is the whole approach of negotiating packages of agreements as comprehensive rounds. Two key issues are noteworthy. First, this approach creates expectations that trade deals must be large-scale, offering deep reform and substantial new commercial opportunities. Over the course of the GATT period, agreements moved ever further in this direction (with the very first round in 1947 being the exception, since it was far more ambitious than anything that would follow for many decades). But these rounds also consequently became harder to conclude and took ever longer to negotiate. The Uruguay round became mired in difficulty, collapsing on multiple occasions, but when eventually concluded formed the most comprehensive trade agreement ever seen (Croome, 1999).[1] The Doha round followed this pattern, although the divisions ultimately proved to be insurmountable. The pressure for rounds that produce significant global aggregate gains is matched by pressure on the negotiating teams of each member-state to secure a domestic 'win' in which their country's gains outweigh any losses.

The second problem of negotiating in rounds is the inevitable tendency to make each one a reaction to its predecessor. In effect, previous experiences shape the demands brought to each negotiation and perceived inequalities in the outcome of previous rounds lead to demands for redress, reducing the latitude for reaching an agreement. This was most clearly seen in the Doha round, which was explicitly framed within a need to deliver disproportionate benefits to developing countries in recognition of the asymmetrical outcomes of the Uruguay round (Ostry, 2002; Wilkinson, 2006). Relatively early in the WTO's existence, J. Michael Finger presciently questioned whether the WTO could get over the iniquitous 'North-South bargain' of the Uruguay round (Finger, 2002). After the tortuous process – and eventual collapse – of the Doha round, his fears have proven well-founded.

The GATT's history of layers of unequal bargains being built one on top of the other has meant that developing countries approach each new negotiation seeking to rectify past inequalities (Gowa & Kim, 2005; Wilkinson & Scott, 2008). The primary agenda for most of the developed world, meanwhile, is to extend trade rules into new, cutting-edge sectors to cement their dominance therein, while protecting uncompetitive industries and agricultural production. Consequently, members are placed at loggerheads from the outset as they seek to reconcile these two opposing positions. That process has typically unfolded into a bargain based on exchanging remedial measures to redress the inequalities generated by previous rounds for expanding the WTO agenda into new areas. It is an approach that is an inevitable outcome of the bargaining character of the multilateral system and the desire for reciprocity that has always been a major foundational principle of the GATT and WTO (Keohane, 1986). When this form of bargaining is combined with the profoundly unequal power distribution that characterizes international politics, it is almost inevitable that each round generates further asymmetries.

In this sense, it is the very negotiating principles of the WTO that are contributing to the difficulties the organization faces. The use of reciprocal exchange as a means of opening, or governing, trade opportunities inevitably entrenches inequalities into the system and creates layers of asymmetry. The imbalances in influence, power and negotiating capacity between members when combined with the reciprocity principle is a potent driving force for unequal outcomes, with the resentment thereby engendered feeding into subsequent rounds. Efforts to attenuate the ensuing problems can only take place within the context of a new round of reciprocally exchanged concessions, beginning the process again.

While it is true that developing countries have been afforded 'less than full reciprocity' and the least developed among them are expected to make considerably fewer concessions, this approach to mitigating the asymmetries among members has proven to be deeply problematic. It has the effect of diminishing the influence of developing countries over the trade agenda (Subramanian & Wei, 2007) and ensures that they receive only whatever hand-outs the rich countries are willing to give. All too often, these hand-outs have proven to be rather limited, with the Doha round a case in point: the concessions made to least developed countries were limited in value (Oxfam, 2005), while those demanded were potentially more significant than often assumed (Chang, 2005).

The WTO's negotiating system, including its modes of operation (negotiating in rounds) and the principles on which it is based (particularly reciprocity), has contributed significantly to the resentments built up toward the organization and consequently the difficulties in securing the original GATT objective of 'mutually advantageous arrangements directed to the substantial reduction of tariffs and other barriers to trade and to the elimination of discriminatory treatment in international trade relations' (GATT, 1994, preamble). It is unlikely that the WTO could be revitalized, or set on a more progressive path, without changes being made to its approach to negotiating.

A simple step forward may be moving to a process of continual negotiations on specific sectors, with stand-alone agreements adopted as and when consensus is achieved. The 2013 TFA – the only multilateral deal the WTO has reached – is an example of this approach. It sought to balance the desires of the developed countries to expedite the movement of goods across borders with the need among developing countries for technical and financial assistance to implement the ensuing obligations and to do so in an internally balanced way. To this end, the Agreement included a ground-breaking clause stipulating that developing countries could only be bound by its requirements if they were provided with sufficient assistance to implement them.

Such stand-alone agreements are tacitly the route adopted at the Buenos Aires Ministerial Conference of 2017, with plurilateral negotiations opened on 'Micro, Small and Medium-size Enterprises' and 'Investment Facilitation for Development' alongside the first steps toward an agreement on e-commerce (Hannah et al., 2018). However, caution is needed with this new approach as it holds significant pitfalls for developing countries. First, plurilateralism may exacerbate the inequalities in negotiating influence between developed and developing countries, leading to agreements that, for all the development rhetoric suffused throughout, continue to be asymmetric in impact. The TFA – despite the clause requiring technical assistance be forthcoming – is a case in point. The TFA demands few regulatory changes from rich countries, being rather a multilateralization of the practices that they already employ. As such, it does little to facilitate exports into the developed countries. It is within the developing world that the TFA's regulatory changes bite, where it is predicted to reduce the costs of importing by around 13–15% among low- and middle-income countries. Overall, then, the TFA will liberalize imports into the developing world, but not into the developed (Perera, 2016).

Second, the practice of negotiating in rounds and concluding multiple sectors together in a combined 'single undertaking' was designed to ensure that the costs associated with liberalizing particularly politically sensitive sectors could be balanced against the benefits of new trade opportunities in other sectors. Without this mechanism, the sectors that the most powerful states find most politically difficult – most notably agriculture – are highly unlikely to see further liberalization (Scott, 2017). More broadly, the areas that will be favoured for plurilateral agreements will be chosen by those with most influence over the agenda-setting process. Weaker states will continue to be marginalized.

Further changes may help to alleviate this problem, such as creating new opportunities for non-state actors to participate in trade governance. The state centrism of the WTO is increasingly problematic and reflective of a rather narrow vision of global governance – a vision that has been transcended by other institutions and moments in time. For instance, when the League of Nations was created following World War I, it was originally intended that the delegates to the General Assembly would not be drawn just from governments but would also represent civil society, business and other such groups, as part of Woodrow Wilson's vision that the Assembly would be there to express 'world public opinion' (Armstrong et al., 2004, p. 57). While this did not come to pass, in the other great institution of world governance created at that time, the International Labour Organization (ILO), non-state actors were given a central part in its decision-making process through a tripartite structure linking governments, labour unions and business representatives (Hughes & Haworth, 2011). Within this context, it is hard not to see the state-centrism of the WTO (mirroring that of the GATT) as being less progressive than these previous conceptions of how global governance might be structured. The result is that the range of voices heard within the organization is limited, with inevitable consequences for the range of ideas being considered.

In 2001, the WTO inaugurated its Public Forum, partly as a means of addressing this problem by creating a space within the WTO for a greater variety of voices and the discussion of ideas. Although a welcome change, the Public Forum has over time become something of a sterile arena, increasingly dominated by business groups and representatives of intergovernmental organizations while excluding heterodox voices (Hannah et al., 2017). Nevertheless, the effective inclusion of non-state actors would help to reverse the narrowing of debate within the organization and move beyond the focus on competitive bargaining that has become so problematic. This may help to ease the negotiating function of the WTO and would also contribute to overcoming the inequalities being generated by the current system. Non-governmental organizations, unions and other such civil society groups have an important role to play in ensuring that the gains from globalization are more equitably distributed and the interests of the marginalized protected.

A more radical step would be to give actors other than states a formal role in decision-making within the WTO. This is unlikely to take place any time soon, but it is clear that the WTO's decision-making processes, particularly around negotiations, have become mired in dysfunction. Neither a shift away from negotiating in rounds nor the inclusion of non-state actors should be seen as a panacea for the problems of the WTO, but they could form part of an incremental shift toward a less dysfunctional institutional politics if the pitfalls can be avoided. Anything more than this incremental type of improvement demands more deep-seated, foundational reform, to which we now turn.

Deeper reform

The suggestions above still see the WTO as largely continuing on a similar path, but one that is less hamstrung by problems generated and one that gives at least some greater recognition of the need to integrate development more fully. They are arguably 'problem solving', rather than 'critical', to use Robert Cox's (1996) distinction. This would also be the case for any adjustments made to the dispute-settlement system in light of the current stasis and US actions in relation to it (Zhou & Gao, 2019). For true reglobalization, we need to go further to bring about a deeper normative shift and address the WTO's current descent. Helpfully, other institutions of global governance provide lessons for how organizational precariousness can be addressed and institutional trajectories altered to secure continued relevance. Numerous such examples exist. One of the most useful is the ILO.

Since its creation in 1919 the ILO has demonstrated a capacity for institutional resilience and innovation that has kept it relevant at times when the organization's very existence has been called into question (Hughes & Haworth, 2011). Much of this resilience and innovation is attributable to the leadership of successive directors-general and the concerted efforts of a secretariat intent on ensuring the organization's continuing relevance. A key component of this strategy has been to undergo a process of periodic rejuvenation at moments when its very existence has been threatened. Certainly, the ensuing changes did not resolve all problems within the ILO. Nonetheless, they enabled the organization to survive the transition from the League of Nations to the United Nations (UN) at a point in time when that transition was far from certain. It was also able to stave off the threat posed by the creation of the United Nations Industrial Development Organization in the 1960s (Cox, 1973, p. 110) and in general has remained relevant in an era when the old sources of its strength and support (largely organized labour) have fallen back. Moreover, the organization has sought to respond to the fundamental changes in the nature of work and the rise of precarious employment to which globalization has given rise (see Standing, 2008 for a critical assessment). As

Robert O'Brien puts it (2013, p. 152), 'the ILO has been able to survive for the past 90+ years due to strategic leadership, an ability to reposition itself to address the challenges of its times and the work of highly technical staff providing policy relevant advice'.

One specific moment in this process is particularly useful for present purposes: that was during the construction of a new world order after the Second World War when the ILO faced being set aside as a relic of old. The ILO was not included in any of the major conferences (Dumbarton Oaks, Bretton Woods and finally San Francisco where the UN was established) and, as a consequence, was not mentioned in the UN Charter (Johnston, 1970, pp. 78–79). Nevertheless, on 14 December 1946 the ILO made the transition from the League of Nations to the UN, securing a place within the latter's framework as a specialized agency (Phelan, 1946).

Three aspects of the ILO's strategy for achieving this are instructive. First, its then director-general, Edward Phelan, convened a conference (in Philadelphia in 1944) designed to re-affirm the organization's credentials and underline its centrality to the post-Second World War reconstruction effort. Second, the outcome of the conference, which was the Declaration of Philadelphia, refined and updated the ILO's aims and objectives, reorienting the work of the organization around the core normative human rights agenda of the nascent United Nations. Third, as a necessary corollary, Phelan paved the way for the ILO to become a UN family institution. In combination, these and other factors 'saved' the institution, ensuring its continued relevance and placing its work squarely within the wider ambit of the United Nations system (Hughes & Haworth, 2011).

This strategy is pertinent to the WTO because it currently lacks the kind of coherence required of contemporary global economic governance (Bernstein & Hannah, 2012) and is frequently at odds with various UN agencies, limiting its effectiveness and creating tensions within the global system. Moreover, the WTO requires a new, socially progressive set of aims and objectives that connects it with the agendas of other global bodies. Embedding it formally within the UN complex would help provide this normative shift. The ILO example illustrates how a restatement of the WTO's purposes could help bring this about, providing a new orientation and ensuring the organization's continued relevance. A key part of this would include the fuller situation of the WTO within the pursuit of wider social goals, with the negotiation of trade openings seen merely a vehicle for their achievement rather than an end in itself. It would also have value in requiring a thorough re-working of the relationships between the WTO and the UN development system (Browne & Weiss, 2020).

What precisely would this mean for the WTO? A new declaration of aims and objectives ought to provide an opportunity to place the realization of trade-led 'development-for-all' (an idea to which we return below) in an environmentally sustainable fashion at the forefront of the purposes of the multilateral trading system, with particular emphasis on helping the least able. The operation of any machinery for that purpose must not be judged on reductions in barriers to trade or estimated projections in the overall contribution that these reductions will make in the aggregate. Rather, the system ought to be judged on its capacity to generate welfare-enhancing opportunities for all (including enabling those most disadvantaged to make use of those advantages).

That said, a reformed WTO cannot be simply and uncritically reinserted into the existing system, stirred, and the problem fixed. What needs to happen simultaneously is a process of wholesale reflection on what it is that our global economic (and other) institutions do, how they do it, and what their purpose is. Indeed, the prolonged stasis in the WTO ought to be turned into an opportunity to contrive an ILO-type 'Philadelphia moment' in which member-states and other relevant actors collectively formulate a strategy and roadmap that offers a coherent and compelling way forward and consequent, thorough reform across the system.

The WTO as a trade-led 'development-for-all' organization

Refreshing the WTO's aims and objectives has to connect smoothly with the necessity of reorienting it as a trade-led 'development-for-all' organization. Here we need to think carefully about what we mean by 'development-for-all' and clearly distinguish this from the negative associations that have long infused, implicitly and explicitly, debates about development. As noted above, the construction of broad categories of states, such as developed and developing, is somewhat arbitrary and often means little beyond helping to leverage a particular kind of politics into a conversation. It is these conversations that infuse the kind of tensions about which Thomas G. Weiss (2009; 2012a) complains.

What is required instead is a way of organizing trade that recognizes the multifaceted nature of the global economy and of states and moves away from a form of governance based on competitive negotiations as the machinery for realizing economic advantage to one that is more focused on fostering trade for all social groups and not just elites across the world. Such a reorientation would ensure that the WTO is much more like a global version of a national department of trade and industry – an idea to which we return momentarily – and much less like a device designed to serve the interests of some and not others. It also offers the conceptual *volte face* required to move the WTO beyond the state it is in.

To be more specific, an approach that recognizes the necessity of trade-led 'development-for-all' would shift the focus of global public policy from states towards people. We know well and understand the contradiction between states negotiating international legal frameworks and economic actors operating under their auspices. A focus on trade-led 'development-for-all' corrects this gaze. It would focus attention on the problems of particular individuals, communities and industries and their capacity, or not, to engage in economic behaviour. It is in targeting them and improving their capacity to make the most of an enabling environment that a more appropriate reorientation of a world trade organization lies.

The key here would be to identify areas wherein special assistance is required and to divert resources and attention accordingly. This, of course, does not mean that leading-edge sectors and new forms of trade should be ignored; it simply means creating an enabling environment within which the poorest and least able receive special attention, distinct from one that has evolved in a fashion that has actively harmed their trade opportunities. These communities should not be identified because they are constituents of poor countries alone. Recognition is also required that resources and knowledge need to transfer to sectors in the developed and middle-income worlds.

A refocus on trade as a means for achieving 'development-for-all', rather than being treated as an end in itself, will also demand a re-examination of the balance within the WTO between trade concerns and other aspects of social and economic well-being. It was a perception that the WTO placed trade concerns above all others that lay at the heart of the civil society backlash that came to the fore in Seattle in 1999 (McMichael, 2000). A process of reglobalization necessitates a return to some of the questions raised then, including the thorny issue of labour regulation. Although this was highly controversial when it first emerged in the late 1990s and rightly resisted by developing countries fearful that it would be used merely as a means of protectionism by developed countries (Hughes & Wilkinson, 1998), circumstances have changed. The WTO is no longer as dominated by its richest members and the voice of developing countries, particularly the likes of Brazil, India and China, cannot now be ignored (Hopewell, 2016), which helps to ensure that the issue will not simply facilitate developed-country protectionism. Furthermore, it has become clear that engagement in trade, even when driving industrialization, does not guarantee improvements in social conditions (Bernhardt &

Pollak, 2016). Inclusion of some form of labour regulation within the WTO may also help to overcome the populist backlash within developed countries against globalization and the perceived loss of jobs through 'unfair' competition from low-wage economies. Similarly, environmental clauses within the WTO need to be revisited, including an urgent need to clarify the legality of measures to combat climate change, such as border-tax adjustments.

A global department of trade and industry

If we understand that, like any national economy, the world economy has areas that are highly advanced, others that are not, others still that languish or are in decline, or else lie somewhere in between, and we marry this to an understanding that the goal of any global organization ought to be to provide welfare gains for all, then the task of a world trade organization ought to be, among other things, to intervene strategically to help those areas of economic activity that require assistance, regulate against abuses (such as monopoly power) and develop purposeful initiatives that assist in the further development of all sectors. While this may seem radical, it is perhaps not as revolutionary as it might at first appear. Since global organizations first became preferred modes of public global governance we have had a system of global regulation that mimics the design of the governmental apparatus of a state. The WTO is unique among global institutions in its deployment of a competitive and adversarial system as the means by which governance is exercised. Most others, despite including elements of political contestation, do not rely upon competition between members for their everyday operation. We have long since made the move away from grand global systems based on explicitly disadvantaging some for the benefit of others (as colonialism did); it is about time we eradicated their last vestiges of disadvantage.

The point here is that global institutions are in some way designed to provide and regulate the provision of global public goods, irrespective of whether they also help cement wider arrangements of political power and advance the interests of the powerful therein. As public-goods providers they have a responsibility to ensure equitable access to those goods, certain restrictions notwithstanding (a condition of restricting access to opportunities for trade-led growth as a global public good would not, for instance, be because a country is poor and inconsequential in global trade, as is currently the case). We should take this commitment seriously and press our global institutions to provide these goods in ways that are as fulsome as possible.

Refashioned in this way, a world trade organization ought to move away from adversarial negotiations as the mechanism of distributing economic opportunity to a form of governance that incentivises and facilitates trade-led growth (an area in which the World Bank actually has more expertise than the WTO currently constituted). In this vision the primary functions of the WTO should be to: (i) develop strategic plans and strategies for assistance that speak to and help realize wider socially progressive global goals; (ii) facilitate the transfer of knowledge about global trade in a way that is genuinely equitable and which speaks to the specific economic circumstances of recipients; and (iii) establish a development fund designed to nurture trade-generating activities in hard-to-realize places.

Other *desiderata* could be included to guard against monopolistic and anti-competitive behaviour. Crucially, the system would not work on the basis of *states* as the primary focus of attention, but rather geographic areas and specific agents within, between and across states. Thus, the 'rust-belt' in the United States and the de-industrialized parts of South Wales and north-east England would be eligible for trade assistance from a refashioned world trade organization, as would subsistence farmers in Burkina Faso or shack-dweller co-operatives in Mumbai. Clearly, need would determine the direction in which assistance flows, as well as the kind of assistance that was offered (finance for trade in one area, knowledge transfer and legal expertise in another and so on), although it remains the case that the lion's share of attention ought to be focused on the least developed.

The deeper institutional reforms suggested here are, of course, unlikely to be realized in the present political climate and a significant change of mind would be required before they could be brought into effect. Furthermore, they are not meant as a crystallized package that we advocate as some sort of finalized solution. They are conceived, rather, as just one input into the process of institutional reinvigoration and reform that is proposed above. If that process is to succeed, a wide range of ideas from diverse stakeholders will be necessary.

Conclusion

Globalization, and the trade expansion that has underpinned it, has been a powerful force for economic change, but the benefits that it has created have been highly unequally distributed and have left some of the most vulnerable even more precarious. The consequences of this can no longer be ignored and have generated a prolonged crisis within the WTO. A new form of globalization is needed, which continues to harness the benefits of a rules-based global economy but which also ensures that moves are made to advance the interests of the marginalized. Without such a renewal, there is a distinct risk of a destructive, disordered deglobalization.

To bring such a renewal about, a profound reflection on the aims, objectives and procedures of the WTO needs to be undertaken that would both secure the necessary inclusivity and help to overcome the WTO's current gridlock. Here, we have drawn from the revitalization of the ILO in its own moments of crisis to sketch a potential path toward the required reglobalization of the WTO. The suggested process of institutional reflection could be a catalyst for an organization that has not looked at what it is and what it does (but has merely got on and done it) since it was first created, that inherited its statement of purpose from an organization that was still-born in the mid-1940s (the proposed International Trade Organization) and that was designed with different aims and objectives in mind, speaking necessarily to different interests. The WTO should be reoriented away from its focus on the removal of barriers to trade as an end in itself to one wherein trade openings drive the achievement of broader social goals as the organization's primary reason for being.

Such a moment of deep reflection may prove to be overly ambitious at this moment in time, but smaller-scale reform may be more immediately achievable and still hold significant potential. We have outlined here two key areas for such transformation. First, the current approach to negotiating trade deals through broad-based rounds finalized through a single undertaking has become unworkable, creating political tensions and underpinning the asymmetric outcomes seen within the trade system since the inception of the GATT. As an alternative, the WTO should move to a mode of continual negotiations on specific sectors, coupled with stand-alone agreements where achievable. Second, the state-centric, competitive trade governance model has, perhaps unsurprisingly, shown itself to be poorly suited to pursuing broad social goals. If we are to expand the agenda, the range of voices that are heard must be expanded concomitantly. Labour unions and other organizations representing the interests of workers can bring a vital balance to the demands of business lobbies. They can offer perspectives from the grassroots concerning the environment, development and other social causes. While there were understandable fears within the WTO after the debacle of the 1999 Seattle Ministerial Conference about any engagement with what were perceived as radical groups, the organization has subsequently navigated successfully a path of constructive engagement with civil society groups (Hopewell, 2015). As such, there already exists a platform on which to build.

The consequences of inaction may prove to be deeply damaging. Already, trade relations between the world's two trading superpowers, the United States and China, have moved largely outside of the existing institutions of multilateral oversight. A continuation of such a trajectory, irrespective of any accommodations reached, is in nobody's interests and risks lasting damage to the principle of a rules-based commercial system. Perhaps that threat will be enough to sharpen focus on the need for substantive reform.

Note

1. This was partly facilitated by the unique circumstances offered by the creation of the WTO. The most powerful countries made it clear that they would pull out of the GATT as soon as the WTO was created (Finger & Nogués, 2002), leaving developing countries with the choice of either being left out of multilateral trade rules or signing up to the WTO.

Disclosure statement

No potential conflict of interest was reported by the author(s).

ORCID

James Scott http://orcid.org/0000-0003-3296-0375
Rorden Wilkinson http://orcid.org/0000-0002-0883-8081

References

Armstrong, D., Lloyd, L., & Redmond, J. (2004). *From Versailles to Maastricht: The making of the twentieth century*. Palgrave.

Autor, D. H., Dorn, D., & Hanson, G. H. (2016). The China shock: Learning from labor-market adjustment to large changes in trade. *Annual Review of Economics*, *8*(1), 205–240. https://doi.org/10.1146/annurev-economics-080315-015041

Azevêdo, R. (2019, July 19). *WTO reform is already happening. WTO News Item*. https://www.wto.org/english/news_e/news19_e/tnc_19jul19_e.htm

Baliño, S. (2019). As members debate WTO reform, what lies ahead for 2019? *International Institute for Sustainable Development blog*. https://www.iisd.org/library/wto-reform-2019

Beattie, A. (2019a, December 16). Free traders in the EU will miss the UK when it's gone. *Financial Times*.

Beattie, A. (2019b, December 9). The unappealing fate of the WTO's appellate body. *Financial Times*.

Bernhardt, T., & Pollak, R. (2016). Economic and social upgrading dynamics in global manufacturing value chains: A comparative analysis. *Environment and Planning A*, *48*(7), 1220–1243. https://doi.org/10.1177/0308518X15614683

Bernstein, S., & Hannah, E. (2012). The WTO and institutional (in)coherence in global economic governance. In A. Narlikar, M. Daunton, & R. Stern (Eds.), *Handbook on the World Trade Organization* (pp. 776–808). Oxford University Press.

Bishop, M. L., & Payne, A. (2020a). The political economies of different globalizations: Theorizing reglobalization. *Globalizations*. doi:10.1080/14747731.2020.1779963
Bishop, M. L., & Payne, A. (2020b). Steering towards reglobalization: Can a reformed G20 rise to the occasion? *Globalizations*. doi:10.1080/14747731.2020.1779964
Browne, S., & Weiss, T. G. (2020). *Routledge handbook on the UN and development*. Routledge.
Chang, H.-J. (2005). *Why developing countries need tariffs: How WTO NAMA negotiations could deny developing countries' right to a future*. South Centre.
Cox, R. W. (1973). ILO: Limited monarchy. In R. Cox & H. Jacobson (Eds.). *The Anatomy of influence: Decision making in international organization* (pp. 102–138). Yale University Press.
Cox, R. W. (1996). *Approaches to world order*. Cambridge University Press.
Croome, J. (1999). *Reshaping the world trading system: A history of the Uruguay round*. 2nd ed. Kluwer Law International.
de Ville, F., & Siles-Brügge, G. (2019). The impact of Brexit on EU trade policy. *Politics and Governance*, *7*(3), 7–18. https://doi.org/10.17645/pag.v7i3.2102
Dicken, P. (2011). *Global shift: Mapping the changing contours of the world economy*. 6th ed. Sage.
Donnan, S., & Baschuk, B. (2018, October 12). Trump's threat to leave the WTO could be a saving grace. *Bloomberg*. https://www.bloomberg.com/news/articles/2018-10-12/trump-s-threat-to-leave-the-wto-could-be-a-saving-grace
Driskill, R. (2012). Deconstructing the argument for free trade: A case study of the role of economists in policy debates. *Economics and Philosophy*, *28*(1), 1–30. https://doi.org/10.1017/S0266267112000090
Finger, J. M. (2002). The Uruguay round north-south bargain: Will the WTO get over it? In D. L. M. Kennedy & J. D. Southwick (Eds.), *The political economy of international trade law: Essays in honor of Robert E. Hudec* (pp. 301–310). Cambridge University Press.
Finger, J. M., & Nogués, J. J. (2002). The unbalanced Uruguay round outcome: The new areas in future WTO negotiations. *The World Economy*, *25*(3), 321–340. https://doi.org/10.1111/1467-9701.00435
Froman, M. (2015, December 13). We are at the end of the line on the Doha round of trade talks. *Financial Times*.
GATT. (1958). *Trends in international trade* (The Haberler report).
Gowa, J., & Kim, S. Y. (2005). An exclusive country club: The effects of the GATT on trade, 1950–94. *World Politics*, *57*(4), 453–478. https://doi.org/10.1353/wp.2006.0010
Hannah, E., Scott, J., & Wilkinson, R. (2017). Reforming WTO-civil society engagement. *World Trade Review*, *16*(3), 427–448. https://doi.org/10.1017/S1474745616000446
Hannah, E., Scott, J., & Wilkinson, R. (2018). The WTO in Buenos Aires: The outcome and its significance for the future of the multilateral trading system. *The World Economy*, *41*(10), 2578–2598. https://doi.org/10.1111/twec.12657
Helleiner, E. (2019). Varieties of American neomercantilism: From the first years of the Republic to Trumpian economic nationalism. *European Review of International Studies*, *6*(3), 7–29.
Hopewell, K. (2015). Multilateral trade governance as social field: Global civil society and the WTO. *Review of International Political Economy*, *22*(6), 1128–1158. https://doi.org/10.1080/09692290.2015.1066696
Hopewell, K. (2016). *Breaking the WTO: How emerging powers disrupted the neoliberal project*. Stanford University Press.
Horner, R., & Nadvi, K. (2018). Global value chains and the rise of the global south: Unpacking twenty-first century polycentric trade. *Global Networks*, *18*(2), 207–237. https://doi.org/10.1111/glob.12180
Hughes, S., & Haworth, N. (2011). *The International Labour Organization (ILO): Coming in from the cold*. Routledge.
Hughes, S., & Wilkinson, R. (1998). International labour standards and world trade: No role for the World Trade Organization? *New Political Economy*, *3*(3), 375–389. https://doi.org/10.1080/13563469808406366
Johnson, S. (2019, December 19). Offshoring slows as wages rise in some emerging economies. *Financial Times*.
Johnston, G. A. (1970). *The International Labour Organization*. Europa.
Keohane, R. O. (1986). Reciprocity in international relations. *International Organization*, *40*(1), 1–27. https://doi.org/10.1017/S0020818300004458
McMichael, P. (2000). Sleepless since Seattle. *Review of International Political Economy*, *7*(3), 466–474. https://doi.org/10.1080/09692290050174033
Milanovic, B. (2016). *Global inequality: A new approach for the age of globalization*. Harvard University Press.

O'Brien, R. (2013). Review of Steve Hughes and Nigel Haworth's "The International Labour Organization (ILO): coming in from the cold". *Global Labour Journal*, *4*(2), 152–154. https://doi.org/10.15173/glj.v4i2.1136

Ostry, S. (2002). The Uruguay round north-south grand bargain: Implications for future negotiations. In D. L. M. Kennedy & J. D. Southwick (Eds.), *The political economy of international trade law: Essays in honor of Robert E. Hudec* (pp. 285–300). Cambridge University Press.

Oxfam. (2005). *What happened in Hong Kong? Initial analysis of the WTO ministerial* (Oxfam briefing paper 85).

Payne, A. (2005). *The global politics of unequal development*. Palgrave Macmillan.

Perera, S. (2016). *Trade facilitation agreement (TFA) – Implementing implications* (Emerging issues briefing note (5)). The Commonwealth Secretariat. thecommonwealth.org/sites/default/files/inline/TradeFacilitationAgreement1008.pdf

Phelan, E. (1946). The ILO and the United Nations: The director-general's address to the Assembly. *International Labour Review*, *54*(5-6), 281–284.

Prabhu, S. P. (2017, December 13). *Statement to the WTO's 2017 Buenos Aires ministerial conference* (WT/MIN(17)/ST/9).

Rodrik, D. (2017). *Straight talk on trade: Ideas for a sane world economy*. Princeton University Press.

Scott, J. (2017). The future of agricultural trade governance in the World Trade Organization. *International Affairs*, *93*(5), 1167–1184. https://doi.org/10.1093/ia/iix157

Selwyn, B. (2019). Poverty chains and global capitalism. *Competition and Change*, *23*(1), 71–97. https://doi.org/10.1177/1024529418809067

Standing, G. (2008). The ILO: An agency for globalization? *Development and Change*, *39*(3), 355–384.

Subramanian, A., & Wei, S.-J. (2007). The WTO promotes trade, strongly but not evenly. *Journal of International Economics*, *72*(1), 151–175. https://doi.org/10.1016/j.jinteco.2006.07.007

Trump, D. (2018, March 2). Twitter, @theRealDonaldTrump, 2:50am.

Weiss, T. G. (2009). *What's wrong with the United Nations and how to fix it*. Polity.

Weiss, T. G. (2012a). ECOSOC and the MDGs: What can be done? In R. Wilkinson & D. Hulme (Eds.), *The millennium development goals and beyond: Global development after 2015* (pp. 117–128). Routledge.

Wilkinson, R. (2006). *The WTO: Crisis and the governance of global trade*. Routledge.

Wilkinson, R. (2014). *What's wrong with the WTO and how to fix it*. Wiley.

Wilkinson, R., Hannah, E., & Scott, J. (2016). The WTO in Nairobi: The demise of the Doha development agenda and the future of the multilateral trading system. *Global Policy*, *7*(2), 247–255. https://doi.org/10.1111/1758-5899.12339

Wilkinson, R., & Scott, J. (2008). Developing country participation in the GATT: A reassessment. *World Trade Review*, *7*(3), 473–510. https://doi.org/10.1017/S1474745608003959

Winters, L. A. (2017). The WTO and regional trading agreements: Is it all over for multilateralism? In M. Elsig, B. Hoekman, & J. Pauwelyn (Eds.), *Assessing the World Trade Organization: Fit for purpose* (pp. 344–375). Cambridge University Press.

Wood, A. (2018). The 1990s trade and wages debate in retrospect. *The World Economy*, *41*(4), 975–999. https://doi.org/10.1111/twec.12619

Zhou, W., & Gao, H. (2019). "Overreaching" or "overreacting"? Reflections on the judicial function and approaches of WTO appellate body. *Journal of World Trade*, *53*(6), 951–978.

Towards a feminist global trade politics

Erin Hannah, Adrienne Roberts and Silke Trommer

ABSTRACT
Socially progressive globalization in a post-neoliberal era must recognize the centrality of gendered and other social hierarchies to the deeper workings of the global political economy and actively seek to dismantle them. In practice, this involves: (i) redefining the purpose of global trade in ways that value, prioritize and support progressive forms of social reproduction; (ii) centreing trade policy on a holistic understanding of the economy; and (iii) democratizing global trade relations. In this article, we outline a feminist International Political Economy theoretical perspective for understanding global trade, take stock of a range of gender and trade initiatives pursued by various trade actors and organizations to show where progressive reforms have already been taken and where these fall short, and make concrete suggestions on how to formulate trade policies in line with globalist, feminist prerogatives.

Introduction

In 2015 United Nations (UN) experts expressed concern about the adverse impacts of free trade and investment agreements on 'the rights to life, food, water and sanitation, health, housing, education, science and culture, improved labour standards, an independent judiciary, a clean environment and the right not to be subjected to forced resettlement' (OHCHR, 2015). Their report points to the potential for trade agreements to undermine civil, cultural, economic, political and/or social rights enshrined in legally binding instruments, including commitments made to support gender equality. It notes that, 'undoubtedly, globalization and the many Bilateral Investment Treaties (BITs) and Free Trade Agreements (FTAs) can have positive but also negative impacts on the promotion of a democratic and equitable international order, which entails practical international solidarity' (OHCHR, 2015). These are key concerns for feminist scholars, as well as a growing number of Non-Governmental Organizations (NGOs), states and international organizations.

In our contribution to this Special Issue on post-neoliberal 'reglobalization', we explore the gendered dynamics of trade and chart a pathway to a feminist trade politics that is more progressive than existing approaches, even where gender concerns are present. This is an important endeavour since trade policy is often presented as neutral – targeting neither men nor women – and policy-making is viewed as the realm of experts. Yet, as the UN report suggests, trade can produce equitable and inequitable outcomes globally. Indeed, feminist research has extensively documented how trade impacts on people in their multiple roles as workers, producers, consumers (of goods and services), providers of unpaid care work, and more. Given that existing gender norms and power relations shape one's relationship with these activities, the outcomes of trade policy are deeply gendered, as well as differing also along the lines of class, race, ethnicity, age, ability, and more (Roberts et al., 2019; van Staveren et al., 2007). The impacts of trade also vary depending on country context.

It has been well established that women are among those most negatively affected by the globally integrated trading system that has been a defining feature of neoliberal globalization (Roberts et al., 2019). Yet, like the editors of this Special Issue (Bishop & Payne, 2002a, 2002b), we do not believe that deglobalization will necessarily bring about a more equitable global order, irrespective of whether this notion refers to the undoing of all or most forms of international cooperation, or to the abandonment of the multilateral trading system in favour of bilateral trade relations whereby the most powerful states are best able to secure their interests. Nonetheless, for reasons we elaborate below, socially progressive globalization necessarily spells the end of neoliberal economic globalization – or what some call 'hyper-globalization' (Rodrik, 2011) – where the elimination of obstacles to trade and financial flows in the name of economic growth constitutes an end in itself. Our position is that globalization[1] can take multiple forms and socially progressive, post-neoliberal reglobalization must prioritize social goods such as equality, progressive social reproduction and sustainability over economic growth.

At the same time, however, we are wary of the editors' suggestion that the inequalities of neoliberal globalization can be addressed by re-regulating or re-embedding liberal ideals within the political sphere (Bishop & Payne, 2019). As we demonstrate in detail, although this may lead to some progressive changes, it risks perpetuating gender-based and other hierarchies that operate within the economic and the political spheres, and in the so-called private sphere of the household. It also reproduces a false distinction between these spheres. This distinction fosters a narrow understanding of the social relations that constitute the economy and leads to forms of policy-making that are ultimately unable to address structural inequalities.

In the following section, we outline a feminist International Political Economy (IPE) theoretical perspective for the study of global trade that elucidates how gendered and other power relations shape and are shaped by trade relations at multiple sites and scales. This offers an alternative theoretical vantage point to more liberally-oriented approaches that focus on greater choice and opportunity in the 'public' sphere (i.e. the economy, politics etc.) (Bishop & Payne, 2019), which is, either implicitly or explicitly, analytically separated from the 'private' sphere of the household. Building on longstanding feminist critiques of liberal thought and economic practice, we seek to place the study of power in its various dimensions (economic, political, social) in the centre of the analysis and call for a radical rethinking of economic policy-making.

Using our feminist lens, in section two we explore a range of gender and trade initiatives pursued in trade governance in recent years. We identify policy initiatives that begin to consider the social basis of economic relations, including how trade policy affects women's (and men's) multiple roles in society and in the economy. However, we also argue that a number of factors limit the progressive potential of existing initiatives, including an adherence to a narrow understanding of economic growth as the primary purpose of trade, a limited understanding of how trade impacts on individuals, households and communities, and a failure to develop meaningful forms of democratization. In section three we outline concrete suggestions for how to formulate trade policies that, among other things, help undermine structural inequalities within the global political economy, prioritize progressive forms of social reproduction, infuse global trade politics with a more holistic understanding of economic activity, and democratize trade policy-making.

Toward a feminist IPE of trade

Trade policy reforms under neoliberal globalization have come with a deepening of gender-based inequalities in many areas. This is evidenced, for instance, in increases in the gender-based pay gap that have accompanied the incorporation of women into export-producing industries. Comparative studies have shown this to be the case in many countries where low-paid female labour constitutes a form of competitive advantage (Busse & Spielmann, 2006). Where trade liberalization increases the cost of food imports, this is disproportionately felt by the poorest households and women who tend to have less access to and control over income while also being primarily responsible for food purchase and preparation (Siddiqui, 2009).

Women, alongside certain racial and minority ethnic groups, are also over-represented among public-services users, partly because they tend to take on greater responsibility for care work. In most countries, they also make up the majority of workers in the health, social work and education sectors. This means that, when trade agreements liberalize public and essential services, these groups are disproportionately affected as users and workers (Williams, 2007). At the same time, loss of government revenue resulting from trade-policy reform – e.g. through tariff reductions – may have knock-on effects on public-services users, as public services fall prey to government cut-backs (Elson et al., 2007). If the gendered nature of public-services usage and the provisioning of paid and unpaid care are not taken into account, trade liberalization also risks decreasing the amount of care work performed overall.

While feminist scholars have been documenting the gendered impacts of trade for several decades (Williams, 2013), we have only recently witnessed a surge of interest on the part of a number of states, international organizations, NGOs and others to introduce gender and trade initiatives in global governance. Surveying different gender and trade initiatives offers us an entry point into thinking about one key question that motivates this Special Issue: what would a socially progressive form of globalization actually entail in practice?

From our perspective, the language of 're-regulating' or 're-embedding' economic relations used by the editors of the Special Issue, even where these are conceived as being 'post-neoliberal', has limited potential for radical transformation. Indeed, going back to John Ruggie's (1982) work, the aim of embedded liberalism is to combine global trade liberalization with domestic interventionism. The goal of the former is to increase wealth within the global economy, while the goal of the latter is to achieve economic stability within nation-states. However, the costs of creating domestic stability in the core capitalist countries were ultimately offloaded onto poorer countries (Muzaka & Bishop, 2015), increasing inequalities globally. Moreover, in a key passage, Ruggie claims that attempts to combine global liberalization and national interventionism necessarily led to the 'geographical, sectoral and institutional concentration' of trade and financial flows of the 1950s and 1960s (Ruggie, 1982, p. 400). Geographically, embedded liberal trade became concentrated among the countries that had designed the rules of the embedded-liberal trading system. This trade increasingly took place within the same economic sectors and among the same corporations. For Ruggie, this meant that the gains from trade were increasingly directed towards a select number of individual sectors and firms, which had the effect of increasing economic inequalities (Ruggie, 1982). Recalling this aspect of Ruggie's argument offers an important point of caution: even where domestic 'post-neoliberal' interventionism accompanies reglobalization, this may still cement and reproduce inequalities globally.

A separate critique of the language of embeddedness comes from feminist scholarship, which has long criticized liberalism for perpetuating a false distinction between the public and the private spheres and for ignoring inequalities in the latter. In their work, political economists such as Ruggie (1987, p. 387) and Karl Polanyi (1944)[2] analytically separate 'the economic' from 'society' (which includes political society and the family). This risks obscuring both the social relations that fundamentally constitute the economy and the hierarchical power relations that constitute society (Ferber & Nelson, 1993). As Nancy Fraser (2014, p. 544) writes with respect to Polanyi:

> Preoccupied exclusively with the corrosive effects of commodification upon communities, it [*The Great Transformation*] neglects injustices within communities, including injustices, such as slavery, serfdom and patriarchy, that depend on social constructions of labour, land and money precisely as non-commodities. Demonizing marketization, the book tends to idealize social protection, as it fails to note that protections have often served to entrench hierarchies and exclusions.

While Polanyi has provided an important contribution to critical political economy, we join Fraser in her wariness of the notion of 're-embedding', precisely because it fails to capture adequately the extent to which 'the economic' *and* 'the social' are themselves imbued with hierarchies. In so doing, it risks reproducing socially constructed injustices.

Building on these observations, we suggest that a feminist IPE perspective is necessary in order to elucidate how gendered and other power relations shape and are shaped by trade relations at multiple sites and scales. In particular, we deploy and extend three key analytical insights of feminist IPE scholarship, all of which are interrelated and have important implications for imagining a more progressive future global trading regime.

First, feminist IPE acknowledges the operation of structural inequalities in the global political economy, showing how existing gender norms and power relations shape one's participation in the economy at multiple sites and scales (Bedford & Rai, 2010; Elias & Roberts, 2018). In terms of trade, this explains, *inter alia*, why export promotion that relies on low-paid feminized labour tends to increase the gender pay gap, and why service liberalization tends to affect women and certain racial and minority ethnic groups most negatively. As Mariama Williams, a pioneer in gender research on trade, explains: 'the work is very clear from feminist economics … Trade liberalization does not create structural gender inequalities, but it may create conditions that can either enhance women's economic situation, or exacerbate their pre-existing gender inequality and bias' (Williams, 2019). Put differently, as trade policies affect people in multiple ways, they may either undermine or reproduce existing structural inequalities. As we will demonstrate below, many of the existing gender and trade initiatives remain committed to economic growth as the main purpose of trade and seem to assume that integrating women into existing economic structures will improve gender outcomes. In contrast, we advocate for the need to document better and dismantle actively structural inequalities. This involves, among other things, prioritizing progressive forms of social reproduction in trade theory and policy-making.

A second and related feminist insight is that there is a need to disturb the distinction between the economy and society perpetuated by liberalism in all its forms. One way that feminists have done this is by analytically centreing the relations of social reproduction that underpin all forms of economic activity. Within feminist IPE, most definitions of social reproduction relate to at least three aspects: the biological reproduction of the species, which includes social constructions of motherhood and the conditions under which this work is performed; the reproduction of the labour force (including subsistence, education and training); and the reproduction and provisioning of caring needs (Bakker, 2007, p. 541). Others add the reproduction of culture and ideology (Hoskyns & Rai, 2007) or, at a more abstract level, the reproduction of the conditions of social production in their totality, which includes the basic structures of production (Edholm et al., 1977). From our perspective, the important point to emphasize is that social reproduction takes place in different sites and spaces including the home and the community, through the state (i.e. in the health, social and education sectors), and in the market (including via paid labour in the formal and informal sectors). The point is not to reify a distinction between production and its outside – or 'the economy' and 'society' – but rather to show how the 'production of goods and services and the production of life are part of one integrated process' (Luxton, 2006, p. 36).

Bringing this insight into analyses of trade draws attention to economic relations and impacts that are ordinarily eclipsed from the purview of global trade, despite the fact that they are inherently part of global trade relations. This means, for example, that trade theory and policy analysis needs to consider the impact of trade on communities and people in their multiple roles as producers, workers, consumers (including consumers of public services), carers, and more – as well as the broader environmental conditions in which social reproduction takes place. Starting from the centrality of social reproduction further leads us to follow feminist IPE scholars in insisting that 'the production of people, meeting human needs, and fostering well-being should be the driving force of economics', rather than production for the purposes of economic growth and capital accumulation (Luxton, 2018, p. 37; see also Rai & Waylen, 2014). A crucial part of fostering well-being further involves a commitment to environmental sustainability.

Finally, feminist IPE provides a third analytical insight: it is essential to acknowledge heterodox and feminist knowledge about global trade and those political and societal actors that represent it as valuable and legitimate in trade policy processes. Orthodox knowledge about global trade cements the idea that open markets and free trade are desirable ends in themselves (Eagleton-Pierce, 2016). It is rooted in modernist and positivist dedications to 'rational economic man', whose self-interested, calculating and competitive behaviour is supposed to act as a model for all human decision-making (Ferber & Nelson, 2003; Folbre, 2001). In legal terms, this logic is locked in through binding and enforceable dispute-settlement mechanisms in trade agreements. In political terms, it performs a gate-keeping function in terms of who is considered a legitimate participant in trade policy-making (Hannah et al., 2015). Feminist scholars have criticized this locking-in of market principles because it locks out the rights of people to participate in democratic decision-making and privileges the rights of capital above those of the population (Bakker & Gill, 2006). Feminist IPE instead centres the experiences and voices of people, particularly women and marginalized groups, above open-market and free-trade prerogatives. Inclusiveness, the recognition of the intersectional dimensions of inequality, public transparency and accountability are key feminist concerns for global policy-making (Prügl & True, 2014) that go against the masculinized, elitist and legalized trade orthodoxy.

The (false) promise of existing gender and trade initiatives

Below, we evaluate existing gender and trade initiatives using the three analytical insights outlined above. Elsewhere, we surveyed global-policy practice in the field of gender and trade. Using total population sampling, we identified 77 initiatives launched since 1991 and coded them along 32 dimensions (Hannah, Roberts, et al., 2018). In this section, we assess four exemplary types of gender and trade initiatives emerging from our typology: women's entrepreneurship programmes, the World Trade Organization (WTO) Declaration on Trade and Women's Economic Empowerment, gender chapters in FTAs, and gender-based impact assessments. For each type of initiative, we ask the same questions: What is the overarching purpose of global trade? Does it recognize the centrality of structural gender inequalities to the global economy and seek actively to dismantle them? Does it adopt a narrow or broad understanding of economic relations, and does it further the democratization of global trade relations? We begin our analysis with a brief overview of these initiatives before assessing their promise of advancing gender equality in and through trade.

Currently, the most popular type of gender and trade initiative in global governance is support for women's entrepreneurship in the Global South (Hannah, Roberts, et al., 2018). The International Trade Centre (ITC)'s so-called 'SheTrades' initiative aims to connect one million women entrepreneurs to global markets by 2021. 'Aid for Trade' initiatives that are often part of official development assistance (concessional government aid designed to promote the economic development and welfare of developing countries) are now explicitly mandated for gender equality (WTO and OECD, 2019). Significant resources have also been dedicated to various micro-interventions in support of women who participate in cross-border trade. These interventions often aim to help women grow their enterprises through the provisioning of loans and/or financial literacy education, and to develop the knowledge and skills necessary to engage in trade.

Within this broader context, 121 WTO member-states and observers signed the WTO Declaration at the 2017 ministerial conference. It marks the first time WTO members have signalled a willingness to engage with what was previously seen as a human-rights issue. Although key members – notably India and the United States – remained outliers, the declaration raised the possibility that multilateral trade governance could connect with global economic and social agendas (Hannah, Scott, et al., 2018). A best-endeavour initiative by like-minded members, the declaration launched a fact-finding agenda intended to bolster the role of women in trade, particularly in new areas such as e-commerce. The Work Programme, in particular, commits signatories to seven multi-stakeholder workshops aimed at economically empowering women and integrating them into global value chains (WTO, 2017).

Outside of the multilateral system, there are currently four FTAs with specific gender chapters, and one with proposed text. They are: the Canada-Chile FTA, the Argentina-Chile FTA, the Chile-Uruguay FTA, the Canada-Israel FTA and the EU-Chile FTA. While there are numerous trade agreements containing gender provisions (Monteiro, 2018), gender chapters are the most recent and far-reaching trend in incorporating gender concerns into trade agreements. Like the WTO Declaration, gender chapters aim at advancing gender equality and increasing the participation of women in trade. They do so by affirming the importance of incorporating a gender perspective in international trade and commit parties to the FTA to redressing trade-related gender discrimination.

Alongside these legal texts, policy-makers have begun assessing the gendered impacts of trade policy. In 2017 Canada committed to applying Gender Based Analysis Plus (GBA+) to all federal budget items, including new FTAs. Canada has conducted one initial GBA+ of the Canada-Mercosur FTA to date (Global Affairs Canada, 2019). The European Union (EU) is also increasingly including a gender analysis under its ordinary Sustainability Impact Assessment procedure for FTAs – for example, for the EU-New Zealand FTA (European Commission, 2019). The United Nations Conference on Trade and Development (UNCTAD) has developed a methodology for gender-based impact assessments, named the Trade and Gender Toolbox (UNCTAD, 2017). It consists of four main components: (1) descriptive analysis of gender inequalities and the economic context of the country at stake; (2) quantitative analysis of the expected consequences of trade policies on the economy (in terms of exports, gross domestic product, sectoral labour demand) and particularly on women's participation in the economy; (3) a checklist for gender-sensitive accompanying measures and monitoring indicators; and (4) a 'Trade and Gender Index' treating female employment and gender gaps as indicators of gender inequalities in the workplace (used for within-country analysis over time).

Existing initiatives are welcome to the extent that they move towards acknowledging the links between social reproduction and trade policy, adopt a more holistic understanding of the impacts of trade and recognize that women's groups hold knowledge about global trade that is relevant for policy-making. However, they also risk cementing and even exacerbating social and economic inequalities in ways we set out below.

(Not) prioritizing social reproduction over economic growth

While some existing gender and trade initiatives show awareness of social reproductive activities, they do not abandon their commitment to economic growth as the purpose of global trade. Those initiatives most wedded to economic liberalism, such as ITC's 'SheTrades' and the WTO Declaration, focus on integrating women into a neoliberal economic model and a technocratic trade regime that prioritizes economic growth. More progressive initiatives, like the UNCTAD gender toolbox or the Argentina-Chile and Chile-Uruguay FTAs, are better attuned to how trade policies affect women's participation in the economy and outline domestic policies to mitigate the negative impacts of trade on workers, public-services users, carers, and more. Nonetheless, all gender chapters are stand-alone and generally not enforceable through dispute settlement (Larouche-Maltais & MacLaren, 2019). This means that their provisions find no application in clauses pertaining to trade in goods, trade in services, trade-related intellectual property rights (IPRs), investment protection, government procurement, micro, small and medium-sized enterprises (MSMEs), and e-commerce. The impacts of FTAs in these areas have been shown to exacerbate pre-existing gender inequalities (Roberts et al., 2019). This raises legitimate concerns that gender and trade initiatives in their present form constitute minor policy adjustments that appear to prioritize social goals, but in effect serve as window-dressing, further entrenching neoliberal trade.

The disagreement playing out among WTO member-states over the WTO Declaration is another example of how gender and trade initiatives may reproduce, rather than undermine existing conflicts and the inequitable power relations of the global trading system. The declaration is designed to push forward liberalization and longstanding items on the WTO agenda, including: the removal of trade barriers, trade financing, public procurement, MSMEs and trade facilitation. By contrast, non-signatories in the WTO claim the key to achieving gender equality lies in fulfilling the abandoned Doha Development Agenda, including the liberalization of agriculture through the elimination of domestic subsidies and the fair use of flexibilities such as the special-safeguard mechanism and public stockholding (Mlumbi-Peter, 2019). Proponents on both sides of the argument criticize what they see as the other side's instrumentalization of the gender and trade nexus in order to push through their pre-existing interests in multilateral negotiations. The distribution of expected gains is not explicitly discussed. Instead, it is assumed that either state or market forces will assure women benefit from the reforms, without recognition of the fact that unequal gendered power relations persist in both spheres, as we explained above.

(Partially) considering the multi-faceted impacts of trade policy

The most progressive potential of existing gender and trade initiatives lies in a general acknowledgement that women feel the impacts of trade policy in their multiple roles in society. For example, the EU's proposed text for a gender chapter in EU-Chile acknowledges that 'trade liberalisation may affect men and women in different ways as workers, producers, traders or consumers' (European Commission, 2018). Other gender chapters recognize the importance of strengthening 'women's enhanced participation in the labour market and their economic independence and access to, and ownership of, economic resources' (Canada-Chile Art N bis-01.5), while Argentina-Chile adds access to 'decent work' to this list (Art. 15.1.4). Canada's GBA+ process for gender-based impact assessments includes a range of intersectional concerns, paying attention to relations based on race, religion, indigenous heritage, socio-economic status, and more (Government of Canada, 2018). The UNCTAD gender toolbox points to the need to assess whether export-promotion policies include support for childcare and whether reductions in public expenditures and increases in taxation affect public-services access and the burden of care work (UNCTAD, 2017, p. 28).

However, there is no coherent or systematic approach to embedding a broad understanding of economic activity in trade policy, owing to the fact that social reproduction remains (at best) a second-order concern for trade policy-makers. This limits well-intentioned approaches. For example, Canada's GBA+ has not been applied to patterns of consumption, public-services access or unpaid care work. The UNCTAD gender toolbox does not consider the intersection of proposed trade policies and pre-existing social and economic hierarchies. Moreover, although gender-based impact assessment and monitoring can be useful in order to identify how trade policy can be combined with appropriate social policy to work to reduce gender inequality, the practice can often be different. Impact-assessment exercises are mainly used to legitimate trade-policy choices in the public debate (George, 2015), rather than to mitigate the adverse anticipated, or demonstrated, effects of trade policies, especially as these impact on consumption, relations of care, leisure time, and so on (Hannah, Roberts, et al., 2018; Roberts et al., 2019).

At the same time, many entrepreneurship initiatives and the WTO Declaration focus exclusively on the benefits of entrepreneurship from the perspective of employment and income, limiting their efforts to integrating women into existing economic relations. On the one hand, the support for women-owned SMEs is much needed in a context where they are among those businesses most negatively impacted by import competition under trade liberalization (Gender and Development Network, 2017, pp. 4–5). However, empowering women through entrepreneurship also requires a consideration of the effects this has on their working conditions and domestic obligations, ensuring that entrepreneurship is not conflated with unpaid and precarious work that increases the double burden on women (Roberts & Zulfiqar, 2019). This needs to be accompanied by attempts to bring about broader structural change since women are more likely to choose entrepreneurship because of poverty, lack of labour market opportunities, discriminatory property and inheritance laws, and social norms that limit their mobility and assign them primary responsibility for care work (Jamali, 2009; Vita et al., 2014).

A similar point can be made about achieving women's economic empowerment through e-commerce and digital trade, which is a popular focus of many initiatives. Treating the digital economy as a panacea for 'inclusive economic growth' and women's economic empowerment will cement existing structural inequalities if policy initiatives are not aimed at ensuring access to connectivity for women and other vulnerable groups in the so-called 'digital divide' (ITC, 2017). There are also concerns regarding corporate power in the field of digital trade and e-commerce. The inclusion of women-owned MSMEs in markets dominated by corporate giants like Amazon and Google is unlikely to yield significant benefits to vulnerable populations (James, 2019).

(Not) democratizing trade politics

While some initiatives recognize that women's groups hold valuable knowledge of global trade, they fall short of prompting further democratization of trade policy formation. Stakeholder consultation is a common mechanism across all gender and trade initiatives; yet there is no indication that this means meaningful participation of civil society and women's groups in the decisions related to the formulation, implementation or impact assessment of trade policy.

Despite campaigning since the Uruguay Round and before, civil society organizations, especially women's organizations, were not consulted in the design and execution of the WTO Declaration. Indeed, 164 women's groups and allied NGOs opposed the declaration because it 'appears to be designed to mask the failures of the WTO and its role in deepening inequality and exploitation' (Our World is Not for Sale, 2017). Some consider the declaration to be a 'Trojan horse' for new issues such as e-commerce, MSMEs and investment protection (Bissio, 2017). Others suggest that the 'proposals on gender, small and medium enterprises, [and] facilitating investment for development belie the determination to abandon [the] promises of a Doha Development Round, with negative impacts on billions of women' (Kelsey, 2017). These criticisms are, in part, reactions to the fact that civil society voices have been marginalized and that the declaration upholds existing trade orthodoxy. This means that the prospects for the work arising from the declaration to achieve gender equality and minimize the adverse impacts of trade policy on women and other vulnerable populations are grim.

The way forward

From our perspective, a progressive reform of the global trade regime requires at least three interrelated moves that map on to our three analytical insights. First, it requires redefining the purpose of global trade in a way that de-prioritizes economic growth and supports progressive forms of social reproduction. Second, it requires broadening our understanding of what constitutes economic activity and therefore which relations need to be considered in trade discourses and trade policy-making. Third, it involves the democratization of global trade relations.

To elaborate, *first*, as environmental activists have argued, formulating trade policies from the perspective of overarching societal goals rather than from the perspective of economic growth would radically alter their form and content (Klein, 2014). Although global trade institutions generally acknowledge that trade expansion is a means to other societal ends, such as sustainable development, full employment, human rights, the rule of law, democracy, and, increasingly, gender equality, substantial trade rules continue to be formulated from the perspective of trade flows (Trommer, 2016).[3] They leave intact a status quo in global trade that aims for economic growth through the expansion of merchandise and services trade and investment, irrespective of the negative impacts that this economic model has on the identified overarching societal goals. In terms of gender relations, prioritizing economic growth invariably leads to a line of thinking whereby women's empowerment means bringing the largest possible number of women into the fold of those societal groups that gain directly from increased trade flows: namely, export-oriented corporations and investors. As we have argued, such approaches uphold, and potentially deepen, many of the structural inequalities in which gender inequalities are embedded, rather than actively dismantle them.

Instead, a feminist global trade politics prioritizes progressive forms of social reproduction as the main purpose of global trade and formulates trade policies from this perspective. This means moving away from a trade regime that confers legal entitlements guaranteed by states to corporations and investors, but only attributes well-intentioned but unenforceable rights to women – and often workers in general – and the environment. To achieve a progressive post-neoliberal trade system, we must think seriously about what trade agreements would look like if we were to inscribe the rights of women and other groups that have the potential to be most negatively impacted by trade directly into law, whether at the WTO or through FTAs (Coleman, 2018).

In order to do so, it is essential to re-introduce a conversation about how trade policy can be designed to improve labour standards. These standards must extend beyond the 'formal' productive sphere to include improved conditions in informal and unpaid forms of work – areas where women are over-represented globally. Several International Labour Organisation (ILO) conventions would go a long way in this regard if they were enforced in a similar way to trade agreements. Specifically, four conventions set standards for equality of opportunity and treatment at work. They are: ILO Convention number 100 on equal remuneration, number 111 on discrimination in respect of employment and occupation, number 156 on workers with family responsibilities, and number 190 on violence and harassment. Alongside the eight ILO Core Labour Standards, as well as compliance with up-to-date ILO conventions and instruments such as the Forced Labour Protocol and ILO Conventions on health and safety at work, these commitments could be made pre-conditions for entering into trade negotiations.

The European Trade Union Confederation (ETUC)'s set of recommendations for how labour rights can be made effective in trade agreements offers another concrete example of how trade policy can be done differently (ETUC, 2017). We welcome the ETUC's demand that 'every part of trade agreements (such as sections on investment protection or service listing) be consistent with human rights commitments' and full and enforceable dispute settlement be applied to such commitments (ETUC, 2017). We see further need also to include specific institutional commitments to addressing gender-based wage gaps, the precarity of part-time work, informal work and entrepreneurship, and poor labour conditions in areas where women are drawn into exploitative work as part of export-driven growth strategies. At the broadest level, there is a need to address the mismatch between core labour standards and the structural causes that drive women and other vulnerable groups into exploitative work.

A *second* intricately related move in the repurposing of global trade involves developing and applying a broader understanding of what constitutes economic activity and therefore which relations need to be considered in trade discourses and trade policy-making. Instead of orienting trade discourses and policies around economic indicators, there is a need to consider how trade is underpinned by and works to impact on relations of social reproduction. From this perspective, the main stakeholders in trade policy-making are not only governments and business – as is often taken to be the case – but rather people who engage with trade in their multiple roles as producers, workers, consumers (including consumers of public services), carers, and so on.

Instead of adding stand-alone gender clauses or chapters to existing trade agreements that are otherwise left unchanged, there is a need to (re-)formulate every commitment in trade agreements from the perspective of progressive forms of social reproduction. As noted above, the current practice involves writing clauses that ensure the maximization of trade flows and casting the balancing exercise into exceptions clauses, which are required to be applied in the least trade-restrictive way (this occurs across the WTO-covered agreements and FTAs). A more progressive way forward requires that market access and national treatment commitments for goods and services, IPRs, investment clauses, and all other clauses in agreements are written in ways that balance the goal of enabling global trade flows with other societal goals. If gender concerns are written into trade rules in this way, it would also resolve the shortcoming that gender chapters are not enforceable at present.

It is further crucial that trade institutions give effect to the Beijing Platform for Action – currently the only international legal instrument on gender equality that addresses global trade relations directly. It asks governments to 'enable women to gain access to full and equal participation in the formulation of policies and definition of structures through such bodies as ministries of finance and trade, national economic commissions, economic research institutes and other key agencies, as well as through their participation in appropriate international bodies' (Article 165.d). It further states that they must 'seek to ensure that national policies related to international and regional trade agreements do not have an adverse impact on women's new and traditional economic activities' (Article 165.k). The Beijing Platform also counts unremunerated, family and community work as part of economic activity and acknowledges that economic activity can be carried out in formal or informal, protected and poorly or unprotected, domestic or migrant settings across production, service delivery, subsistence agriculture and entrepreneurship.

In order to meet the requirements of the Beijing Platform, there is a need to engage in much more robust impact assessment and monitoring. In existing human rights impact assessments of trade policy, 'some impacts that would undoubtedly be considered serious from a human rights perspective do seem to be apparent', but they remain unidentified or are viewed as insignificant in reports commissioned, compiled and consumed from the dominant trade perspective (Harrison & Goller, 2008, p. 599). The central purpose of *ex ante* and *ex post* impact assessments has to be to inform trade policy-making, rather than to legitimate trade policy choices in the public debate, as is currently the case. There are a number of progressive methodologies that could form the basis of a comprehensive gender-based impact assessment framework, including the UNCTAD toolbox, as well as proposals made by other UN agencies (e.g. UNEP, 2001) and in the scholarship (e.g. Fontana, 2016; Walker, 2005). In our view, there is a need to go even further than many of these suggestions. As we have elaborated elsewhere (Hannah, Roberts, et al., 2018), gender-based impact assessments can contribute to a progressive, feminist post-neoliberal trade system *if* they are based on several key principles. For one, all parties to an agreement must assess the broader context, undertaking a broad survey before beginning gender-impact modelling in order to understand how existing gender norms and power relations shape forms of economic participation at multiple sites and scales within the territories entering into the agreement. Gendered computable general equilibrium modelling may be helpful in predicting the effects of a proposed trade agreement on men and women in their various roles (Fontana, 2004) if they make use of existing feminist methodologies such as Social Accountability Matrices and model varying degrees of liberalization. Additional, qualitative modes of inquiry are required to capture changes in the quality of employment, control over resources, and the effects of rules governing investment protections, IPRs, procurement, and more. These methods include engagement with women's groups and civil society actors in the areas under investigation.

This brings us to the *third* interrelated move that is necessary for a more equitable post-neoliberal trading system. This entails the democratization of trade policy-making, which requires that we take seriously the voices of women's groups, trade unions and civil society organizations. The dominant model at present for civil society inclusion in trade policy-making is *de facto* a one-way street where informal advocacy channels are largely closed to non-business civil-society groups and where policy elites consider the ideas and knowledge about global trade that non-business civil-society groups provide to be ill-informed about the workings of the global economy (Hannah, 2016; Hannah et al., 2015). As our discussion has made clear, global trade affects people in their multiple roles and representatives of different groups of people and sectors of society have to have a say when trade-policy choices are made.

In order to make civil-society representation in global trade decision-making effective, three governance trends of the past decade have to be reversed. First, the shift towards FTAs as preferred trade governance venues has undermined many of the transparency and accountability gains made at the WTO following the 1999 Seattle protests. In particular, so-called 'mega-regionals' and 'twenty-first century trade agreements', which contain many of the problematic rules on services, IP, investment and government procurement, have been carried out with virtually no access to information outside of trade ministries.

Second, diversity in civil-society representation has been lost in core countries due to funding cuts in the austerity era, and in particular when it comes to women's groups' engagement in trade advocacy (Macdonald et al., 2018). These groups bring not only important knowledge about how trade affects women's (and other minorities') lives to the attention of trade policy-makers, but their knowledge about the global trade system can bridge the divide between trade-policy circles and the broader public, which often sees trade policy as technocratic, complex and abstract.

Third, and in contrast with the inclusion of civil-society representation in the failed International Trade Organisation charter negotiated in the 1940s, the view that direct and formal involvement of civil-society groups in the work of trade institutions is 'not possible' has been further entrenched among policy-makers in the embedded liberal and neoliberal eras (WTO, 1996). While dominant trade institutions by and large continue to subscribe to the view that civil society has a second-order role to play at best (Hannah, Janzwood, et al., 2018), there are examples of more inclusive and participatory models at the fringes of the global economy. In Sub-Saharan Africa, South Africa's tripartite model of trade policy-making and the Economic Community of West African States' participatory model for negotiating its Economic Partnership Agreement with the EU stand as concrete examples (Trommer, 2014). In the United Kingdom, the House of Commons International Trade Committee outlined its policy on transparency and scrutiny in December 2018 (House of Commons International Trade Committee, 2018). The report highlights the important role for business and civil society and for parliamentary oversight in trade policy-making and implementation.

This article has set out a project of reform that we believe to be necessary in order to build a feminist post-neoliberal trading system. We have suggested that, if trade policy is to be used as a means of achieving gender equality, it must be designed in a way that addresses structural inequalities. Reforming the rules of global trade in ways that afford states greater domestic policy space is not sufficient in this regard, as the state may itself work to reproduce inequalities. There is therefore a need for a more thorough shift in macroeconomic policy-making at the national and global levels so that structural inequalities are redressed and progressive forms of social reproduction prioritized above economic growth, which is currently 'locked in' to trade agreements and global institutions. Second, creating a more gender-equitable trading system requires looking beyond economic indicators to consider the ways in which relations of social reproduction underpin and are impacted by trade. This means that trade policy-makers need to have a holistic understanding of what constitutes the economy and consider the impacts of trade on households, care work, unpaid labour, the informal economy, and the broader ecological conditions under which social reproduction takes place. Finally, we need to democratize governance structures. This means not only widening the scope of social and political actors who meaningfully participate in trade policy-making, but also widening the scope of ideas and lived experiences that count as legitimate trade concerns. While we have pointed to a number of concrete steps that can and should be taken in support of these objectives, we must also remain open about the direction of change if we are to take the principle of democratic decision-making seriously.

Notes

1. We understand globalization to refer to any historical process marked by the existence of economic, political, social and cultural exchanges among different political communities across the world.
2. Ruggie (1982, p. 387) credits Polanyi (1944) with developing the distinction between 'embedded' and 'disembedded' economic orders.
3. Where trade rules are formulated to provide for a balancing exercise between trade flows and ulterior societal ends, as under the General Agreement on Tariffs and Trade (GATT) Article XX, they stipulate that those ulterior ends need to be pursued in ways that are least trade-restrictive.

Disclosure statement

No potential conflict of interest was reported by the author(s).

Funding

This work was supported by the Social Sciences and Humanities Research Council of Canada (SSHRC) [grant number 430-2018-00349] and the SSHRC-Economic and Social Research Council Knowledge Synthesis [grant number 872-2018-0012].

ORCID

Erin Hannah http://orcid.org/0000-0001-8062-6035
Adrienne Roberts http://orcid.org/0000-0002-0204-5152
Silke Trommer http://orcid.org/0000-0001-9719-8065

References

Bakker, I. (2007). Social reproduction and the constitution of a gendered political economy. *New Political Economy, 12*(4), 541–556. https://doi.org/10.1080/13563460701661561

Bakker, I., & Gill, S. (2006). New constitutionalism and the social reproduction of caring institutions. *Theoretical Medicine and Bioethics, 27*(1), 35–57. https://doi.org/10.1007/s11017-005-5756-z

Bedford, K., & Rai, S. (2010). Feminists theorize international political economy. *Signs: Journal of Women in Culture and Society, 36*(1), https://doi.org/10.1086/652910

Bishop, M. L., & Payne, A. (2019, October 15). Reglobalisation in action – part 1: Rehearsing the concept. SPERI.Comment: The political economy blog. https://speri.dept.shef.ac.uk/2019/10/15/reglobalisation-in-action-part-1-rehearsing-the-concept/

Bishop, M. L., & Payne, A. (2020a). The political economies of different globalizations: Theorizing reglobalization. *Globalizations*. doi:10.1080/14747731.2020.1779963

Bishop, M. L., & Payne, A. (2020b). Steering towards reglobalization: Can a reformed G20 rise to the occasion? *Globalizations*. doi:10.1080/14747731.2020.1779964

Bissio, R. (2017, December 11). Is 'gender' a Trojan horse to introduce new issues at WTO? Third world network. https://twnetwork.org/wto/%E2%80%9Cgender%E2%80%9D-trojan-horse-introduce-new-issues-wto

Busse, M., & Spielmann, C. (2006). Gender inequality and trade. *Review of International Economics*, *14*(3), 362–379. https://doi.org/10.1111/j.1467-9396.2006.00589.x

Coleman, L. M. (2018). Global social fascism: Violence, law and twenty-first century plunder, CGPE Working Paper, University of Sussex. https://www.sussex.ac.uk/webteam/gateway/file.php?name=global-social-fascism-wp15-coleman-montesinos.pdf&site=359

Eagleton-Pierce, M. (2016). *Neoliberalism: The key concepts*. Routledge.

Edholm, F., Harris, O., & Young, K. (1977). Conceptualising women. *Critique of Anthropology*, *3*(9–10), 101–130. https://journals.sagepub.com/doi/10.1177/0308275X7800300905

Elias, J., & Roberts, A. (Eds.). (2018). *Handbook on the international political economy of gender*. Edward Elgar.

Elson, D., Grown, C., & Cağatay, N. (2007). Mainstream, heterodox and feminist trade theory. In I. van Staveren, C. G. Elson, & N. Çağatay (Eds.), *The feminist economics of trade* (pp. 33–52). London: Routledge.

ETUC. (2017). ETUC submission on the non-paper of the commission services and trade and sustainable development (TSD) chapters in EU Free Trade Agreements (FTA). https://www.etuc.org/en/document/etuc-submission-non-paper-commission-services-trade-and-sustainable-development-tsd

European Commission. (2018, June 22). Draft provisions on trade and gender equality in the context of the modernisation of the EU-Chile Association Agreement. https //trade.ec.europa.eu/doclib/docs/2018/june/tradoc_156962.pdf

European Commission. (2019). Trade sustainability impact assessment in support of FTA negotiations between the European Union and New Zealand, Draft Inception Report. https://trade-sia-new-zealand.eu/images/reports/EU-NZ_SIA_Draft_Inception_Report.pdf

Ferber, M. A., & Nelson, J. A. (1993). *Beyond economic man: Feminist theory and economics*. The University of Chicago Press.

Ferber, M. A., & Nelson, J. A. (2003). *Feminist economics today: Beyond economic man*. Chicago: The University of Chicago Press.

Folbre, N. (2001). *The invisible heart: Economics and family values*. The New Press.

Fontana, M. (2004). Modelling the effects of trade on women, at work and at home: Comparative perspectives. *Economie Internationale*, *3*(99), 49–80.

Fontana, M. (2016). *Gender equality in trade agreements. Study commissioned by the policy department for citizen's rights and constitutional affairs*. European Union.

Fraser, N. (2014). Can societies be commodities all the way down?: Post-Polanyian reflections on capitalist crisis. *Economy and Society*, *43*(4), 541–558. https://doi.org/10.1080/03085147.2014.898822

Gender & Development Network. (2017). *Making trade work for gender equality*. https://gadnetwork.org/gadn-resources/2017/7/4/making-trade-work-for-gender-equality-1

George, C. (2015). Numbers: The role of computable general equilibrium modeling in legitimizing trade policy. In E. Hannah, S. Scott, & S. Trommer (Eds.), *Expert knowledge in global trade* (pp. 107–123). Routledge.

Global Affairs Canada. (2019). *Summary of initial gender-based analysis plus for Canada-Mercosur free trade agreement negotiations*. https://www.international.gc.ca/trade-commerce/assets/pdfs/gba_plus_summary-acs_plus_resume_eng.pdf

Government of Canada. (2018). *Gender-based analysis plus*. https://cfc-swc.gc.ca/gba-acs/approach-approche-en.html

Hannah, E. (2016). *NGOs and global trade: Non-state voices in EU trade policymaking*. Routledge.

Hannah, E., Janzwood, A., Scott, J., & Wilkinson, R. (2018). What kind of civil society? The changing complexion of public engagement at the WTO. *Journal of World Trade*, *52*(1), 113–141. https://kluwerlawonline.com/journalarticle/Journal+of+World+Trade/52.1/TRAD2018006

Hannah, E., Roberts, A., & Trommer, S. (2018). *Gendering global trade governance through Canada-UK trade relations*. Knowledge synthesis grant: Final report. https://www.kings.uwo.ca/kings/assets/File/academics/polisci/bios/hannah/KSG-Final-Report.pdf

Hannah, E., Scott, J., & Trommer, S. (2015). *Expert knowledge in global trade*. Routledge.

Hannah, E., Scott, J., & Wilkinson, R. (2018). The WTO in Buenos Aires: The outcome and its significance for the future of the multilateral trading system. *World Economy*, *41*(10), 2578–2598. https://doi.org/10.1111/twec.12657

Harrison, J., & Goller, A. (2008). Trade and human rights: What does 'impact assessment' have to offer? *Human Rights Law Review*, *8*(4), 587–615. https://doi.org/10.1093/hrlr/ngn026

Hoskyns, C., & Rai, S. M. (2007). Recasting the global political economy: Counting women's unpaid work. *New Political Economy, 12*(3), 297–317. https://doi.org/10.1080/13563460701485268

House of Commons International Trade Committee. (2018). *UK trade policy transparency and scrutiny. Sixth report of session 2017–2019. HC 1043.*

ITC. (2017). *New pathways to e-commerce: A global MSMEs competitiveness survey*. https://www.intracen.org/uploadedFiles/intracenorg/Content/Publications/New%20Pathways%20to%20E-commerce_Low%20res(2).pdf

Jamali, D. (2009). Constraints and opportunities facing women entrepreneurs in developing countries: A relational perspective. *Gender in Management: An International Journal, 24*(4), 232–251. https://doi.org/10.1108/17542410910961532

James, D. (2019). Anti-development impacts of tax-related provisions in proposed rules on digital trade in the WTO. *Development, 62*(1-4), 58–65. https://doi.org/10.1057/s41301-019-00205-4

Kelsey, J. (2017, December 13). Gender 'Pinkwashing' at the WTO bodes ill. *Scoop Independent News*. https://www.scoop.co.nz/stories/PO1712/S00117/gender-pinkwashing-at-the-wto-bodes-ill.htm

Klein, N. (2014). *This changes everything: Capitalism vs the climate*. Simon & Schuster.

Larouche-Maltais, A., & MacLaren, B. (2019). *Making gender responsive free trade agreements*. Conference Board of Canada.

Luxton, M. (2006). Feminist political economy in Canada and the politics of social reproduction. In K. Bezanson & M. Luxton (Eds.), *Social reproduction: Feminist political economy challenges neo-liberalism* (pp. 11–44). Queens University Press.

Luxton, M. (2018). The production of life itself: Gender, social reproduction and IPE. In J. Elias & A. Roberts (Eds.), *Handbook on the international political economy of gender* (pp. 37–49). Edward Elgar.

Macdonald, L., Ibrahim N. & Sinclair, S. (2018, July–August). Gender, trade and austerity. *The Monitor*, Canadian Centre for Policy Alternatives, pp. 38–39.

Mlumbi-Peter, X. (2019, October 10). *Speaking on the panel 'what do women need? WTO reform for a comprehensive gender-friendly trading system, WTO public forum.* World Trade Organization.

Monteiro, J.-A. (2018). *Gender-related provisions in regional trade agreements* (Staff Working Paper ERSD-2018-15). World Trade Organization.

Muzaka, V., & Bishop, M. (2015). Doha stalemate: The end of trade multilateralism? *Review of International Studies, 41*(2), 383–406. https://doi.org/10.1017/S0260210514000266

OHCHR. (2015). *UN experts voice concern over adverse impact of free trade and investment agreements on human rights*. https://ohchr.org/EN/NewsEvents/Pages/DisplayNews.aspx?NewsID=16031

Our World is Not for Sale. (2017, December 13). *Women's rights groups call on governments to reject the WTO Declaration on Women's Economic Empowerment*. https://ourworldisnotforsale.net/2017/Feminist_stmt.pdf

Polanyi, K. (1944). *The great transformation: The political and economic origins of our time*. Beacon Press.

Prügl, E., & True, J. (2014). Equality means business? Governing gender through transnational public-private partnerships. *Review of International Political Economy, 21*(6), 1137–1169. https://www.tandfonline.com/doi/abs/10.1080/09692290.2013.849277

Rai, S. M., & Waylen, G. (2014). *New frontiers in feminist political economy*. Routledge.

Roberts, A., Trommer, S., & Hannah, E. (2019). *Gender impacts of trade and investment agreements*. Policy briefing prepared for the UK Women's Budget Group. https://wbg.org.uk/analysis/uk-policy-briefings/gender-impacts-of-trade-and-investment-agreements/

Roberts, A., & Zulfiqar, G. (2019). The political economy of women's entrepreneurship initiatives in Pakistan: Reflections on gender, class, and 'development'. *Review of International Political Economy, 26*(3), 410–435. https://doi.org/10.1080/09692290.2018.1554538

Rodrik, D. (2011). *The globalization paradox: Democracy and the future of the world economy*. WW Norton & Company.

Ruggie, J. G. (1982). International regimes, transactions and change: Embedded liberalism in the postwar economic order. *International Organization, 36*(2), 379–415. https://doi.org/10.1017/S0020818300018993

Siddiqui, R. (2009). Modeling gender effects of Pakistan's trade liberalization. *Feminist Economics, 15*(3), 287–321. https://doi.org/10.1080/13545700902964295

Trommer, S. (2014). *Transformations in trade politics: Participatory trade politics in West Africa*. Routledge.

Trommer, S. (2016). Trade policy communities, expert language and the de-humanization of world trade. In E. Hannah, J. Scott, & S. Trommer (Eds.), *Expert knowledge in global trade* (pp. 63–82). Routledge.

UNCTAD. (2017). *Trade and gender toolbox: How will the economic partnership agreement between the European Union and the East African community affect Kenyan women?*.
UNEP. (2001). *Reference manual for the integrated assessment of trade-related policies*. United Nations.
van Staveren, I., Elson, C. G., & Çağatay, N. (Eds.). (2007). *The feminist economics of trade*. Routledge.
Vita, L. D., Mari, M., & Poggesi, S. (2014). Women entrepreneurs in and from developing countries: Evidence from the literature. *European Management Journal, 32*(3), 451–460. https://doi.org/10.1016/j.emj.2013.07.009
Walker, S. (2005). Human rights impact assessments of trade-related policies. In M. Gehring & M.-C. Segger (Eds.), *Sustainable development in world trade law* (pp. 217–256). Kluwer Law International.
Williams, M. (2007). Gender issues in the multilateral trading system. In I. van Staveren, C. G. Elson, & N. Çağatay (Eds.), *The feminist economics of trade* (pp. 277–291). London: Routledge.
Williams, M. (2013). A perspective on feminist international organizing from the bottom up: The case of the ITGN and the WTO. In G. Caglar, E. Prugl, & S. Zwingel (Eds.), *Feminist strategies in international governance* (pp. 92–108). Routledge.
Williams, M. (2019, October 10). *Speaking on the panel "what do women need? WTO reform for a comprehensive gender-friendly trading system", WTO public forum*. World Trade Organization.
WTO. (1996). *Guidelines for arrangements on relations with non-governmental organizations*. WT/L/162. World Trade Organization.
WTO. (2017, December). Joint declaration on trade and women's economic empowerment on the occasion of the WTO Ministerial Conference in Buenos Aires. https://www.wto.org/english/thewto_e/minist_e/mc11_e/genderdeclarationmc11_e.pdf
WTO and OECD. (2019). *Aid for trade at a glance 2019: Supporting economic diversification and empowerment*. https://www.oecd.org/dac/aft/aid-for-trade-at-a-glance-22234411.htm

Reforming global climate governance in an age of bullshit

Hayley Stevenson

ABSTRACT
There is a significant deficit of 'ecological integrity' in contemporary climate change governance, defined as explicit recognition of the mismatch between rhetoric, intentions and actions. This deficit is not unique to climate governance: we live in an age of bullshit (indifference to the truth). Philosopher Harry Frankfurt (*On bullshit*, 2005, Princeton University Press) identifies this as 'one of the most salient features of our culture'. In this article, I argue that the concept captures the inconsistencies we observe in global climate governance. I begin by conceptualizing it and identifying the various forms it can take. I then provide an overview of the past three decades of global climate governance, before analysing illustrative examples of bullshit. I conclude by proposing reforms to the climate regime's accountability arrangements to enhance the integrity and limit the harmful effects of bullshit in global climate governance.

1. Introduction

Globalization and climate change are intimately and inextricably related. Of course, countries were emitting greenhouse gas (GHG) emissions long before globalization became a defining characteristic of the international order. But the 'widening, deepening and speeding up of worldwide interconnectedness' (Held et al., 1999, p. 2) has magnified the scope of the capitalist growth imperative, and created and consolidated highly polluting practices and processes (such as high volumes of extraction, trade and transportation). But, as the editors of this special issue note, globalization has not been all bad, even for climate change (Bishop & Payne, 2020a, 2020b). It has strengthened the potential for multilateral cooperation on climate change and enabled new forms of cooperation among state and non-state actors (as well as exclusively among non-state actors). But, in a context of *neoliberal* globalization, the global climate regime has produced norms and rules that tend to privilege and protect the interests of global elites over the needs of the global majority. The climate regime has proven more effective in protecting neoliberal globalization than in resolving the climate crisis. This regime is increasingly unfit for purpose and in urgent need of reform.

In this article, I focus on one particular problem within global climate governance: the prevalence of bullshit. I argue that efforts to reform and 'reglobalize' international cooperation on climate change need to address the deficit of ecological integrity, defined as explicit recognition of the mismatch between rhetoric, intentions and actions. There is no shortage of declarations, pledges, and policies promising ambitious emissions reductions. And yet, emissions continue to rise and mitigation actions fall far short of the ambition required to ensure a stable climate. Words are rarely supported by sincere ambition and serious action. Scholarship critical of environmental and climate politics is, of course, plentiful, but scholars have yet to come to terms with the challenges posed by insincerity. It is a theme only recently coming under scrutiny. Barry and Blühdorn (2018, p. 249) observe that environmental decision-making is characterized by 'half-heartedness, pretending and delay'. Such 'symbolic politics', they argue, is a common strategy that '(i)n contexts of uncertainty or lacking resources … may maintain political momentum until more information has become available, or more resources and support have been mobilized for the implementation of more satisfactory solutions'. Hudson (2019), by contrast, is concerned that insincerity undermines the potential for real victories: 'Taking fake victories at face value strengthens the fakers, reassures the waverers that they don't need to get involved, and does *nothing* to build our own capacity to tell the truth and expose lies'. Geden (2016, p. 1) observes that climate change policy and research communities tend to assume 'consistency between talk, decisions, and actions'. But 'real-world policymaking', he argues, is inherently inconsistent. To deal with inconsistency between progressive rhetoric and cautious action, most governments resort to hypocrisy (Geden, 2016, p. 5). Gunster et al. (2018) show that charges of hypocrisy can be used to undermine the credibility of climate advocates, but are more commonly invoked by progressives seeking more ambitious climate action. The impact of insincerity and hypocrisy on global climate and environmental governance, as well as citizens' efforts to hold actors to account, clearly warrants greater research.

In this article, I argue that the concept of bullshit captures the mistruths and inconsistencies we observe in global climate governance, draws our attention to the insidious effects of deceit and helps us grasp the kinds of reform needed. As awareness of the climate crisis spreads, citizens are increasingly demanding action, but the complexity of climate change science and policy makes this domain particularly vulnerable to insincerity and hypocrisy. Few citizens have the capacity to readily distinguish truth from bullshit in the pronouncements of political leaders and policy actors. It is, therefore, an urgent, albeit difficult, problem to address in reforming the climate regime. In the following section, I conceptualize bullshit and identify the various forms it can take. I then provide an overview of the past three decades of global climate governance, before analysing illustrative examples of bullshit. I conclude by proposing ways to reform and reglobalize the climate regime. Subjecting the regime to greater public scrutiny and accountability could enhance the integrity and limit the harmful effects of bullshit on global climate governance.

2. Conceptualizing bullshit

Harry Frankfurt's 1986 essay 'On Bullshit, later reprinted as a short book (Frankfurt, 2005), was the first work to trigger interest in the nature and role of bullshit in public life. Political theorists have conceptualized bullshit as both an activity (verb) and a product (noun). Analysing bullshit as an activity (bullshitting) focuses more on the actor (the bull) and their motives while focusing on bullshit as a product (the shit) minimizes the importance of prior motives (Cohen, 2002). The former is best illustrated in the work of Harry Frankfurt (2005, 2007), while the latter is developed by G.A. Cohen (2002).

Frankfurt was one of the first to theorize bullshit, although his work owes much to Black's prior (1985) work on humbug, which he saw as distinct from bullshit only in its more polite tone (Frankfurt, 2005, pp. 4–5). Frankfurt argued that the bullshitter speaks and acts 'without any regard for how things really are' (Frankfurt, 2005, p. 30). It is this indifference to the truth which Frankfurt argues is the 'essence' of bullshit and is ultimately more pernicious that straight-out lying (Frankfurt, 2005, p. 34).

Fifteen years ago, he saw this as 'one of the most salient features of our culture' (Ibid., 1); it is even more salient today in the era of 'fake news' and 'post-truth'.

Bridgeman and Sandrik's (2008) study of bullshit in contract law illustrates the difference between lying and bullshitting. Lying is akin to promissory fraud whereby 'a party makes a promise that it has no intention to keep, and it does so in order to deceive the promisee about its intentions (Ibid., 1). A 'bullshit promise', by contrast, is made when a party 'uses promissory language but elsewhere reserves the right not to perform'. The party in this case may not have a specific plan to change the terms but keeps their options open such that the promise is insincere, even though the party may end up keeping it.

As conceptualized by Frankfurt, bullshit reveals a carelessness with the truth; it is not a lapse into laziness but rather intentionally saying whatever will advance one's interests (Belfiore, 2009, p. 345). The content may be true or false; what matters is that it leaves a favorable impression. Bullshit, Frankfurt (2005, pp. 42–43) argued, is hot air: 'mere vapor … without substance or content … Just as hot air is speech that has been emptied of all informative content, so excrement is matter from which everything nutritive has been removed'. The bullshitter is indifferent to whether the words they articulate reflect reality or not, they only want the audience to believe it is true. No attempt is made to confirm the accuracy of the words or attend to all relevant facts. Bullshit 'is closer to bluffing than it is to lying' (Belfiore, 2009, p. 345).

In his product-focused theorization, Cohen (2002) defined bullshit as nonsensical talk or writing. He delineated three types. The first is the unclarifiable discourse, 'that is not only obscure but which cannot be rendered unobscure, where any apparent success in rendering it unobscured creates something that is not recognizable as a version of what is said' (Cohen, 2002, p. 6). Cohen was mainly concerned with this type of bullshit because it is so prevalent in the academy. The other two types are rubbish or arguments that are 'grossly deficient either in logic or in sensitivity to empirical evidence'; and irretrievably speculative comments that simply cannot be verified one way or the other (Ibid., 6–7). The motives for producing bullshit are not of primary interest for Cohen because they do not define the concept. One might innocently repeat bullshit under the false belief that it is true; such a person is not indifferent to the truth, just mistaken about it. For Cohen (2002, p. 5), it does not make an utterance any less bullshit simply because the speaker did not aim to deceive. Equally, a bullshitter may be deliberate in their actions; they may 'have reason to want what they say to be unintelligible, for example, in order to impress, or in order to give spurious support to a claim' (Ibid., 8).

A further type of bullshit, or at least a very close cousin, is hypocrisy (Dovi, 2001; Finnemore, 2009; Krasner, 1999; Runciman, 2008; Seymour, 2014; Shklar, 1984; Weaver, 2008). Hypocrisy can be understood as an act performed by someone who does not really believe what they are saying, thereby manifesting as an inconsistency between stated principles and actual behaviour. The stated principles can be understood as bullshit in the absence of a genuine attempt to align practice with them; the principles are then shown to be 'hot air' designed to affect an audience in the actor's favour. This may occur at the individual level, but also at the institutional level. As Thompson (1995, p. 176) explains, '(i)nstitutional hypocrisy involves a disparity between the publicly avowed purposes of an institution and its actual performance or function. This form of bullshit is pervasive and harmful in politics. In international relations, this has been studied mostly in the context of states' responses to humanitarian crises (Dovi, 2001; Lipson, 2007; Seymour, 2014), as well as bureaucratic hypocrisy in the World Bank (Weaver, 2008). Some consider it insignificant or benign (Mearsheimer, 2011; Shklar, 1984). However, others argue that it erodes trust and promotes cynicism (Dovi, 2001; Thompson, 1995). I agree with this latter assessment and, by examining the case of climate change, will show that bullshit also undermines our collective ability to respond to problems of public concern.

2. Global climate governance: an overview

Since multilateral climate negotiations began three decades ago, rhetoric and action on climate change have been misaligned. A recent *Nature* editorial observed that 'many policymakers who argue that emissions must be curbed, and fast, don't seem to appreciate the scale of what's required' (Nature, 2018, p. 404). This is as true today as it was 30 years ago. By the 1980s scientists were confident that increasing concentrations of greenhouse gases in the atmosphere posed a threat to climate stability, which in turn would threaten the stability and even survival of human societies. At the behest of scientific 'knowledge brokers' who stepped out of the academy to advocate political action to reduce GHG emissions, international leaders began crafting declarations in 1988 and the United Nations Framework Convention on Climate Change (UNFCCC) was agreed in 1992 (see Bodansky, 2001). Over time, norms emerged about *who* should take responsibility for mitigating climate change, and *how* such mitigation should be pursued. The first norm held that international efforts to reduce emissions should be based on the universal participation of states, but guided by the principle of common but differentiated responsibilities and respective capabilities (CBDR). This put the primary responsibility on industrialized countries based on their historical contribution to pollution and/or their greater capacity to bear the costs incurred. The second norm held that climate change mitigation should be achieved through domestic emission reduction targets and timetables (Stevenson, 2013). Until the collapse of talks in Copenhagen in 2009, states negotiated the substance of these norms in a top-down fashion in the UNFCCC. The Kyoto Protocol distributed responsibility for emissions cuts and limitations so as to deliver a 5% reduction in the emissions of industrialized countries by 2012, relative to 1990 levels. But, as these states pursued their national targets, the challenge of matching pledges with practice became apparent. This pushed some states to abandon the Kyoto Protocol (most famously, the United States (US), but also Russia, Canada and Japan in the second commitment period). Other states rhetorically maintained the commitments but sought creative techniques such as emissions trading that allowed them to comply without undermining economic growth ambitions nor transforming unsustainable development practices. Over time, responsibility was reframed as requiring emission cuts in the developing world on the basis of their projected emissions. The practice of offsetting allowed many industrialized countries to make the virtuous claim that they were meeting their own national targets while simultaneously promoting low-carbon development in poorer countries. Offsetting involves a high-emitting country or company investing in emissions reduction (reforestation, energy efficiency, renewable energy, etc.) in a developing country, and claiming the reduction towards their targets.

By the time states came to negotiate a post-2012 climate change agreement, it was clear that genuine mitigation of the scale called for by scientists exceeded political will and capacity. Disagreements over how to distribute responsibility and reduce emissions resulted in a shift from top-down negotiated targets to a bottom-up process whereby each state determines the scale and style of their commitment. The 2015 Paris Agreement therefore has an aspirational collective goal of limiting global warming to 2°C, and possibly 1.5°C, but there is no way to ensure consistency between the goal and individual commitments. Unsurprisingly, national targets and actual policies are insufficiently ambitious to deliver this result (Climate Action Tracker, n.d.).

Impatience with the slow pace and low ambition of UN processes has pushed non-state actors to construct parallel governance initiatives. Of course, climate concern was not the only or indeed primary motivation; the market-based mechanisms of the Kyoto Protocol had already awakened businesses to the profit potential of mitigation, and advancing voluntary regulation was preferable to accepting potentially more stringent public regulation in the future. Some, like Hoffmann (2011, 5) argue that the 'centre of gravity' in global climate governance shifted away from the UN after the failed Copenhagen summit of 2009 and now lies in voluntary transnational experiments led by market and subnational actors and civil society. Such experiments involve sharing information, tools for disclosing and monitoring emissions, offsetting, municipal-based targets, and subnational emissions trading. Advocates argue that these experiments are valuable not only for the emissions they directly reduce but also for signalling to states that society is willing to take action, which indirectly may push up the level of ambition (Chan et al., 2015). But, while many non-state actors are committing to voluntary action, the vast majority is not. And, among those who are, there are very few who are accountable for their pledges (Bulkeley & Newell, 2010, p. 66). Whether or not transnational governance can make a genuine difference to global GHG emissions, this style of governance is here to stay. Indeed, the 2015 Paris Agreement recognizes and incorporates voluntary commitments and actions by non-state actors and sees cooperation between states and non-state actors as the path to higher ambition. As Geden (2016) observes, this bottom-up process has secured a higher level of participation, but its ability to produce the desired outcome is taken as a matter of faith.

3. Bullshit in global climate governance

As we saw above, bullshit can manifest in various forms: saying whatever will advance one's interests, irrespective of whether it reflects reality; making a promise while implicitly or explicitly reserving the right not to perform accordingly; nonsense statements; unclarifiable discourse; illogical arguments that are insensitive to empirical evidence; irretrievably speculative comments; and an inconsistency between statements and practice produced by the lack of genuine effort to ensure consistency. Bullshit is pervasive in global climate change governance and manifests in several, and potentially all, these forms. A vast literature on global climate governance has already captured the problem of inadequate action. The value of conceptualizing this in terms of bullshit is that it draws our attention to mistruths and inconsistencies, as well as their potential impacts. Detecting bullshit is difficult for non-specialists. If undetected, bullshit undermines the likelihood of stabilizing the climate system. But undetected bullshit is also dangerous because suspicions that it is pervasive will further erode public trust in political institutions. The erosion of trust will make it even harder to get democratic mandates to take ambitious action on climate change. Beyond helping to grasp the presence and consequences of mistruths and inconsistencies, the concept of bullshit also helps us to understand better the types of reforms needed in the global climate regime. There is a vast literature on accountability in climate governance, but the particular problem of insincerity and hypocrisy is not adequately addressed by existing reform proposals. In the next section, I address this challenge, but first I analyse the nature and scope of climate bullshit in greater detail.

The analysis in this section draws attention to illustrative examples in state-based climate governance. A fuller account would encompass the transnational experiments that are now proliferating and are likely to be a strong source of climate bullshit given the prominence of corporate greenwashing. I start with two examples drawn from the UN's principal climate body, the United Nations Framework Convention on Climate Change. As Geden (2016, 3) observed of the UNFCCC, there are 'numerous instances of disconnect between decisions and actions'. This is enabled by the fact that policy-makers come and go; unless there is close scrutiny, they can repeat their unfulfilled promises *ad nauseum*. Year after year, the annual climate convention repeats its promise 'to reach global peaking of greenhouse gas emissions as soon as possible', and year after year 'as soon as possible' is projected further into the future. Decisions are not taken, nor actions implemented, that will genuinely produce a peaking of emissions in anything close to the timeline scientists tell us is necessary. The truth that nobody wants to admit is that climate change negotiations are driven by political feasibility, not environmental desirability (Geden, 2016). This results in various instances of bullshit. Two instances are selected for illustration to highlight what may become the most dangerous form of bullshit in climate governance (the growing reliance on 'negative emissions') and a form of bullshit that has been sustained for over two decades (the omission of politically sensitive emissions). Designing more effective and sincere multilateral agreements requires ambitious participation by states. I, therefore, follow the UNFCCC cases with a national case to illustrate the gap between rhetoric and action at the national level. I selected Germany not because this country's climate record is particularly egregious but because it presents itself, and is widely seen, as a climate leader. The gap between rhetoric and action is therefore particularly large. In the absence of progress in the UNFCCC, observers often highlight the potential leadership role of the Group of 20 (G20). I, therefore, complete my analysis with this case to show that climate bullshit is also prominent in this multilateral space.

3.1. Negative emissions

Emissions modelling, including that informing the Paris Agreement, now tends to include large-scale use of 'negative emissions technologies' (Larkin et al., 2018). Most scenarios developed by the Intergovernmental Panel on Climate Change (IPCC) for limiting warming to 1.5 or 2°C are based on large-scale deployment of negative emissions technologies from 2020 onwards (van Vuuren et al., 2017). While still unproven, these technologies are expected to remove carbon dioxide from the atmosphere. Scenarios that exclude these technologies are based on a much larger reduction of greenhouse emissions by 2050: 60–75% reduction relative to 2010 levels, compared to 40–60% reduction if negative emissions technologies are used (van Vuuren et al., 2017, p. 902). The assumption that this technology will be deployed and will work therefore injects considerable wriggle room into emissions-pathway planning (Anderson & Peters, 2016). It is the equivalent of adopting a drastic weight-loss goal while only moderately reducing calorie intake because future medical innovations should be able to offset the excess brownies and burgers. Yet, despite their 'pivotal role' in mitigation scenarios, negative emissions technologies are 'almost completely absent from climate policy discussions' (Anderson & Peters, 2016, p. 183). Some negative emissions technologies are benign and mundane: many countries already discount the emissions absorbed by afforestation and reforestation. But modelling for 1.5°C and 2°C depends on a technology known as BECCS, bioenergy combined with carbon capture and storage. It assumes that carbon will be absorbed during the growth of biomass (trees), then captured before or during the burning of biomass for energy, and finally stored permanently in underground deposits. As of February 2019, only one pilot demonstration plant is in existence (Drax, 2019), but lack of investment in technological development and still nascent technological demonstration are not deterring its use in emissions planning. It is not simply that we are at an early stage of research; according to Anderson and Peters (2016, p. 183), '(t)wo decades of research and pilot plants have struggled to demonstrate the technical and economic viability of power regeneration with CCS, even when combusting relatively homogenous fossil fuels. Substituting for heterogenous biomass feedstock adds to the already considerable challenges'. Geological storage of the captured CO_2 presents the greatest technical problem because 'the subsurface does not contain any empty space' (Scott et al., 2013, p. 107). Many depleted oil and gas fields have been filled with water in the process of extracting more energy. Others find that the technical feasibility is promising, but the likelihood of implementation is undermined by a lack of societal and political support, as well as concerns about trade-offs. Deploying BECCS would require covering a land area of between one and two times the size of India with biomass, which would undermine other land uses such as food production. Existing surveys do not show high levels of disapproval, but rather ignorance: most people simply do not know anything about this technology (Perdan et al., 2017; Yang et al., 2016). As one study admits, 'public views expressed in our survey could be classified as largely uninformed opinions' (Perdan et al., 2017, p. 82). Such 'pseudo-opinions' are often considered 'weak and unstable, and as such regarded as unsuitable for predicting future public support or opposition to a technology' (Ibid.). Evidence from Germany shows that public acceptance of CCS is low and that it decreases further when additional information is provided (Braun et al., 2017). In the absence of more solid evidence about the technical viability of this negative emissions technology, and of its public acceptability, its inclusion in mitigation scenarios is bullshit. It reveals an indifference to truth, as well as a mismatch between the stated urgency of mitigating climate change and actions to reduce emissions. Geden (2016, pp. 4–5) describes it as 'magical thinking that has the effect of 'masking the growing inconsistency between political talk, decisions, and actions'.

3.2. Omitted emissions

Two sources of greenhouse gas emissions are fully or partially omitted under the measuring, reporting and mitigating rules of the UNFCCC: military emissions and international aviation. Military emissions are patchy and opaque, while international aviation has been the focus of a new, separate UN agreement consistent with the contemporary age of bullshit.

Military emissions are never openly talked about in climate negotiations.[1] Concerns that global climate policy would undermine state sovereignty and national security led to loopholes in the UNFCCC reporting rules that would make it almost impossible to know the true scale of military GHG emissions, and impossible to ensure states reduce these emissions. Recent estimates suggest that the Pentagon in the US is the world's largest institutional emitter of GHG (Nuttall et al., 2017, p. 3). Based on fuel usage, only 46 countries emit more than the US military (Belcher et al., 2020, 8). Given the scale of these emissions, their patchy inclusion in inventories and absence from mitigation plans advances the interests of powerful actors at the expense of the truth.

The US did not, as sometimes claimed (Nelson, 2015), secure a blanket exemption on reporting military emissions during the Kyoto Protocol negotiations; it sought this (Eizenstat, 1998), but only secured partial exemption and flexibility that renders it difficult to determine precisely which emissions are included and excluded from national accounts. The fact that the Pentagon was 'fully satisfied' (Ibid.) with the reporting rules agreed in the late 1990s makes it clear is that there is no intention to address the enormous emissions arising from military activity. National reports include domestically consumed military jet fuel. International bunker fuels (fuel used in commercial and strategic international aviation and marine transportation) are included but subtracted (e.g. EPA, 2019, Tables 3-1 and 3-13). For a long time, the difficulty of assigning responsibility was resolved by holding no one responsible. Multilateral operations consistent with the UN Charter are also excluded from emission totals, but *should* be reported for information purposes in line with 'good practice' (UNFCCC, 2006, p. 8.2.1; UNFCCC, 2018, Table 1D, Note 2). Few countries conform to good practice; the vast majority artfully deploys notation keys to deflect attention.[2] But reported data only includes fuel purchased in-country and used abroad in operations, rather than fuel purchased abroad mid-operation (namely, international bunker fuel).[3] Further ambiguity is introduced by the vagueness of the reference to 'multilateral operations pursuant to the Charter of the United Nations' (UNFCCC, 2006, p. 8.2.1), which should presumably mean operations approved by the Security Council but has been interpreted more broadly to limit mitigation action. A US State Department official told the Senate Foreign Relations Committee in 1998 that:

> The parties in Kyoto took a position to exempt key overseas military activities from any emissions targets, including exemptions for bunker fuels we used in international aviation and maritime transport and from emissions resulting from multilateral operations, such as self-defense, peacekeeping, and humanitarian relief. This would include everything from Grenada to U.N.-sanctioned activities. Thus, it exempts from our national targets not only multilateral operations authorized by the Security Council, like Desert Storm or Bosnia, but importantly it also exempts multilateral operations initiated pursuant to the charter but without the express authorization of the Council, such as Grenada. (Eizenstat, 1998)

The Paris Agreement neither reaffirms nor modifies rules and expectations on military emissions. The reporting guidelines used by the UNFCCC have not changed. What has changed is the enhanced flexibility for countries to choose the degree and nature of their domestic emission reductions.

After three decades of inaction on international aviation, a separate UN agreement (outside the UNFCCC) was agreed in 2018. However, the CORSIA (Carbon Offsetting and Reduction Scheme for International Aviation) agreement is riddled with weaknesses that confirm that the international community remains unwilling to curb emissions from this sector. Firstly, it is an agreement of the International Civil Aviation Organization (ICAO), whose remit excludes international flights from police, military, customs and state aircraft (ICAO, 2018a, p. 28). The aviation industry underplays the significance of its emissions by stressing that they account for only 2% of global GHG emissions. However, this figure only includes civil aviation, and this is growing at an annual rate of nearly 5%. If the CORSIA objectives are achieved as well as targets on biofuels and technological improvements, the sector will account for some 12% of total emissions in 2050, but if it falls short the sector may account for over 25% of all emissions (CarbonBrief, 2016). The aviation industry's statements are therefore bullshit in the sense of being insensitive to empirical evidence.

Secondly, the agreement is not based on limiting aviation and thereby reducing emissions, but rather provides a system for offsetting emission increases from 2020 levels. It is a plan for 'carbon-neutral growth'. This entails investing in tree planting or a technological innovation to absorb emissions from the atmosphere or avoid emissions growth in another sector. But carbon offsets are a classic case of bullshit that practice has disproven as an effective mitigation measure. Their inclusion is then another case of insensitivity to empirical evidence or bullshit. An evaluation of the European Commission's offset projects under the Kyoto Protocol's Clean Development Mechanism found that 85% had a low likelihood of reducing emissions; only 2% had a high likelihood of doing so (Cames et al., 2016, pp. 10–11). The limitations and problems with offsetting are widely known (Song, 2019; Stevenson, 2013); an agreement based exclusively on their use can only be considered bullshit. As Lyle (2018, p. 10) summarizes: 'Offsets carry the risk of encouraging people to believe that they need not change their behaviour, thus creating irreversibility in consumption and production patterns. Offsetting often lacks due diligence on effectiveness and requires costly management and administration'.

Thirdly, the agreement measures are voluntary until 2027 (ICAO, 2018b, p. 3), by which time the international community will have been debating climate change for nearly 50 years. The voluntary provision requires that both the departure and arrival countries of a route agree to participate, although it is the carriers, not the countries, which are responsible for offsetting the emissions. The countries are responsible for monitoring, verifying and reporting the emissions data (Lyle, 2018, p. 6). But the voluntary provision is not replaced with a mandatory one after 2027: ICAO has no authority over its member-states and can only encourage them to comply with the scheme through its completion in 2035 (Ibid., 7).

3.3. Germany

The case of Germany reflects bullshit in the sense of inconsistency between stated principles and actual performance. Germany has long positioned itself as a leader in global efforts to address climate change. Perhaps less well known outside climate policy circles is just how convenient this position was for Germany, at least in the initial years of negotiating the UN climate convention and its Kyoto Protocol. Following unification in 1990, many heavily polluting and inefficient industries and coal-fired power plants in the east were shut down. By insisting on 1990 as an emissions baseline, Germany was able to earn environmental credit through economically-motivated actions. By the time the Kyoto Protocol was agreed in 1997, Germany was already below its 1990 level of emissions (Harrison & McIntosh Sundstrom, 2007, p. 4). But little progress has been made further and deliberately to reduce GHG emissions since that time. Germany's emissions in 2018 were similar to their 1992 level (Appunn & Wettengel, 2019). While *per capita* emissions have decreased from 11.6 metric tons in 1991–8.8 metric tons in 2018, they remain nearly double the world average of 4.9 (and nearly three times the estimated sustainable level of 3 tons per capita) (World Bank, 2019a).

Germany has consistently and vocally stressed the importance of ambitious emissions cuts and criticized regressive steps by the United States. This occurred in the 1990s, first under the leadership of Sigmar Gabriel and since then under the leadership of the media-dubbed 'Climate Chancellor' Angela Merkel (Keating, 2008). But Germany has not been immune to short-termism. Despite its strong rhetoric, 'the history of German climate policy shows that short-term economic interests have frequently won key political battles' (Michaelowa, 2008, p. 160). If Germany was genuinely 'leading by example', as Jänicke (2017, p. 114) suggests, we should have seen progress to transition away from its dependence on lignite (brown coal) and hard coal. Instead, these sources still account for 35.4% of Germany's power production, which is more than all renewable sources combined (Appunn et al., 2019). Moreover, the energy company RWE recently advanced with plans to clear the 12,000-year-old Hambach Forest to expand lignite mining (DW, 2018). The federal energy secretary supported the clearing, arguing that 'we still need lignite for our reliable coal supply' (quoted in Vaughan, 2018). This contradicts the *Energiewende*, a national plan to move to an energy system based almost entirely on renewable sources.

As a result of failures to cut lignite dependence, Germany has fallen far short of its renewable energy target of 20% in 2020 (reaching just 13% in 2017) (Wilkes et al., 2018). This figure is well below the world average of 18% and puts Germany in the company of Turkey, Venezuela, and Moldova, countries hardly known for their ambitious climate change policies (World Bank, 2019b). Partly for this reason, Germany is set to miss its 2020 goal of reducing emissions by 40% by 2020 (relative to 1990 levels) (Ibid.). This explains the country's opposition to increasing the European Union (EU)'s 2030 emissions pledge under the Paris Agreement, with Merkel now saying: 'I think we should first stick to the goals we have already set for ourselves. I don't think permanently setting ourselves new goals makes any sense.' (quoted in Stam, 2018). Beyond the coal industry, the car industry also wields considerable influence over Germany's climate policy, as evidenced by

Merkel's efforts to delay the introduction of stronger EU-wide CO_2 standards for cars (Schreurs, 2016, pp. 115–116).

Much is made of Germany's renewable electricity production, but this praise hides two problems. The first is that electricity is just one part of the energy system (heating, cooling, and transport are the other components). Renewable sources account for 38.2% of electricity consumption (roughly the same as lignite and coal), but, when we look at total energy supply, Germany's profile is much less impressive. Renewables provide just 5.6% of transport energy and 13.9% of heating and cooling (Renewable Energies Agency, 2019).

The second problem is that, if Germany is going to meet its climate change targets, it will need to continue expanding renewable electricity production and consumption. However, investment gaps cast doubt over this. Most renewable electricity is produced from wind in the north and needs to be transported to the industrial south and west, but doing so requires new high-voltage connectors between these regions. The current grid lacks the capacity to deliver high volumes of electricity across the country, which results in switching off wind turbines and a lost opportunity to avoid GHG emissions (Appunn, 2018). The European Court of Auditors describes the situation as 'urgent'; just 10% of the planned extension of 7900 km had been completed by the end of 2017 and grid operators express doubt that it will be achieved by 2025 (Appunn, 2018; ECA, 2019).

3.4. The Group of 20

Every year, the world's largest 20 economies meet and agree to a raft of principles and actions on economic development and financial stability. Every year from 2009 until President Trump joined the annual meeting in 2017, the G20 repeated its commitment to phase out inefficient fossil fuel subsidies. It took the election of a climate-change-denying US president to bring the G20's words more closely into alignment with its actions, which effectively deny the urgency of climate change. But this has not removed the bullshit from the annual G20 Summit declaration. The inclusion of climate change and, more recently, reference to the Paris Agreement is typically met with cheer among concerned observers, but this will remain empty rhetoric until member-states cease propping up the fossil-fuel sector with large subsidies. Estimates of the scale of subsidies vary because different actors use different definitions of subsidies. Industrialized countries frequently claim that they provide no fossil-fuel subsidies, but this claim rests on a definition of subsidies as payments to consumers. Broader definitions include any public support that reduces the consumer price of coal, petrol, or gas, lowers production costs, or increases producing companies' profits. This includes payments to producers, fiscal benefits, low-interest loans, free or reduced access to water, land, and infrastructure, price controls, and public investment in research and development. The International Monetary Fund (IMF) includes in its definition the absence of a carbon price by arguing that unless the pollution carries a price tag it is effectively subsidized. Based on the latest data available, the IMF estimates that US$4.7 trillion (6.3% of global gross domestic product) was spent on fossil-fuel subsidies in 2015 and projects this number to rise US$5.2 trillion in 2017. It identified China as the largest subsidizer (US$1.4 billion), followed by the US ($649 billion), Russia ($551 billion), the EU ($289 billion) and India ($209 billion) (Coady et al., 2019, p. 1).

The most comprehensive study of G20 countries estimates the value of their coal, oil and gas subsidies at US$147 billion annually (Climate Transparency, 2018, p. 7). Saudi Arabia is unsurprisingly the largest subsidizer, at US$30 billion, followed by Italy (US$14 billion), Australia (US$7 billion) and Brazil (US$16 billion). According to a European Commission report, annual fossil fuel subsidies in the EU total EUR 55 billion (nearly US$62 billion) and have not decreased despite commitments to the UNFCCC and G20 (EC, 2019, p. 10). However, we should take this data with a grain of salt since governments typically underestimate their subsidies. Germany, for example, identified 22 tax breaks and budgetary transfers that favour fossil fuels to the value of US$17.6 billion annually (GSI, 2017). Civil society estimates put the value of German fossil-fuel subsidies at between US$40 and 50 billion (GermanWatch, 2017).

4. Enhancing integrity in global climate governance

In the context of neoliberal globalization, bullshit has thrived in the climate regime. Reform is unavoidable if the international community is to respond successfully to the global climate crisis, but the challenge is to identify forms of reform that are immediately politically feasible. I argue that the most promising forms of reform lie within the realm of 'democratic reglobalization'. Democratic reglobalization could harness worldwide interconnectedness to bring the climate regime under greater public scrutiny and control, with the aim of producing better outcomes. This would not require shrinking the role of either state or non-state actors, but rather bringing their decisions and actions under greater democratic control. One key element of this, and the one on which I focus in this section, is to reform the climate regime's accountability mechanisms to make it harder for powerful actors to get away with climate bullshit.[4]

When the Paris Agreement entered into force in November 2016, attention began turning towards the challenge of ensuring that it is effectively implemented. Its standing as a piece of international law requires states to take steps to fulfil their own commitments (although the commitments themselves are not legally binding) and to ensure the agreement fulfils its overall objectives. Unfortunately, enforcement and accountability mechanisms remain weak at the international level, largely because states were keen to ensure they remained so (Karlsson-Vinkhuyzen et al., 2018). The Paris Agreement anchors accountability in a transparency framework on the premise that 'peer and public pressure can be as effective as legal obligation in influencing behavior' (Bodansky, 2016, p. 311). This requires states to submit regular GHG emissions inventories and provide 'information necessary to track progress in implementing and achieving its nationally determined contribution' (Article 13.7). A technical review panel is then to review submissions and make 'non-intrusive, non-punitive' suggestions for improving performance (Article 15). Whether such a mechanism can induce compliance is debatable. What is clear, however, is that such a polite, peer-review approach will not reveal the bullshit in states' policies and practices. Throughout three decades, the UNFCCC has proven incapable of recognizing and rectifying inconsistencies and contradictions in its approach to governing climate change. Rather than abandoning the accountability architecture of the Paris Agreement, I propose reforms based on an expanded notion of accountability. My reform proposal expands both the *audience* of accountability (to whom states and the UNFCCC ought to be accountable) and the *means* by which this is achieved. It retains the UNFCCC's notion of communicative-based (as opposed to punitive-based) accountability but strengthens this by aligning it with the principles of deliberative democracy (Dryzek et al., 2019; Stevenson & Dryzek, 2014).

The Paris Agreement's transparency mechanism makes the states themselves the audience of accountability. It is based on the traditional institutionalist assumption that international institutions can best facilitate cooperation by reducing asymmetries of information, thereby limiting uncertainty and building trust between states (Keohane, 1984). Certainly, we do need to ensure that the climate regime continues to promote cooperation. But, with a problem as grave as climate change, this is clearly insufficient. We need a functioning institution that also resolves the climate crisis. This latter understanding of institutional effectiveness requires holding states to a higher standard than they will typically hold each other. There is evidence to suggest that citizens have a higher level of climate ambition than that pursued by their states in international negotiations (Stevenson & Dryzek, 2014, p. 20). Making citizens and civil society part of the accountability audience, therefore, has pragmatic merit (in addition to normative merit, if one accepts democratic principles). Arguably, citizens already constitute part of the accountability audience. After all, in democratic states, they can punish underperforming governments at the ballot box. In practice, though, citizens vote on the basis of a portfolio of preferences, of which climate change is only one. Accountability will remain diluted if we make do with this existing punitive option.

The existing accountability architecture of the Paris Agreement reflects what Jane Mansbridge (2009) calls 'narrative accountability' whereby actors provide an account of their actions and decisions. The anticipated exchanges with a technical panel potentially present an opportunity for two-way based dialogue, but diplomatic norms and respect for state sovereignty are unlikely to promote a robust process of questioning and answering. A more deliberative approach to accountability could be constructed by nesting the existing 'technical chamber' in a 'public chamber' constituted by civil-society representatives. Detecting and publicizing bullshit requires sustained scrutiny by actors unconstrained by diplomatic decorum and committed to minimizing the impacts of climate change. Civil society is best placed to perform this function. This nested-accountability arrangement could work by requiring parties to respond to questions from a technical panel *and* to engage in a two-way dialogue of questions and answers with civil society. Thousands of organizations are already accredited observers of the UNFCCC, many of which are aware of the nuances of existing and evolving climate policies. Populating the public chamber would not be a challenge.

However, to be most effective in holding states to account for their bullshit, the public chamber of a reformed accountability institution would have to be connected to a wider public sphere. For concerned citizens, it is easy to demand 'Climate Action Now', but they are poorly equipped to critique the subtleties of national pledges and plans. For the average citizen, it is exceedingly difficult to detect climate bullshit. The cynical and the savvy among them may assume that political rhetoric on climate change is laden with bullshit, but pointing it out with confidence and substantiation requires contact with actors dedicated to scrutinizing the UNFCCC. Stronger channels of communication between well-informed civil society organizations and the broader public would develop citizens' capacity to detect and denounce climate bullshit. Of course, civil society organizations engaged in the UNFCCC are not a homogeneous group. However, a diversity of views can be a strength, not a weakness, in helping citizens to discriminate between truth and nonsense, but only if arguments and their implications are clearly explained.

The idea of a 'citizen broker' moving between the multilateral/global and local levels is found in the Swedish schoolgirl, Greta Thunberg. She is well-informed and speaks eloquently and passionately to the powerful and the ordinary alike. Greta goes beyond the usual exaltations for greater action by pinpointing precisely where leaders are failing, and where their words are inconsistent with their actions. Exposure of her words has had an extraordinary impact on public consciousness, triggering protests by schoolchildren in cities across the world and inducing 'flight shame', which has led to an 8% rise in Swedish rail travel.

In the absence of institutional reform, informal accountability arrangements would still be beneficial. A nested approach would be ideal in the formal realm too and could require UNFCCC-accredited civil society groups and activist scientists to make their observations and analyses more accessible to nationally- and locally-based citizen groups. For example, greater exposure of the 'Fossil of the Day' activist ceremonies that take place at UN meetings could sensitize citizens to bullshit. A performance is played out to recognize the countries deemed to have behaved most reprehensibly in each day of negotiations. Argentina, for example, won a 'fossil award' at the 2015 Paris summit for simultaneously supporting a goal of 1.5°C and investing in the fossil-fuel industry by passing a law to nationalize a coal company (GreenTV, 2015). Existing civil-society initiatives, such as Climate Action Tracker and the Universal Ecological Fund, aim to make climate science and policy accessible and help non-specialists understand whether the rhetoric and substance of national mitigation plans match up.

5. Conclusion

Harry Frankfurt (2007, p. 72) concluded that human society cannot flourish in the face of pervasive bullshit unless we heighten our ability 'to discriminate reliably between instances in which people are misrepresenting things to us and instances in which they are dealing with us straight'. Until we can better detect bullshit about climate change policies, more nuanced democratic debate about how we can effectively confront this challenge will continue to be repressed. There are no easy solutions for mitigating bullshit in global climate governance, but the most promising options lie in nested accountability arrangements that stretch from the local to the global levels.

Many states are likely to resist such a reform. However, norms of civil society engagement are constantly being renegotiated. The UNFCCC is a living institution that has proven capable of adapting to changing expectations of who should mitigate climate change and how they should do so. In global governance more generally, civil society contributes to the legitimation and delegitimation of international institutions through various forms of discursive, institutional and behavioural practices (Bäckstrand & Söderbaum, 2018). It is up to civil society to incorporate enhanced accountability into its narratives of what constitutes legitimate global climate governance. Celebrating weak achievements merely confers unwarranted legitimacy and gives the impression that 'the solution to climate change is now at hand' (Allan, 2019, p. 5).

Public pressure has been the key to getting climate change on the political agenda and keeping it there. Now that nearly all states and an increasing number of non-state actors have pledged to reduce their greenhouse gas emissions, the challenge is to ensure the integrity of these pledges. I have proposed nested accountability arrangements to enhance our collective capacity to detect and denounce bullshit and thereby hold political leaders to account. However, there is a clear need still for more research to be done on bullshit mitigation in environmental and climate change governance.

Notes

1. This can be confirmed by searching the meeting reports of the Earth Negotiations Bulletin.
2. NE: not estimated; IE: included elsewhere (precisely where is unknowable because the data is protected); C: confidential; NA: not applicable; NO: not occurring. I verified this by checking data submitted to UNFCCC in 2006, a year which captured key conflicts in Iraq and Afghanistan, available at: http://unfccc.int/di/DetailedByCategory/Event.do?event=go Only three countries, France, Sweden and Slovenia, transparently reported emissions from their participation in multilateral operations.
3. See the Swedish explanation: 'These emissions are calculated based on information from the military on the amount of fuel purchased in Sweden but used abroad by Swedish forces participating in international operations.' (Swedish Environmental Protection Agency, 2017, p. 126).
4. For a fuller account of reforms consistent with democratic reglobalization, see Stevenson and Dryzek (2014).

Disclosure statement

No potential conflict of interest was reported by the author(s).

ORCID

Hayley Stevenson http://orcid.org/0000-0002-4876-1496

References

Allan, J. I. (2019). Dangerous incrementalism of the Paris Agreement. *Global Environmental Politics, 19*(1), 4–11. https://doi.org/10.1162/glep_a_00488

Anderson, K., & Peters, G. (2016). The trouble with negative emissions. *Science, 354*(6309), 182–183. https://doi.org/10.1126/science.aah4567

Appunn, K. (2018, April 10). *Energiewende hinges on unblocking the power grid.* https://www.cleanenergywire.org/dossiers/energy-transition-and-germanys-power-grid

Appunn, K., Bieler, F., Haas, Y., & Wettengel, J. (2019, June 26). *Germany's energy consumption and power mix in charts.* https://www.cleanenergywire.org/factsheets/germanys-energy-consumption-and-power-mix-charts

Appunn, K., & Wettengel, J. (2019, June 6). Germany's greenhouse gas emissions and climate targets. *Clean Energy Wire.* https://www.cleanenergywire.org/factsheets/germanys-greenhouse-gas-emissions-and-climate-targets

Barry, M., & Blühdorn, I. (2018). Symbolic environmental politics. In N. Castree, M. Hulme, & J. Proctor (Eds.), *Companion to environmental studies* (pp. 249–253). Routledge.

Bäckstrand, K., & Söderbaum, F. (2018). Legitimation and delegitimation in global governance. In J. Tallberg, K. Bäckstrand, & J. A. Scholte (Eds.), *Legitimacy in global governance* (pp. 101–118). Oxford University Press.

Belcher, O., Bigger, P., Neimark, B., & Kennelly, C. (2020). Hidden carbon costs of the "everywhere war". *Transactions of the Institute of British Geographers, 45*(1), 65–80. https://doi.org/10.1111/tran.12319

Belfiore, E. (2009). On bullshit in cultural policy practice and research. *International Journal of Cultural Policy, 15*(3), 343–359. https://doi.org/10.1080/10286630902806080

Bishop, M. L., & Payne, A. (2020a). The political economies of different globalizations: Theorizing reglobalization. *Globalizations.* doi:10.1080/14747731.2020.1779963

Bishop, M. L., & Payne, A. (2020b). Steering towards reglobalization: Can a reformed G20 rise to the occasion? *Globalizations.* doi:10.1080/14747731.2020.1779964

Black, M. (1985). *The prevalence of humbug.* Cornell University Press.

Bodansky, D. (2001). The history of the global climate change regime. In U. Luterbacher, & D. Sprinz (Eds.), *International relations and global climate change* (pp. 23–40). MIT Press.

Bodansky, D. (2016). The Paris climate change agreement: A new hope. *American Journal of International Law, 110*(2), 288–319. https://doi.org/10.5305/amerjintelaw.110.2.0288

Braun, C., Merk, C., Pönitzsch, T. G., Rehdanz, K., & Schmidt, U. (2017). Public perception of climate engineering and carbon capture and storage in Germany: Survey evidence. *Climate Policy, 18*(4), 471–484. https://doi.org/10.1080/14693062.2017.1304883

Bridgeman, C., & Sandrik, K. (2008). *Bullshit promises.* FSU College of Law, Public Law Research Paper No. 314. doi:10.2139/ssrn.1262477.

Bulkeley, H., & Newell, P. (2010). *Governing climate change.* Routledge.

Cames, M., Harthan, R. O., Füssler, J., Lazarus, M., Lee, C. M., Erickson, P., & Spalding-Fecher, R. (2016). How additional is the clean development mechanism? Study prepared for DG CLIMA Reference: CLIMA.B.3/SERl2013/0026r. https://ec.europa.eu/clima/sites/clima/files/ets/docs/clean_dev_mechanism_en.pdf

CarbonBrief. (2016, August 8). Analysis: Aviation could consume a quarter of 1.5C carbon budget by 2050. https://www.carbonbrief.org/aviation-consume-quarter-carbon-budget

Chan, S., van Asselt, H., Hale, T., Abbott, K.W., Beisheim, M., Hoffmann, M., Guy, B., Höhne, N., Hsu, A., Pattberg, P., Pauw, P., Ramstein, C., & Widerberg, O. (2015). Reinvigorating international climate policy: A comprehensive framework for effective nonstate action. *Global Policy*, *6*(4), 466–473. https://doi.org/10.1111/1758-5899.12294

Climate Action Tracker. (n.d.). https://climateactiontracker.org

Climate Transparency. (2018). *The G20 transition to a low-carbon economy*. https://newclimate.org/wp-content/uploads/2018/11/B2G_2018_rev.pdf

Coady, D., Parry, I., Le, N. P., & Shang, B. (2019). *Global fossil fuel subsidies remain large: an update based on country-level estimates*. IMF Working Paper. https://www.imf.org/~/media/Files/Publications/WP/2019/WPIEA2019089.ashx

Cohen, G. A. (2002). *Deeper into bullshit*. https://learning.hccs.edu/faculty/robert.tierney/phil1301-6/bullshit/g.a.-cohen-deeper-into-bullshit/at_download/file

Dovi, S. (2001). Making the world safe for hypocrisy? *Polity*, *34*(1), 3–30. https://doi.org/10.2307/3235505

Drax. (2019, February 7). *Carbon dioxide now being captured in first of its kind BECCS pilot*. https://www.drax.com/press_release/world-first-co2-beccs-ccus/

Dryzek, J. S., Bohman, Q., Kuyper, J., Pickering, J., Sass, J., & Stevenson, H. (2019). *Deliberative global governance*. Cambridge University Press.

DW. (2018, September 30). No chance of saving Hambach Forest, says RWE boss. *DW*. https://www.dw.com/en/no-chance-of-saving-hambach-forest-says-rwe-boss/a-45698266

Eizenstat, S. (1998, May 13). Statement of Hon. Stuart Eizenstat, Under Secretary of State For Economic, Business And Agricultural Affairs, Department of State. 2nd session13. http://commdocs.house.gov/committees/intlrel/hfa49425.000/hfa49425_0f.htm

Environmental Protection Agency, US. (2019). Inventory of US Greenhouse Gas Emissions and Sinks. 1990-2017. https://www.epa.gov/sites/production/files/2019-04/documents/us-ghg-inventory-2019-main-text.pdf

European Commission. (2019, January 9). Report from the Commission to the European Parliament, the Council, the European Economic and Social Committee and the Committee of the Regions: Energy prices and costs in Europe. https://eur-lex.europa.eu/legal-content/EN/TXT/PDF/?uri=COM:2019:1:FIN&from=EN

European Court of Auditors. (2019). Special Report No 08/2019: Wind and solar power for electricity generation. http://publications.europa.eu/webpub/eca/special-reports/wind-solar-power-generation-8-2019/en/

Finnemore, M. (2009). Legitimacy, hypocrisy, and the social structure of unipolarity. *World Politics*, *61*(1), 58–95. https://doi.org/10.1017/S0043887109000082

Frankfurt, H. (2005). *On bullshit*. Princeton University Press.

Frankfurt, H. (2007). *On truth*. Princeton University Press.

Geden, O. (2016). The Paris agreement and the inherent inconsistency of climate policymaking. *WIRES Climate Change*, *6*(7), 790–797. https://doi.org/10.1002/wcc.427

Germanwatch. (2017, November 17). Germany fails at G20 fossil fuel subsidy review. https://germanwatch.org/en/14750

Global Subsidies Initiative. (2017, November 16). Germany and Mexico publish peer reviews of fossil fuel subsidies Under G-20. https://www.iisd.org/gsi/subsidy-watch-blog/germany-mexico-peer-reviews-ffs-g20

GreenTV. (2015). COP21 Fossil of the Day 9 Winner: Australia and Argentina. https://www.youtube.com/watch?v=MYEP38EXEeY

Gunster, S., Fleet, D., Paterson, M., & Saurette, P. (2018). Climate hypocrisies: A comparative study of news discourse. *Environmental Communication*, *12*(6), 773–793. https://doi.org/10.1080/17524032.2018.1474784

Harrison, K., & McIntosh Sundstrom, L. (2007). The comparative politics of climate change. *Global Environmental Politics*, *7*(4), 1–18. https://doi.org/10.1162/glep.2007.7.4.1

Held, D., McGrew, A. G., Goldblatt, D., & Perraton, J. (1999). *Global transformations*. Stanford University Press.

Hoffmann, M. (2011). *Climate governance at the crossroads*. Oxford University Press.

Hudson, M. (2019, June 13). The morality of morale maintenance. https://marchudson.net/2019/06/13/the-morality-of-morale-maintenance-of-days-off-nihilism-4-1-23-and-oldfartclimateadvice/

ICAO. (2018a). Carbon Offsetting and Reduction Scheme for International Aviation (CORSIA). FAQs. Retrieved August 9. https://www.icao.int/environmental-protection/CORSIA/Documents/CORSIA_FAQs_Update_9Aug18.pdf
ICAO. (2018b). Resolution A39-3: Consolidated statement of continuing ICAO policies and practices related to environmental protection. https://www.icao.int/environmental-protection/Documents/Resolution_A39_3.pdf
Jänicke, M. (2017). Germany: Innovation and climate leadership. In R. K. W. Wurzel, J. Connelly, & D. Liefferink (Eds.), *The European Union in international climate change politics* (pp. 114–130). Routledge.
Karlsson-Vinkhuyzen, S., Groff, M., Tamás, P., Dahl, A., Harder, M., & Hassall, G. (2018). Entry into force and then? The Paris agreement and state accountability. *Climate Policy*, *18*(5), 593–599. https://doi.org/10.1080/14693062.2017.1331904
Keating, J. (2008, April 17). Quotable: Bush's neanderthal speech. *Foreign Policy* https://foreignpolicy.com/2008/04/17/quotable-bushs-neanderthal-speech/
Keohane, R. O. (1984). *Beyond hegemony*. Princeton University Press.
Krasner, S. D. (1999). *Sovereignty: Organized hypocrisy*. Princeton University Press.
Larkin, A., Kuriakose, J., Sharmina, M., & Anderson, K. (2018). What if negative emission technologies fail at scale? *Climate Policy*, *18*(6), 690–714. https://doi.org/10.1080/14693062.2017.1346498
Lipson, M. (2007). Peacekeeping: Organized hypocrisy? *European Journal of International Relations*, *13*(1), 5–34. https://doi.org/10.1177/1354066107074283
Lyle, C. (2018). Beyond the ICAO's CORSIA. *Climate Law*, *8*(1-2), 1–20. https://doi.org/10.1163/18786561-00801004
Mansbridge, J. (2009). A "Selection Model" of political representation. *Journal of Political Philosophy*, *17*(4), 369–398. https://doi.org/10.1111/j.1467-9760.2009.00337.x
Mearsheimer, J. J. (2011). *Why leaders lie: The truth about lying in international politics*. Oxford University Press.
Michaelowa, A. (2008). German climate policy between global leadership and muddling through. In H. Compston, & I. Bailey (Eds.), *Turning down the heat* (pp. 144–163). Palgrave.
Nature. (2018). Negative thinking. *Nature*, *554*(22 February), 404. https://media.nature.com/original/magazine-assets/d41586-018-02184-x/d41586-018-02184-x.pdf
Nelson, J. (2015, December 4). The pentagon's carbon boot print. https://www.counterpunch.org/2015/12/04/the-pentagons-carbon-boot-print/
Nuttall, W., Samaras, C., & Bazilian, M. (2017). Energy and the military. University of Cambridge Energy Policy Research Group, 1717: 1–29. https://www.repository.cam.ac.uk/bitstream/handle/1810/270620/cwpe1752.pdf?sequence=1&isAllowed=y
Perdan, S., Jones, C., & Azapagic, A. (2017). Public awareness and acceptance of carbon capture and utilisation in the UK. *Sustainable Production and Consumption*, *10*(April), 74–84. https://doi.org/10.1016/j.spc.2017.01.001
Renewable Energies Agency. (2019). Key facts about the energy transition in Germany. https://2019.energydialogue.berlin/wp-content/uploads/2019/04/betd_press_factsheet.pdf
Runciman, D. (2008). *Political hypocrisy*. Princeton University Press.
Schreurs, M. (2016). Is Germany really an environmental leader? *Current History*, *115*(779), 114–116. https://doi.org/10.1525/curh.2016.115.779.114
Scott, V., Gilfillan, S., Markusson, N., Chalmers, H., & Haszeldine, R. S. (2013). Last chance for carbon capture and storage. *Nature Climate Change*, *3*(February), 105–111. https://doi.org/10.1038/nclimate1695
Seymour, L. (2014). Let's bullshit! Arguing, bargaining and dissembling over Darfur. *European Journal of International Relations*, *20*(3), 571–595. https://doi.org/10.1177/1354066113476118
Shklar, J. (1984). *Ordinary vices*. Harvard University Press.
Song, L. (2019, May 22). An even more inconvenient truth. *ProPublica*. https://features.propublica.org/brazil-carbon-offsets/inconvenient-truth-carbon-credits-dont-work-deforestation-redd-acre-cambodia/
Stam, C. (2018, October 2). European Commission abandons plans to raise climate ambition. *EURACTV*. https://www.euractiv.com/section/climate-environment/news/european-commission-to-abandon-plans-for-rising-climate-ambition/
Stevenson, H. (2013). *Institutionalizing unsustainability: The paradox of global climate governance*. University of California Press.

Stevenson, H., & Dryzek, J. S. (2014). *Democratizing global climate governance*. Cambridge University Press.
Swedish Environmental Protection Agency. (2017). National Inventory Report. https://www.naturvardsverket.se/upload/sa-mar-miljon/statistik-a-till-o/vaxthusgaser/2016/data-metoder/nir-se-submission-2017.pdf
Thompson, D. (1995). Hypocrisy and democracy. In B. Yack (Ed.), *Liberalism without illusions* (pp. 173–190). Chicago University Press.
UNFCCC. (2006). https://www.ipcc-nggip.iges.or.jp/public/2006gl/pdf/1_Volume1/V1_8_Ch8_Reporting_Guidance.pdf
UNFCCC. (2018). United States of America CRF 2018. https://unfccc.int/documents/65782
van Vuuren, D., Hof, A., van Sluisveld, M., & Riahi, K. (2017). Open discussion of negative emissions is urgently needed. *Nature Energy*, *2*(12), 902–904. https://doi.org/10.1038/s41560-017-0055-2
Vaughan, A. (2018, October 1). German energy secretary backs forest clearance to build coal mine. *The Guardian*. https://www.theguardian.com/business/2018/oct/01/german-minister-backs-plan-to-cut-down-forest-to-build-coal-mine
Weaver, C. (2008). *Hypocrisy trap*. Princeton University Press.
Wilkes, W., Warren, H., & Parkin, B. (2018, August 15). Germany's failed climate goals. *Bloomberg*. https://www.bloomberg.com/graphics/2018-germany-emissions/
World Bank. (2019a). CO2 emissions (metric tons per capita). https://data.worldbank.org/indicator/EN.ATM.CO2E.PC?locations=DE-1W
World Bank. (2019b). Renewable energy consumption (% of total final energy consumption). https://data.worldbank.org/indicator/EG.FEC.RNEW.ZS?locations=DE-1W&most_recent_value_desc=true
Yang, L., Zhang, X., & McAlinden, K. J. (2016). The effect of trust on people's acceptance of CCS (carbon capture and storage) technologies. *Energy Policy*, *96*(1), 69–79. https://doi.org/10.1016/j.energy.2015.12.044

Philosophies of migration governance in a globalizing world

Antoine Pécoud

ABSTRACT

International migration is a key feature of globalization. Yet there is no international migration regime that would support cooperation and governance at the global level. This makes for enduring and worldwide migration crises. This article identifies five distinct patterns of migration governance: (1) national/sovereign migration governance, according to which migration is an issue of state sovereignty; (2) global anti-migrant governance, which posits that cooperation and governance exist in practice, but either to control migration (global forced immobility governance) or to exploit migrant labour (global labour exploitation governance); (3) global rights-based migration governance, grounded in human rights and international norms; (4) managerial/developmental global migration governance, which aims at steering migration flows to optimize their utility; and (5) the free (non)-governance of migration, premised on ethical and utilitarian arguments in favour of free movement. The article discusses the implications of this typology for understanding current and future prospects of migration governance.

1. Introduction

In her 1996 book, *Losing Control*, Saskia Sassen (1996, p. 59) wrote that

> there is a growing consensus in the community of states to lift border controls for the flow of capital, information, and services and, more broadly, to further globalisation. But when it comes to immigrants and refugees … the national state claims all its old splendour in asserting its sovereign right to control its borders.

At the time, with the collapse of the Soviet Union and other geopolitical developments (such as the war in the Balkans), governments were facing what Myron Weiner (1995) first called a 'global migration crisis'. This prompted largely unilateral efforts to strengthen border control – turning migration governance into a high-politics security issue.

More than twenty years later, in 2018, some 160 states adopted the United Nations (UN)-sponsored *Global Compact for Safe, Orderly and Regular Migration*, whose tone is quite different: affirming that 'migration has been part of the human experience throughout history' and is 'a source of prosperity, innovation and sustainable development in our globalized world', it argues that 'no State can address migration on its own due to the inherently transnational nature of the phenomenon' and calls for 'international, regional and bilateral cooperation and dialogue' in the governance of migration (United Nations, 2018, pp. 3–4).

Yet, despite the recognition of the normalcy of migration and of the need for inter-state concertation, migration dynamics remain associated with a climate of 'crisis', according to which peoples' mobility is a challenge to state sovereignty and a destabilizing factor for governments and societies. The on-going 'migration/refugee crisis' in the euro-Mediterranean region has, for example, illustrated both Western governments' emphasis on border control and the human cost of this political approach, as thousands of migrants have lost their lives in trying to reach Europe. This is not an isolated case: throughout the world the movement of migrants and refugees generates political and humanitarian crises (Menjivar et al., 2019).

While migration is a longstanding and structural feature of globalization, there remain major uncertainties regarding how it should be governed. This article contributes to this discussion by identifying different philosophies of (global) migration governance, each of which refer to a specific understanding of how migration is, should be, or could be, governed. 'Governance' is here defined by two key attributes: first, it extends beyond the state and posits that migration is not governed by governments only, but also by non-state actors like the private sector, civil society and inter- or supranational entities; second, governance is understood as a multi-level process in which political strategies designed at the national level coexist with international, regional and local dynamics (such as global capitalism, multilateral regimes or international norms).

The article outlines five distinct patterns of migration governance, which are described in the following sections: (1) national/sovereign migration governance, according to which migration is an issue of strict state sovereignty; (2) global anti-migrant governance, which posits that cooperation exists, but either to control migration (global forced immobility governance) or to exploit migrant labour (global labour exploitation governance); (3) global rights-based migration governance, grounded in human rights and international norms; (4) managerial/developmental global migration governance, which aims at steering migration flows to optimize their utility; and (5) the free (non-) governance of migration, premised on ethical and utilitarian arguments in favour of free movement. The final section discusses the implications, biases and limits of this typology in the context of the broader concern with 'reglobalization' (Bishop & Payne, 2020a, 2020b). Put simply: any substantive process of reglobalization is a long way off in the area of migration, simply because neither the globalization *of* governance nor its subsequent deglobalization has happened in what is an undeveloped governing regime.

2. National/sovereign migration governance

As made clear by Sassen, states are keen on their sovereign right to control the admission and treatment of non-nationals. This attitude contrasts with their commitment to inter-state cooperation over other transnational issues such as trade, climate change, development and human rights. Despite the current crisis of multilateralism, globalization has come along with the emergence of international regimes that define 'principles, norms, rules, and decision-making procedures around which actor expectations converge in a given issue-area' (Krasner, 1982, p. 185). Regimes enable states to cooperate over certain issues and therefore lessen the costs stemming from anarchy and non-cooperation.

When it comes to human mobility, only refugees are the object of a regime. The 1951 *Convention Relating to the Status of Refugees* (Geneva Convention) details its key legal and political principles (right to seek asylum, *non-refoulement*, etc.), while the Office of the UN High Commissioner for Refugees (UNHCR) is mandated to translate these principles into practice. No comparable regime exists for other types of human mobility. This highlights the influence of national/sovereign migration governance, which is based on the principle that the governance of migration is not a global/international issue but should remain an object of national sovereignty.

National/sovereign migration governance fits into a Westphalian tradition, according to which statehood rests upon the authority over a territory and its people. The implementation of sovereignty over human mobility has played a key role in state-building. Since the nineteenth century, governments have strived to achieve a monopoly over the legitimate control of migration through administrative and bureaucratic means (Torpey, 2000). Noiriel (1991) argues that immigration and immigration policy are therefore characterized historically by the 'tyranny of the national', while Zolberg (1997) shows how already in the late nineteenth century the United States took measures to halt Chinese immigration. Later on, states progressively opened up to transnational flows of goods and investments and agreed to their liberalization, but people remained outside this process. This makes for today's imbalanced governance of globalization, marked by the contrast between the free circulation of capital and the unfree circulation of labour.

In the second half of the twentieth century, the rise of multilateralism was accompanied by the creation of international and inter-governmental organizations (IOs) to address a wide range of transnational issues, but migration remained largely outside this process. Labour migration is included in the mandate of the International Labour Organization (ILO), but has rarely figured prominently in its activities. The only IO with an exclusive migration mandate – the International Organization for Migration (IOM) – went through a chaotic and fragile history, and only joined the UN in 2016 (Pécoud, 2018). Betts (2011) shows how the global governance of migration is composed of a heterogeneous set of treaties and non-binding norms, which pertain to different aspects of migration (labour migration, human trafficking and smuggling, disaster-induced displacement, internally-displaced people) and remain disconnected from each other; the result is a fragmented field with little overarching logic in which governments go venue-shopping. Even the European Union (EU), despite its highly-advanced cooperation experience, finds it difficult to craft a genuinely regional immigration policy – a problem that also arises in other world regions and with other regional organizations (Nita et al., 2017).

National/sovereign migration governance further rests upon the premise that migration constitutes a security threat and that the control of migration is therefore of key strategic importance. While this is a longstanding issue, particularly in times of war and conflict, the securitization of migration has gained prominence since the end of the Cold War gave rise to new security concerns, and even more so in the wake of the terrorist attacks of September 11 in the United States (Adamson, 2006).

Sovereignty does not necessarily mean that states are closed to migration. They organize peoples' mobility through all kinds of policies (guest-worker programmes, selective immigration policies, family reunification, student mobility, etc.) and migration has been rising over the past decades: while there were 84 million migrants in 1970, this figure climbed to 272 million in 2019; this represents an increase from 2.3 to 3.5 per cent of the world population (IOM, 2019, p. 21). In historical and proportional terms, however, and contrary to widespread beliefs, migration flows have not skyrocketed: in 1910, migrants already made for 2 per cent of the world population (McKeown, 2004, p. 184). Neither does sovereignty imply that states achieve 'real-world' control over migration: there is a significant gap between what they want to achieve (namely, control over their borders) and actual migration dynamics, like the persistence of unauthorized migration (Hollifield et al., 2014).

3. Global anti-migrant governance

According to the second interpretation, while in the absence of a regime migration remains formally under the realm of state sovereignty, there are actually patterns of global migration governance. These take the form of 'global anti-migrant governance' because they are geared towards either the forced immobility of people and/or the exploitation of migrant labour. In both cases, states cooperate with each other while also cooperating with non-state actors, which is why one can justifiably speak of global governance mechanisms. This section distinguishes between 'global forced immobility governance' (based on the objective of controlling migration) and 'global labour exploitation governance' (which aspires at facilitating employers' access to cheap migrant labour).

3.1. Global forced immobility governance

Global forced immobility governance takes the form of intense inter-state cooperation to enhance border control and expulse unwanted migrants (Cassarino, 2010). Faced with growing migration pressure and with the interdependencies that stem from migration dynamics, governments in the Global North aim at regulating migration flows before they reach their borders and therefore externalize control 'away from the border and outside the state' (Lahav & Guiraudon, 2000, p. 55). In Europe, such delegation of surveillance to non-Western governments started across the East–West divide, as the end of the ban on exit that characterized the Soviet bloc led to fears over massive migration. Remote control later developed towards North and West Africa, as well as to other countries such as Turkey. In North America, this mostly concerns transit migration from Central America to the United States through Mexico (Zaiotti, 2016).

Cooperation is necessary to ensure that governments in the Global South are financially and materially equipped to control their borders (with biometric technology, for example). It also entails the training of local actors (like policymakers and border guards) and the diffusion of norms to change policy and legislation in sending and transit regions. Because migration flows are asymmetrical, cooperation often resorts to issue-linkages: in exchange for their cooperation over irregular migration, less-developed states secure development support or legal migration channels for their citizens. The practical, political and legal complexity of this process has favoured the creation and development of specialized inter-governmental agencies, such as the International Centre for Migration Policy Development (ICMPD) and the IOM (Hess, 2010; Pécoud, 2018).

Global forced immobility governance also relies on private actors. Airline carriers are tasked to control passengers' right to travel to destination before boarding and also work closely with governments when it comes to expulsing undocumented migrants. There is evidence that migration detention centres are sometimes operated by private security companies, while border control relies on the services provided by enterprises that specialize in biometrics and other technologies of surveillance. To some extent, global anti-migrant governance also involves cooperation with civil society: even though many non-governmental organizations (NGOs) contest global forced immobility governance, some of them take part in it; in the case of expulsions, for instance, they may be solicited to support migrants' reintegration in their home country (Dini & Giusa, 2020).

Global forced immobility governance thus corresponds to a traditional pattern of multi-level and multi-actor governance. Yet such governance is not based on explicit principles. From the analysis of states' strategies, one can conclude that the overall objective is to 'keep people in their place', a political objective that is rooted in a long history of defiance towards the mobility and agency of the poor (Bakewell, 2008, p. 1341). But there is no formal commitment to such a principle in the form of, say, a UN-sponsored declaration in favour of immobility. Rather, it is the multitude of *ad hoc* and often disconnected initiatives that, taken together, make for an implicit regime (Punter et al., 2019).

3.2. Global labour-exploitation governance

Concomitantly with forced immobility governance, another pattern of global anti-migrants governance takes the form of the generalized exploitation of migrant labour. There is longstanding evidence that foreign workers concentrate in secondary labour markets, such as agriculture, construction and domestic work, which are characterized by precarity, under-protection and low wages (Piore, 1979). There is also ample evidence that strict border control enhances migrants' vulnerability (by depriving them of a legal status or by making them deportable), thereby facilitating migrant workers' exploitation and contributing to a reserve army of cheap and flexible labour (Anderson, 2010). While the casualization of labour is above all a consequence of Post-Fordism and the spread of neoliberalism in a globalizing economy, migration policy plays a role therein, in particular by creating the conditions for renewed forms of unfree labour.

Global labour-exploitation governance takes different forms, out of which two clear-cut scenarios can be outlined. The first is the tacit tolerance, by governments, of large populations of undocumented migrants, coupled with low efforts towards workplace control. Employers' need for foreign labour is therefore met informally, often through reliance on all kinds of intermediaries and brokers. Such a pattern of governance is implicit, as governments do not usually acknowledge the dependence of their economy upon such workers. The second scenario takes the form of state-sponsored recruitment programmes, which imply formal cooperation between sending and receiving countries and were once common in both Western Europe and North America (the guest-worker system in postwar Europe, the Bracero programme between 1942 and 1964 in the United States). Today, while such policies have been the object of renewed policy interest, they are less state-regulated and mostly rely upon intermediaries, which range from formal labour recruitment agencies to illegal traffic by smugglers and traffickers (Martin, 2017). While guest workers enjoy greater protection than undocumented migrant workers, temporary labour migration still provides migrant workers with less rights than their non-migrant counterparts (as, for example, when foreign workers are precluded from changing employers).

The general principle behind global labour-exploitation governance is the need for foreign labour and the necessary circulation of labour in a globalizing economy. This principle may be implicit (as in the case of the *de facto* tolerance of undocumented migrant workers) or explicit (in the case of proactive recruitment policies). In all cases, such governance relies upon the cooperation between governments, employers and private intermediaries. It also fits into the broader imbalances that characterize the governance of globalization: first, because it is embedded in an uneven migration diplomacy between (stronger/richer) receiving and (weaker/poorer) sending states (Adamson & Tsourapas, 2019) and, second, because global labour-exploitation governance rests directly upon the discrepancy between the free circulation of capital and the unfree circulation of people/labour.

Global forced immobility governance and global labour-exploitation governance share certain common points. They display illiberal governance patterns and generally unfold into situations characterized by human and labour rights abuses. Moreover, both patterns have deep historical roots: in particular, the mobility of people during colonial times already displayed the mix of control and exploitation that characterize today's global anti-migrants governance. Although they seemingly pursue two different objectives (border control and labour mobility respectively), they are also complementary – as increased border control makes migrants more readily exploitable. What is unclear is whether this complementarity is deliberate and the outcome of an explicit (but unpublicized) political strategy, or whether it is the product of the coincidental convergence of different political objectives. Taken together however, global forced immobility governance and global labour-exploitation governance make for a robust pattern of global anti-migrant governance, in which virtually all states and large segments of the private sector are directly involved.

4. Global rights-based migration governance

In light of these abuses, a third approach to global migration governance focuses on human and labour rights standards. At first sight, global rights-based migration governance rests upon firm ground. By definition, human rights are designed to protect everybody – and hence also apply to migrants, whether in a regular or irregular situation. It follows that human rights law – and especially its codification in international law – should provide a sound basis for migration governance. But, in practice, implementation of migrants' human rights is problematic: as Groenendijk (2004, p. xix) recalls,

> it took lawyers and judges in most European countries several decades to accept that "everyone" in the European Convention on Human Rights … really means every human being, that non-citizens are covered and protected by most of the provisions of human rights instruments, and that these instruments also apply to immigration law.

In 1990 the UN adopted the *Convention on the Rights of Migrant Workers and Members of Their Families*. While part of international human-rights law (and hence monitored by the Office of the High Commissioner for Human Rights), this convention finds its roots in labour protection. It built upon previous conventions adopted under the auspices of the ILO, an agency that, upon its creation in 1919, was already concerned with the 'the protection of the interests of workers when employed in countries other than their own'.[1] The regulation and protection of migrant workers were understood as a strategy to lessen the competition between nationals and foreigners within the labour market – and hence to protect all workers, irrespective of their nationality; this was a major concern for unions, which, along with employers, are members of the ILO (Cholewinski et al., 2009).

Global rights-based migration governance is thus a century old. This qualifies the first philosophy of governance discussed above, according to which immigration policy would have always remained under the realm of strict national sovereignty. Already at the beginning of the twentieth century, governments were aware of the interdependencies generated by migration and explored ways to establish international standards (Rosental, 2006). Yet these efforts found little support: the UN Convention has been ratified by 55 states only, and by no major Western receiving state. The reasons for such low ratification record include the arguments discussed above, namely: (1) states' scepticism towards multilateral interventions in their sovereign corner; and (2) the dependence of many economies upon unprotected migrant labour (and the consequent reluctance to adopt binding protective measures). In addition, ratification faces a reciprocity problem: given that migrants concentrate in a fairly small number of receiving states, an international standard designed to protect them affects above all those states that host foreign populations.

This does not mean that human rights play no role in migration governance. Rights – and more generally, the liberal principles upon which Western democracies are grounded – exert significant influence on the admission and treatment of foreigners. Commitment to rights makes for 'self-limiting sovereignty' as it constrains the ways in which governments control migration (Joppke, 1998, p.

292). Similarly, welfare states have progressively extended social rights to migrants, albeit in an unpublicized manner (Guiraudon, 2000). It remains the case, however, that states' reluctance towards international legal standards hinders the establishment of migrants' rights as an issue of genuine state cooperation.

Global rights-based migration governance is grounded in international standards and based on multilateral cooperation and on IOs' involvement, thereby corresponding to a standard pattern of global governance. It also relies on cooperation with civil-society organizations (CSOs), whose role in ensuring human rights protection is well-established. As far as key principles are concerned, global rights-based migration governance rests upon the strong normative role of human rights in global governance. That said, the major human rights abuses that take place in the context of migration testify to the challenges faced by global rights-based migration governance, which is not therefore the dominant pattern of governance shaping migration policy.

5. Managerial/developmental global migration governance

In 2015 the international community adopted the Sustainable Developments Goals (SDGs), which replaced the Millennium Development Goals (MDGs). One of the innovations of the SDGs is that they explicitly address migration, a topic that was absent from the MDGs. Indeed, target 10.7 of the SDGs reads as follows: 'Facilitate orderly, safe, regular and responsible migration and mobility of people, including through the implementation of planned and well-managed migration policies'.[2]

This objective reflects the philosophy behind the managerial/developmental global migration governance that currently dominates the international agenda and the work of IOs. Its key inspiration is of a utilitarian nature: as made clear in target 10.7, the keyword is *management*, which conveys the idea that migration should be properly 'managed' to yield optimal results. This leads to a technocratic focus on the ways in which migration can be governed as a tool for development (through remittances in particular), as well as an emphasis on the benefits of 'well-managed' migration to address labour market shortages in receiving countries. According to managerial/developmental global migration governance, migration is a normal and potentially desirable feature of a globalizing world. Given the systemic nature of migration flows, states can no longer claim to control them in a sovereign manner, but should rather cooperate to make the most of them. This implies 'facilitating' migration, but in an 'orderly' and 'planned' manner – that is to say, in a way respectful of state sovereignty (Geiger & Pécoud, 2010).

Aware of the challenges faced by global rights-based migration governance, managerial/developmental global migration governance tends to downplay the issue of rights and to call merely for 'safe' migration – a wording that takes into account migrants' well-being, but arguably in a light and non-binding fashion. In the context of the migrant/refugee crisis, this wording rather favours humanitarian considerations, centred on the need to protect vulnerable migrants (like victims of human smuggling and trafficking). This soft and apparently consensual protection agenda is also associated with more controversial practices, such as so-called 'voluntary' return programmes or the setting up of information campaigns to dissuade would-be migrants from leaving their country (see, for example, Collyer, 2012).

As far as actors are concerned, while certain governments have relied upon the notion of migration management (see Balch, 2009 for the case of the UK), it is above all IOs that have contributed to its popularity. Since the 1990s, the issues raised by migration have gained visibility within the international community and inside IOs, with the above-mentioned 2018 Global Compact constituting one of the outcomes of this process. The IOM has played a particularly salient role here, having popularized the notion of 'migration management' and having played a key role in the drafting of the Compact (Pécoud, 2018). Other IOs, like the World Bank, also play an important role, especially when it comes to remittances and the migration and development nexus.

From a political economy perspective, managerial/developmental global migration governance can be understood as a 'third way' between the first and second patterns of governance discussed above. As argued, states cling to their control over human mobility, in a unilateral (Section 2) or cooperative manner (Section 3.1), while also ensuring access to flexible migrant labour (Section 3.2). This mechanically leads to irregular migration, which (apart from human/labour rights abuses) raises security problems: undeclared/shadow economies, smuggling/trafficking networks, etc. 'Managed' migration strives to overcome this contradiction by promoting patterns of 'regulated openness' that conciliate the need for labour mobility and respect for state sovereignty (Ghosh, 2000, p. 25).

From a geopolitical perspective, and in line with IOs' federating role at the world level, managerial/developmental global migration governance also aims at conciliating the diverging interests of governments along the sending/receiving states divide. By promoting development and including humanitarian considerations, migration management favours a comprehensive approach, based around another of its keywords, namely, the 'triple-win' objective and the aspiration to make migration beneficial for receiving countries, sending countries and migrants themselves. In the absence of a widely-accepted regime, this all-inclusive political agenda enables IOs and governments both to work together and with other actors such as civil society and the private sector.

6. The free (non-)governance of migration

The last philosophy of migration governance is based on the free movement of people. Authorizing people to move freely across borders amounts to a kind of non-governance, since it presupposes that states and other controlling actors no longer monitor human mobility. Yet free movement is also the outcome of a governance strategy, which is why one may speak of the free (non-)governance of migration. In addition, free movement presupposes inter-state cooperation because it implies reciprocity: no state would unilaterally open its borders and such decisions can therefore only be taken in concertation with other states.

There are at least three manifestations of the free (non-)governance of migration. The first is the actual implementation of this pattern of governance within regional integration processes. The best-known case is Europe, in which EU citizens enjoy the right to move and settle down freely across the continent. Other regions, like West Africa or Latin America, have designed somewhat similar policy strategies, but with fairly different outcomes on the ground. By contrast, other regional integration processes (like the North American Free Trade Agreement (NAFTA)) reproduce at the regional level the well-established patterns of governance discussed above, with a free market but closely-monitored borders. In general terms, the free (non-)governance of migration at the regional level is designed to foster growth by enabling the free circulation of labour, while also strengthening a regional identity (Lavenex et al., 2016).

While a legitimate political issue at the regional level, free movement is completely absent from policy discussions at the global level. This is a peculiar situation, as many other regional objectives (such as free trade) are also global objectives. Even the UN, which regularly expresses bold and visionary ambitions, has never addressed free movement, not even to reject it. The second and third manifestations of the free (non-)governance of migration are therefore of a speculative nature and consist of calls for alternative migration policies, rather than actual political processes.

The second take on the free (non-)governance of migration is based on an ethical argument. Following Carens (1987, p. 252), it posits that restricting access to migration on the basis of nationality amounts to a 'feudal privilege' that is at odds with modern liberal values because it treats people differently on the basis of their unchosen and inherited country of birth. Apart from a handful of researchers, this position is sometimes advocated by activists and CSOs concerned with global justice and migrants' rights. The third take follows a utilitarian argument and posits that the free circulation of labour (and hence people) would massively favour growth and prosperity worldwide. According to a simple neoclassical model, free movement is the condition for the perfect allocation of labour. Without going so far, Rodrik (2005) argues that even a modest liberalization of immigration would yield much higher benefits than free trade (see also Clemens, 2011). This argument is supported by certain market-friendly media organizations: in a 1984 editorial, the *Wall Street Journal* (1984) wrote that, 'if Washington still wants to "do something" about immigration, we propose a five-word constitutional amendment: There shall be open borders', while the *Financial Times* journalist Martin Wolf (2004, p. 117) wrote that 'controls on migration create the world's biggest economic distortion – the discrepancy in rewards to labour – but nobody seems to be suggesting the obvious answer: free migration'.

Both ethical and utilitarian arguments can be challenged: the first because it tends to overlook the necessary closure that enables societies to develop meaningful community life and solidarity mechanisms (such as democracy or welfare states); the second because most models think in terms of aggregate effects, which says nothing of the gains and losses for particular countries or groups. It remains the case that both arguments envisage a pattern of migration governance based on free movement and that, in certain regions at least, states have taken concrete steps to implement such a model.

7. Discussion

Five philosophies of global migration governance have been outlined. Table 1 provides an overview of each governance pattern, in terms of key principles, involvement of non-state actors and levels of implementation.

The first pattern (national/sovereign migration governance) sees migration as an issue of state sovereignty and does not therefore leave much space to non-state actors or inter-state cooperation. In this respect, one may wonder whether it actually corresponds to a pattern of governance, as defined in the introduction. All other patterns, however, involve non-state actors (private sector, civil society) and entail some kind of cooperation with other states in a more or less formalized way. They also imply multi-level policymaking processes, not least because domestic immigration policy is coupled with inter-state cooperation.

Table 1. Overview of governance patterns.

	Key principle	Non-state Actors involved	Level
Sovereignty	State sovereignty, security	private sector	National
Forced immobility	Control of borders and of mobility	private sector, certain NGOs, IOs	Global
Exploitation	Labour cost/flexibility	private sector, brokers/intermediaries	Global
Rights	Human/labour rights	IOs, NGOs, unions, courts	Global
Management	Utilitarianism	IOs, private sector, NGOs	Global
Free movement	Freedom, human agency	Individuals, private sector	Global/regional

These philosophies of migration governance differ in terms of their more or less explicit nature. Sovereignty, human rights and free movement are explicit principles that rely on well-established arguments and can easily be defended by their respective promoters. Managerial/developmental governance is less clear, as it pursues a confusing set of often contradictory objectives (border control, migrant protection, development, growth) that makes for a heterogeneous and less robust narrative (Pécoud, 2015). Global anti-migrant governance tends to be much more implicit, as it contradicts some of the core liberal values that underlie (Western) *Etats de droits* – hence the often unpublicized nature of inter-state cooperation in this field, as well as the structural gap between rhetoric and practice.

As argued above, there is no international migration regime. By nature, the first pattern of governance (national/sovereign migration governance) cannot serve as a regime, as it is explicitly about sovereignty and non-cooperation. The second one (global anti-migrant governance) is a *de facto* regime: from a functional perspective, it works quite well – but to the detriment of migrants, and in a way that exposes it to normative criticisms. The next three patterns of governance could, in principle, serve as the basis for a formal regime. The third one (global rights-based migration governance) relies on well-established hard-law standards and institutional monitoring mechanisms, but faces deep resistance as it runs against some of the core structural forces that have been shaping the global economy for decades. The fourth one (managerial/developmental global migration governance) is designed as a consensual, catch-all policy agenda: this makes it relatively easy to promote, but qualifies its actual impact. According to its detractors, 'migration management' would be nothing more than a vibrant plea for the *status quo*, that is to say, the codification (or formalization) of the second governance pattern (global anti-migrant governance, based on both control and exploitation) in just a slightly more 'human' fashion. The fifth scenario (the free (non-)governance of migration) partially corresponds to an actual regime in certain world regions, but despite its fairly strong ethical or economic grounds remains a utopia at the global level.

7.1. Opposition, continuity and/or complementarity

There are tensions and incompatibilities between these five patterns of governance. For example, the emphasis on labour/human rights is difficult to conciliate with strict state sovereignty, with migrant labour exploitation, with the forced immobilization of migrants, or with migration management. These philosophies are therefore often opposed to each other: Piper and Rother (2012), for instance, argue that international debates on migration are pervaded by an opposition between rights-based and managerial/development governance; Punter et al. (2019) contrast the sovereign-national governance pattern (according to which there cannot be a migration regime) with the global anti-migrant governance regime.

On the other hand, one may conceive these different philosophies of governance as displaying continuities, overlaps and even complementarity. For example, global forced immobility governance can be understood as a continuation of national/sovereign migration governance: faced with the difficulty of asserting their sovereignty over migration, states would resort to other strategies to pursue the same goal of controlling migration – even if this implies actually engaging in cooperation with other states and non-state actors (and therefore nuancing the strict national character of migration policy). As suggested above, managerial/developmental governance can be understood as a compromise between diverging philosophies of governance, as it aspires to respect state sovereignty over borders, maximize the benefits of migrant labour, protect migrants from abuses, and so on.

In practice, the five patterns of migration governance coexist with each other, albeit with different weights. In the current state of affairs, states resort to all of them to craft migration policy, making for a kind of policy *bricolage* in which different patterns of governance sometimes complement each other (for example, when rights-based mechanisms counterbalance the border-control measures) or are applied to different groups of people or different situations (for example, when certain people are granted free movement while others are not). From this perspective, no single pattern of governance can serve as the unique basis for migration governance and, if a single migration regime was to be adopted, it would likely build upon all philosophies. This nevertheless leaves open the delicate issue of the balancing (or fine-tuning) of the different philosophies in such a regime.

7.2. Migration governance and the global class structure

As it is fundamentally about distinguishing between nationals and foreigners, migration policy is usually associated with states, citizenship and national borders – at the risk of downplaying the essential role played by class. Bauman (1998, p. 9) argues that globalization entails the emergence of a global society in which 'mobility has become the most powerful and most coveted stratifying factor': the rich of all countries enjoy widespread mobility opportunities, which (given the unequal distribution of wealth across the globe) further contributes to their privileged situation; wherever they come from, the poor remain trapped in the disadvantaged segments of their country.

This global class structure is central in global anti-migrant governance, which applies above all to unskilled people: they are confined to precarious and unattractive working conditions whereas skilled workers, who are the object of a 'global hunt for talent' (Kapur & McHale, 2005), are granted more rights and enjoy greater access to migration opportunities. In certain cases, the free (non-)governance of migration also includes class-differentiated approaches: NAFTA, for example, provides facilitated mobility opportunities to investors, entrepreneurs or expatriates. At the world level, the governance of trade similarly foresees the liberalization of the 'movement of natural persons' for professionals providing services, notably under the so-called 'Mode 4' of the World Trade Organization GATS agreements.[3] Global rights-based migration governance, by contrast, envisages the horizontal distribution of human rights to all, while the emphasis on nationality that characterizes national/sovereign migration governance lessens the weight of class factors.

7.3. Governing complex migration dynamics

All philosophies of governance face the challenge of the complexity of migration dynamics. They explain *how* migration should be governed without checking *whether* it can be governed. Migration is a multifaceted process that is connected, *inter alia*, to development, conflict, environmental change, labour markets and, not least, peoples' and households' strategies. There is evidence that migration policies – whatever their orientations – regularly fail to reach their stated objectives, mainly because market dynamics challenge states' regulatory mechanisms and legal norms (in democratic countries at least) constrain governments' strategies (Castles, 2004).

Another challenge is human agency. Irregular migration testifies to migrants' capacity to circumvent border control and to stay and work in receiving societies regardless of whether or not they are formally authorized to do so: this is a problem for all the philosophies of governance that aspire at steering peoples' behaviour (except for global labour-exploitation governance, which relies on this state of affairs). Yet global labour-exploitation governance can be contested by migrants' claims for rights and protection, through collective action and the support of CSOs and courts. In the case of managerial/developmental global migration governance, attempts to turn migrants into development-friendly actors may run into their reluctance to behave as such. In a different way, free movement strategies sometimes face the obstacle of peoples' reticence to move: in the EU, for instance, free movement was born out of a strategy to facilitate the circulation of labour for the sake of economic competitiveness, but people have long displayed a reluctance towards such mobility, especially as far as low-skilled workers are concerned (Kunz & Leinonen, 2007).

7.4. 'Global' or 'Western' migration governance?

This article concentrates on South–North migration flows and on the attitudes of Northern receiving countries towards these flows. But there is empirical evidence that South-South migration is equally important in global migration dynamics. The issue therefore is whether this Northern (or Western) bias questions the very idea of 'global' migration governance. While a thorough analysis of this issue is beyond the scope of this article, research on the Global South shows that less-developed states display strategies that echo the different philosophies of governance identified in this article.

For example, Adamson and Tsourapas (2020) argue that migration policies in the Global South can be divided into three types. The first is a 'nationalizing' pattern, according to which migration is governed to support state-building and national identity: this posits a strong connection between migration and sovereignty and thus presents some similarity with national/sovereign migration governance. The second pattern consists of 'developmental' policies, which are concerned with the economic benefits reaped by emigration (remittances, outflow of excess domestic workforce) and are therefore in line with managerial/developmental global migration governance. Lastly, neoliberal strategies see states in the Global South using migrants as a commodity to generate revenues – for example, by asking for financial support or development aid in exchange of cooperation over migration control: as argued, this is one of the pillars of global forced immobility governance.

In the same vein, Thiollet (2019) analyses migration policy in the Arab Gulf and highlights a convergence towards illiberal migration governance between this region and the Global North. This would indicate that global anti-migrant governance is not specific to Western states but also characterizes, albeit in different ways, the migration strategies of governments outside the West. In another world region, Piper (2004) observes that certain sending states, such as the Philippines, strive to develop a rights-based policy to protect their emigrants working abroad and that, to do so, they rely on the international standards that are characteristic of global rights-based migration governance. Lastly, and as noted above, the free (non-)governance of migration is best exemplified by Europe, but also exists in other world regions.

7.5. Economic versus forced migration governance

A related bias concerns the focus on labour/economic migration. The philosophies of governance identified in this article are mostly concerned with the attitude of Western industrial states towards foreign workers; this ignores forced or conflict-induced migration (including for environmental reasons) which plays a key role in certain regions of the Global South, such as Africa. To some extent, this makes sense because the premise of the analysis is precisely that migration governance lacks a proper regime, whereas there does exist a regime for refugees and forced migration. Yet this simple observation leaves open the question of the relevance of (narrowly-defined) labour/economic migration governance in a world characterized by 'survival migration', that is to say, patterns of mobility linked to 'an existential threat for which [people] have no access to a domestic remedy or resolution' (Betts, 2013, pp. 4–5) and that fall outside the (equally narrowly-defined) governance of refugee protection.

None of the five philosophies of governance discussed above seems fit to cater to the needs of migrants forced to live and work in a country other than their own (or, sometimes, in another region of their own country), under very fragile conditions and without benefiting from the protection deriving from the refugee regime. National/sovereign migration governance and global anti-migrant governance are irrelevant here: they may well aggravate (or even cause) such situations of vulnerability. Rights-based governance is about protection, but in its current form it has been criticized for being excessively oriented towards migrant *workers* (as the name of the aforementioned UN Convention makes clear), and hence insensitive to other patterns of migration in which labour is less central. To some extent, the catch-all nature of managerial/developmental migration governance makes reference to situations of vulnerability (for example, by emphasizing the need to protect victims of trafficking), but it fails to provide a comprehensive framework to address forced migration. Likewise, crossing borders under conditions of free movement is of little use for people whose livelihood is threatened in both sending and receiving countries.

On that basis, two strategies can be outlined. The first is to design new humanitarian and protection-oriented philosophies of governance that focus on forced migration connected to conflict, climate change and environmental threats and found specifically in weak or under-developed states that lack the capacity to address this challenge. This is the underlying rationale behind recent initiatives taken by the international community, like the 1998 Guiding Principles on Internal Displacement or the Nansen Initiative on disaster-related displacement (launched in 2012). The second strategy is to reemphasize the centrality of labour in all migration patterns, irrespective of their root causes: as Long (2013) recalls, before the adoption of the refugee regime in the 1950s, refugees were treated as economic migrants; while this threatened their access to protection, it helped them find long-term secure livelihood opportunities outside their country of origin. There have been recent calls for a paradigmatic policy shift that would turn refugees from passive beneficiaries of humanitarian aid into full economic actors, as workers (or even entrepreneurs), thereby granting them autonomy and facilitating their durable settlement in receiving countries (Betts & Collier, 2017). While a thorough discussion of this issue is again beyond the scope of this article, the nuancing of the refugee/migrant divide is a central argument in thinking about global patterns of migration governance.

7.6. Crises and philosophies of governance

Philosophies of governance do not develop in a vacuum, but respond to particular socio-economic and geopolitical contexts. In this respect, two contexts are particularly salient to understand the possible evolutions affecting migration governance: the 2008 financial/economic crisis because it affected economic conditions in all countries, including the advanced economies that attract most labour migrants; and the migration/refugee crisis that emerged from 2013 onwards in Europe, which highlighted the shortcomings of immigration policies and their inability to regulate migration flows successfully.

The 2008 crisis had profound implications for international migration flows, as well as for the social and political context in which they take place. Tilly (2011) shows that it led to a reduction of labour migration in response to fewer job opportunities: this concerns in particular irregular migration flows, even though it has been demonstrated that institutional (and not only economic) factors play an important role in guiding migrants' behaviour (for example, in determining their decision to return to their country of origin). In addition, the crisis affected the reception of migrants, both because it increased hostility towards migrants on the part of host populations and because it incited governments to tighten admission requirements. Yet such political developments fit into broader trends that date back to the 1990s and cannot be solely attributed to the crisis. In terms of philosophies of governance, therefore, the crisis is clearly unsupportive of (already weak) rights-based or free movement approaches, but it is unclear whether it really modifies the overall political architecture of migration politics.

In a different way, the same can be said of the ongoing refugee/migration crisis in the euro-Mediterranean region. Since the beginning of the Arab Spring in 2011, Europe has been facing increased migration pressure on its southern and south-eastern border. This has raised major political and humanitarian challenges, not least because thousands of people have lost their lives in shipwrecks a few miles away from European shores. This crisis has both reinforced and challenged the national/sovereign pattern of migration governance. Faced with increased irregular migration, states have reacted through well-established strategies of unilateral border control, which in some cases implied erecting border walls (such as in Hungary in 2015). On the other hand, the crisis highlighted the inadequacy of this pattern of governance, leading states to develop other strategies. Global forced immobility governance, in particular, was reinforced: the 2015 agreement between the EU and Turkey, whereby the Turkish government agreed to retain Syrian refugees in exchange for financial and logistic support, was a clear example. The crisis also favoured managed/developmental migration governance. At the global scale, the UN adopted two Global Compacts (on refugees and migrants respectively) that were directly born out of the crisis (Ferris & Donato, 2020). At the regional level, IOs were solicited to help governments: for example, the IOM and the UNHCR were among the key beneficiaries of the EU-Turkey deal, as they received financial support to take care of Syrian refugees in Turkey.

By showcasing the limits of national/sovereign migration governance, the crisis has contributed to globalizing migration governance. But this is equivocal, because it has prompted both formal globalization (by leading to new soft-law instruments pertaining to migration, like the Global Compact) and informal globalization (through heightened forced immobility governance). These different patterns of governance, however, preceded the crisis, which does not therefore constitute a fundamental turning point that would have seen the emergence of new political philosophies. Rather, the crisis led to a reorientation of already-existing patterns of governance.

8. Conclusion

This article started with Saskia Sassen's argument that the current governance of migration is an illiberal anomaly: illiberal, because it rests upon values of national closure and control, and an anomaly, because these values contradict the ongoing globalizing forces that make all countries and economies ever more interdependent. In the absence of a regime, and even more so in the current context of migration crises and rising populism in the Global North, governments convey the idea that they should retain full control over their borders. As this article has made clear, such rhetoric contrasts with reality, and with the many competing patterns of governance that shape migration policy.

At times, migration appears like an excessively 'unglobal' issue, heavily embedded in a national framework, and therefore at risk of displaying some of the traditional characteristics of nationalism (such as the 'us versus them' divide or the scapegoating of foreigners). Yet migration is at the same time excessively global because, as global anti-migrant governance illustrates, it is characterized by a kind of global police and a globally-competitive labour market, both of which favour exploitation and abuses at a global scale and lead to a highly deregulated neoliberal *laissez-faire*.

In both cases, migration appears as a dark hole – or perhaps the 'last frontier' (Moses, 2006) – within the current governance of globalization, with the result that the future of global migration governance therefore appears as quite undecided. It may indicate a combination of the excesses of both nationalism and free markets, which would not only characterize migration governance but, more broadly, the ongoing tendencies inside Western democracies towards what is often called neo-liberal authoritarian statehood. By contrast, if states were to agree on a regime to better govern labour migration, this would signal their commitment to address global inequalities by regulating one of their key symptoms, to respect human rights in a genuine way and to recognize the need for a kind of 'cosmopolitics' (Cheah & Robbins, 1998) that takes into account the embeddedness of nations in a world context and the interdependencies between countries. In terms of reglobalization, we have further to go in migration than many other policy arenas, in large measure because governance of this global problem was never adequately globalized in the first place. Recognizing that interdependence, it seems, would be a good place to start.

Notes

1. See https://www.ilo.org/global/topics/labour-migration/fair-migration-agenda/lang--en/index.htm
2. See https://sustainabledevelopment.un.org/
3. See https://www.wto.org/english/tratop_e/serv_e/mouvement_persons_e/mouvement_persons_e.htm

Disclosure statement

No potential conflict of interest was reported by the author(s).

ORCID

Antoine Pécoud http://orcid.org/0000-0002-3159-8338

References

Adamson, F. B. (2006). Crossing borders: International migration and national security. *International Security*, *31*(1), 165–199. https://doi.org/10.1162/isec.2006.31.1.165

Adamson, F. B., & Tsourapas, G. (2019). Migration diplomacy in world politics. *International Studies Perspectives*, *20*(2), 113–128. https://doi.org/10.1093/isp/eky015

Adamson, F. B., & Tsourapas, G. (2020). The migration state in the global south: Nationalizing, developmental and neoliberal models of migration management. *International Migration Review*, https://doi.org/10.1177/0197918319879057

Anderson, B. (2010). Migration, immigration controls and the fashioning of precarious workers. *Work, Employment and Society*, *24*(2), 300–317. https://doi.org/10.1177/0950017010362141

Bakewell, O. (2008). 'Keeping them in their place': The ambivalent relationship between development and migration in Africa. *Third World Quarterly*, *29*(7), 1341–1358. https://doi.org/10.1080/01436590802386492

Balch, A. (2009). Labour and epistemic communities: The case of 'managed migration' in the UK. *The British Journal of Politics and International Relations*, *11*(4), 613–633. https://doi.org/10.1111/j.1467-856X.2009.00384.x
Bauman, Z. (1998). *Globalisation: The human consequences*. Polity Press.
Betts, A. (Ed.). (2011). *Global migration governance*. Oxford University Press.
Betts, A. (2013). *Survival migration: Failed governance and the crisis of displacement*. Cornell University Press.
Betts, A., & Collier, P. (2017). *Refuge: Transforming a broken refugee system*. Penguin Random House.
Bishop, M. L., & Payne, A. (2020a). The political economies of different globalizations: Conceptualizing reglobalization? *Globalizations*. doi:10.1080/14747731.2020.1779963
Bishop, M. L., & Payne, A. (2020b). Steering towards reglobalization: Can a reformed G20 rise to the occasion? *Globalizations*. doi:10.1080/14747731.2020.1779964
Carens, J. H. (1987). Aliens and citizens: The case for open borders. *The Review of Politics*, *49*(2), 251–273. https://doi.org/10.1017/S0034670500033817
Cassarino, J.-P. (2010). *Unbalanced Reciprocities: Cooperation on readmission in the Euro-mediterranean area*. The Middle East Institute.
Castles, S. (2004). Why migration policies fail. *Ethnic and Racial Studies*, *27*(2), 205–227. https://doi.org/10.1080/0141987042000177306
Cheah, P., & Robbins, B. (1998). *Cosmopolitics: Thinking and feeling beyond the nation*. University of Minnesota Press.
Cholewinski, R., de Guchteneire, P., & Pécoud, A. (Eds.). (2009). *Migration and human rights: The United Nations convention on migrant workers' rights*. Cambridge University Press.
Clemens, M. A. (2011). Economics and emigration: Trillion-dollar bills on the sidewalk? *Journal of Economic Perspectives*, *25*(3), 83–106. https://doi.org/10.1257/jep.25.3.83
Collyer, M. (2012). Deportation and the micropolitics of exclusion: The rise of removals from the UK to Sri Lanka. *Geopolitics*, *17*(2), 276–292. https://doi.org/10.1080/14650045.2011.562940
Dini, S., & Giusa, C. (2020). *Externalising migration governance through civil society. Tunisia as a case study*. Palgrave.
Ferris, E. G., & Donato, K. M. (2020). *Refugees, migration and global governance: Negotiating the Global Compacts*. Routledge.
Geiger, M., & Pécoud, A. (Eds.). (2010). *The politics of international migration management*. Palgrave.
Ghosh, B. (Ed.). (2000). *Managing migration: Time for a new international regime?* Oxford University Press.
Groenendijk, K. (2004). Introduction. In B. Bogusz, R. Cholewinski, A. Cygan, & E. Szyszczak (Eds.), *Irregular migration and human rights: Theoretical, European, and international perspectives* (pp. xvii–xxii). Martinus Nijhoff.
Guiraudon, V. (2000). The Marshallian triptych reordered: The role of courts and bureaucracies in furthering migrants' social rights. In M. Bommes & A. Geddes (Eds.), *Immigration and welfare: Challenging the borders of the welfare state* (pp. 72–89). Routldege.
Hess, S. (2010). We are facilitating states! An ethnographic analysis of the ICMPD. In M. Geiger & A. Pécoud (Eds.), *The politics of international migration management* (pp. 96–118). Palgrave.
Hollifield, J. F., Martin, P. L., & Orrenius, P. M. (2014). *Controlling migration: A global perspective* (3rd ed.). Stanford University Press.
International Organization for Migration. (2019). *World migration report 2020*. IOM.
Joppke, C. (1998). Why liberal states accept unwanted immigration. *World Politics*, *50*(2), 266–293. https://doi.org/10.1017/S004388710000811X
Kapur, D., & McHale, J. (2005). *Give us your best and brightest: The global hunt for talent and its impact on the developing world*. Centre for Global Development.
Krasner, S. D. (1982). Structural causes and regime consequences: Regimes as intervening variables. *International Organization*, *36*(2), 185–205. https://doi.org/10.1017/S0020818300018920
Kunz, J., & Leinonen, M. (2007). Europe without borders – rhetoric, reality or utopia? In A. Pécoud & P. de Guchteneire (Eds.), *Migration without borders: Essays on the free movement of people* (pp. 137–159). Berghahn.
Lahav, G., & Guiraudon, V. (2000). Comparative perspectives on border control: Away for the border and outside the state. In P. Andreas & T. Snyder (Eds.), *Wall around the west: State borders and immigration controls in North America and Europe* (pp. 55–80). Rowman & Littlefield Publishers.

Lavenex, S., Givens, T. E., Jurje, F., & Buchanan, R. (2016). Regional migration governance. In T. A. Börzel & T. Risse (Eds.), *The Oxford handbook of comparative regionalism* (pp. 457–485). Oxford University Press.

Long, K. (2013). When refugees stopped being migrants: Movement, labour and humanitarian protection. *Migration Studies, 1*(1), 4–26. https://doi.org/10.1093/migration/mns001

Martin, P. L. (2017). *Merchants of labor: Recruiters and international labor migration*. Oxford University Press.

McKeown, A. (2004). Global migration, 1846–1940. *Journal of World History, 15*(2), 155–189. https://doi.org/10.1353/jwh.2004.0026

Menjivar, C., Ruiz, M., & Ness, I. (Eds.). (2019). *The Oxford handbook of migration crises*. Oxford University Press.

Moses, J. W. (2006). *Migration: Globalization's last frontier*. Zed Books.

Nita, S., Pécoud, A., De Lombaerde, P., de Guchteneire, P., Neyts, K., & Gartland, J. (Eds.). (2017). *Migration, free movement and regional integration*. UNESCO & United Nations University.

Noiriel, G. (1991). *La tyrannie du national. Le droit d'asile en Europe (1793–1993)*. Calmann-Lévy.

Pécoud, A. (2015). *Depoliticising migration: Global governance and international migration narratives*. Palgrave.

Pécoud, A. (2018). What do we know about the International Organization for Migration? *Journal of Ethnic and Migration Studies, 44*(10), 1621–1638. https://doi.org/10.1080/1369183X.2017.1354028

Piore, M. J. (1979). *Birds of passage: Migrant labour and industrial societies*. Cambridge University Press.

Piper, N. (2004). Rights of foreign workers and the politics of migration in South-East and East Asia. *International Migration, 42*(5), 71–97. https://doi.org/10.1111/j.0020-7985.2004.00302.x

Piper, N., & Rother, S. (2012). Let's argue about migration: Advancing a right(s) discourse via communicative opportunities. *Third World Quarterly, 33*(9), 1735–1750. https://doi.org/10.1080/01436597.2012.721271

Punter, D. E., van der Veen, H., van Wingerden, E., & Vigneswaran, D. (2019). A 'distributive regime': Rethinking global migration control. *Political Geography, 70*, 117–126. https://doi.org/10.1016/j.polgeo.2019.01.014

Rodrik, D. (2005). Feasible globalizations. In M. Weinstein (Ed.), *Globalisation: What's new?* (pp. 196–213). Columbia University Press.

Rosental, P.-A. (2006). Géopolitique et Etat-providence. Le BIT et la Politique Mondiale des Migrations dans l'Entre-Deux-Guerres. *Annales. Histoire, Sciences Sociales, 61*(61), 99–134. https://doi.org/10.1017/S0395264900030900

Sassen, S. (1996). *Losing control? Sovereignty in an age of globalisation*. Columbia University Press.

Thiollet, H. (2019). *Immigrants, markets, brokers, and states: The politics of illiberal migration governance in the Arab Gulf*. International Migration Institute Working Paper 155.

Tilly, C. (2011). The impact of the economic crisis on international migration: A review. *Work, Employment and Society, 25*(4), 675–692. https://doi.org/10.1177/0950017011421799

Torpey, J. (2000). *The invention of the passport: Surveillance, citizenship and the state*. Cambridge University Press.

United Nations. (2018). *Draft outcome document of the intergovernmental conference to adopt the global compact for safe, orderly and regular migration*, UN: General Assembly A/CONF.231/3.

Wall Street Journal. (1984, July 3). In praise of huddled masses. p. 1.

Weiner, M. (1995). *The global migration crisis: Challenge to states and to human rights*. Harper Collins College Publishers.

Wolf, M. (2004). *Why globalisation works*. Yale University Press.

Zaiotti, R. (Ed.). (2016). *Externalizing migration management: Europe, North America and the spread of remote control practices*. Routledge.

Zolberg, A. (1997). The great wall against China: Responses to the first immigration crisis, 1885–1925. In J. Lucassen & L. Lucassen (Eds.), *Migration, migration history, history. Old paradigms and new perspectives* (pp. 291–315). Peter Lang.

Steering towards reglobalization: can a reformed G20 rise to the occasion?

Matthew Louis Bishop and Anthony Payne

ABSTRACT

This paper makes three arguments. First, it provides an embryonic blueprint for 'reglobalization' by crystallizing the insights of the special issue. We *can* and *should* build a better globalization that addresses enduring inequality, based on a radical analysis cognizant of the partiality, fragility and incompleteness of the existing global governance architecture, and which seeks to expand, upgrade and democratize the multilateral order. Second, following a post-financial crisis interregnum replete with morbid symptoms, the Covid-19 shock potentially represents the dénouement of a long period of neoliberal decay, after which different approaches to globalization will be necessary. Finally, only a reformed G20 can provide the crucial coordinating function that any process of progressive reglobalization requires, with three necessary reforms: its proper institutionalization with a permanent Secretariat; a widening of its remit to cover all aspects of contemporary globalization; and a concomitant narrowing of its focus to discharge aggressively that specific coordinating function.

Two broad arguments have underpinned our analysis in this special issue. First, despite the many real-life travails faced by 'actually-existing' neoliberal globalization, those that advocate 'deglobalization' from both right and left are misguided. The former offer few answers to neoliberal decay: they are, in fact, only deglobalizers insofar as they seek a neo-nationalist retreat from the multilateral order. For all the characteristic, anti-globalist, Trumpian rhetoric, they embody a contradictory mix of authoritarian populism and economic libertarianism, seeking simultaneously to extend and intensify the worst excesses of the neoliberal era via the destabilization of the very global institutions that underpinned its expansion previously, and to entrench the most malign of its current tendencies. The latter offer undeniably purposeful critique: they are right that neoliberal globalization was and remains deeply problematic in many respects, and they have unquestionably catalogued to great effect its many failures which have only intensified in the era of financialized rentier capitalism. But they are wrong to advocate retreat. Not only does this dance to the hard-right's bidding, but it is based on a faulty misreading of globalization itself. Put simply, as we have: globalization as a process is here to stay, but the 'actually-existing' neoliberal variant is just that, a particular expression of a distinct time and space that was possessed of positives as well as negatives. Since the major challenges we face as global citizens remain transboundary in nature – and will certainly continue to be so – the only thing worth debating is how globalization is shaped, by whom, and to what ends.

Second, and consequently, any truly progressive agenda in the contemporary era has to think globally: all politics fundamentally plays out on a global stage and it is, above all, our institutions operating at that level that urgently need to be refocused, recast and in some areas even created, so that they can better serve the interests of the great mass of humanity. By choosing to vacate this stage – and holding existing regional and multilateral global governance bodies to impossibly utopian standards – leftist deglobalizers are culpable in several respects. They risk throwing out all that is good about globalization with its accompanying neoliberal bathwater; they are complicit in hard-right attempts to de-legitimize, de-regulate and de-democratize globalization; and, above all, they evade the difficult job of generating plausible visions of incremental change to the global order. We already know what is wrong with the World Bank, the International Monetary Fund (IMF), the European Union (EU) and so on. Although refining the mountains of extant critique is undoubtedly important, it is just too easy, and ultimately empty, to conclude that in the face of this we must abandon them altogether. The harder, utterly unheroic, but necessary task is instead to grapple with mundane realities and seek to engineer small improvements to the existing institutional architecture. Globalization will be maintained in some form: those on the left who claim to be internationalist can either work through the institutions that we currently have and bolster them by building complementary ones (Adler, 2019) or they can support withdrawal.

We doubt that, by taking the latter course, a socialist phoenix will rise from the ashes of leftist deglobalization; it is more likely that the right will simply develop a form of globalization that is even more hyper-neoliberal and even worse governed (Bishop & Payne, 2019). So, although it might be somewhat drier and less sexy, we have advocated strongly in this special issue for the construction of a politics that staunchly defends the global order and rebuilds it purposively. We have argued specifically – and our contributing authors have demonstrated – that this process of 'reglobalization' needs to be undertaken on distinctly 'post-neoliberal' lines and 're-embedded' once more in enhanced multilateral institutions. We already have much in place in respect of global governance. But it is, and will remain, imperfect, since every period of multilateral institution-building – including Bretton Woods itself – has inevitably disappointed and come up short against the lofty ambitions of its most imaginative architects, in part thanks to the inertia of resistant political forces (see, *inter alia*, Buzdugan & Payne, 2016; Helleiner, 2014a, 2014b; Ruggie, 1992). For all that, we still have what we have in institutional terms and, crucially, it is not static: if deglobalizing tendencies are already doing great damage to this apparatus, it stands to reason that reglobalizing forces can have a contrarily positive effect too.

The task at hand, then, is it to envision how that might happen. In the remainder of this article, therefore, we seek to define the initial steps on a road that may lead to such a future. First, we revisit the articles in the special issue: we do not reiterate in any detail their specific insights regarding particular arenas of global governance, but we do attempt to tease out their common implications – as well as admit the gaps, omissions and policy domains requiring of similar analysis – for both the political economy of reglobalization in practice and future research on the subject. Second, we build on the argument made in our opening article (Bishop & Payne, 2020) regarding the political bargain necessary to underpin the process and seek to undertake the thornier job of explaining how the real-world politics of realizing such a bargain might be effected. This is unarguably a difficult task, but it must be attempted if the malign forces ranged against better management of the global order are to be faced down. This is especially so given the myriad questions posed by the Covid-19 crisis that unfolded in early 2020 as we were finishing the issue: will what comes next be a shot in the arm for reglobalization – a genuine opportunity to transcend the Gramscian 'interregnum' – or will the deglobalizing tendencies we have identified here intensify? Finally, we suggest that the Group of 20

(G20) is the only game in town for coordinating and managing such an endeavour: what, then, needs to be done to this organization by way of reform to ensure that it can do that job?

An embryonic blueprint for reglobalization

We *can* build a better kind of globalization. Every article in this special issue has demonstrated this, pointing us towards the sorts of initiatives that would be required in specific realms of governance. All of our authors consider reglobalization a worthy goal and, crucially, recognize that it is both possible and plausible: in a range of policy areas running from finance to trade and from the environment to migration they suggest that we live in more fertile times than we might realize for embedding progressive norms about what a 'good' globalization could look like. The case of tax is instructive: as Andrew Baker and Richard Murphy (2020) suggest, much can be done via 'spillover' assessments to encourage a 'race to the top' in tax practices. At present, harmful competition between countries forces a narrowing of the tax base and shrinking of public investment, the costs of which fall most heavily on poorer states which are less able to resist competitive deregulatory pressure. By effectively shaming those with the most negative spillovers – and altering norms around what constitutes acceptable practice – this can be redressed to the benefit of all. The first insight from the special issue, then, is that in every policy arena there are some things that can be preserved from the existing global order, but there also exist a range of meaningful improvements that can be both envisioned and outlined in practical ways, such that they might be brought into being. This may seem obvious, but it is worth making the point explicitly: our entire agenda of reglobalization only works in general if we can conceive of specific innovations that might be realized in both theory and action.

The second insight is that our authors all generally recognize a key tension at the heart of decaying neoliberal globalization: namely, that the substantial wealth that has been generated in this period has been distributed grotesquely unequally, leading to marked patterns of exclusion. However, it is not only critical scholars who have become exercised about this (they have, of course, been sounding the tocsin for many years). Rather, many in the heartland institutions of global capitalism have come to realize the importance of assuaging what are now deeply destabilizing concentrations of capital, and disfiguring apparatuses of ideological power underpinning them (Piketty, 2014, 2020). What this means, moreover, is that traditional readings of those institutions as unflinchingly neoliberal and beyond redress appear outdated. As Ben Clift and Te-Anne Robles (2020) demonstrate in the case of finance, the IMF has come to view redressing global imbalances of wealth and generating better social protection as a central part of its mission, and this increasingly underpins its pursuit of greater global legitimacy. However, because it functions 'within restrictive economistic parameters that flow from its technocratic compulsions', it cannot yet fully realize that greater legitimacy (see also Clift, 2018). The implications for reformers are clear: we are pushing at an open door; the objective has to be to find the language and analysis that permits those within global institutions to go further.

This brings us to the third point: if we are able to reshape globalization, and there exists a latent desire for such change, even amongst (elements of) the powerful, recognition of its many accompanying problems does not constitute an argument for making the world any less 'global', but rather for making globalization *work better*. Economists have recently noted how trade liberalization throughout the 1990s and beyond caused substantial dislocations in Western countries as production was increasingly offshored: net aggregate growth masked the distributional costs paid by laid-off workers, and the overall cost may even have been net negative when we factor in the multiplier effect in depressed industrial regions, poor health outcomes and so on (Banerjee & Duflo, 2019). The continued pursuit of ever-deeper free trade agreements (FTAs) was based less on good economics and more on winning an ideological battle against protectionist backsliding (Rodrik, 2017). Yet these arguments are not new: critical political economists have long argued that growth rates were generally higher during the post-1945 era, when capital was subjected to stronger state control, than during the subsequent neoliberal period. Even then – where the international dimension of such national interventionism was Ruggie's (1982) 'embedded liberalism' compromise discussed in our opening article (Bishop & Payne, 2020) – domestic stability in Western countries was balanced on the backs of poorer states, a problem that only intensified under neoliberalism when the benefits from global free trade accrued disproportionately to developed and 'emerging', rather than poorer developing countries, and to capital, rather than labour (Muzaka & Bishop, 2015). Neoliberals championed greater openness while it served the interests of powerful Western actors, but it is now paradoxically left to globalization's critics to defend it as many neoliberals become neo-nationalists and threaten to jettison the good along with the bad. We cannot risk this: while continuing to recognize globalization's many problems, we need to assuage them by improving its functioning, not dispensing with it and failing to solve (and worsening) the many transboundary challenges we face.

The fourth point is that we need to think truly globally when tallying up the pros and cons of globalization. None of our authors put it quite so explicitly, but a certain Eurocentrism pervades (otherwise well-meaning) critiques that inadvertently privilege the negative consequences for Western societies and elide the sheer diversity of worldwide experience under a constantly evolving global capitalism (Hobson, 2012, 2020). This is not to underplay the crucial class-based analysis that identifies how, on the whole, neoliberal globalization has largely benefitted the wealthy, wherever they may be, with workers – especially labourers in the very poorest countries, but also those with white-collar jobs in the West – seeing their relative incomes decline precipitously (Milanović, 2016). In fact, this insight only makes a 'global' analysis even more important. When it comes to trade, painful industrial decline in one place has been offset by massive increases in wealth, and therefore reductions in poverty, elsewhere, especially amongst the expanding Chinese middle classes. So, while critics are right to decry the distributional costs of greater integration, that does not constitute an argument against globalization itself. Rather, it should open up other questions about ensuring that the *global* benefits can be spread more evenly and *local* losers can be compensated (Rodrik, 2017). Moreover, a relatively open global trading system is intrinsically a public good worth defending. But openness should not be considered an end in itself, as under neoliberalism; it should be a means to other (developmental) ends. The level of openness or integration consequently matters far less than the quality of the architecture underpinning it and the way this embeds marked differences of power and interests, resolves the conflicts that arise in consequence, and facilitates a necessary politics of redistribution.

Our fifth point is that such a 'social purpose' (Bishop & Muzaka, 2018) has frayed in many areas of globalization. This is particularly noticeable in trade, as the sheer relentless growth in cross-border activity has reached the limits of acceptable domestic dislocations, something further intensified by the gigantic scale of China's economic miracle and its ability to dominate many global markets, with troubling implications for developing countries especially (Hopewell, 2019; Kaplinsky, 2013; Phillips, 2009). At present, the WTO appears unable to re-embed these conflicts and resolve this challenge. Moreover, this essential lack of a social purpose is pervasive throughout the institutional settlements that shape the global economy and the policy agendas to which they give rise (Baker, 2018). There is no doubt that, since Trump came to power in the US, the WTO has found itself in the mire, although its many travails long pre-date his election and reflect the broader disharmony of interests between developing and developed countries (Wilkinson, 2014). Indeed, as James Scott and Rorden

Wilkinson (2020) put it in their article in the special issue, 'globalization has unquestionably helped to generate significant economic wealth, but the distribution of those gains has not been sufficiently equitable and the resulting tensions are increasingly unsustainable politically'. However, they also go on to suggest that these challenges can be overcome with the right kind of recasting of the global (trade) agenda to assuage the raw cleavages with which it is associated. What matters, then, is not the pursuit of a rigid ideal of globalization, but rather the existence of set of shared norms and flexible rules underpinning the regime to manage legitimate derogations within it, thereby facilitating greater collective wellbeing and commitment to it.

Erin Hannah, Adrienne Roberts and Silke Trommer (2020) go even further: there is substantial hidden labour in the global economy – or, rather, much very visible but unpaid labour tends to be overlooked in conventional conceptualizations of what constitutes 'work' – which is revealed by deploying a feminist lens. As such, they argue, it should be recognized and taken into far better account when working out where and how value is created if we are to generate meaningful transformations of economic and social relations (see also Elias & Roberts, 2016; Hannah et al., 2017). By re-historicizing Ruggie's 'embedded liberalism', they suggest that the 're-embedded post-neoliberalism' for which we have called does not offer sufficient radical potential. Yet, to our minds, this is not a fundamental divergence of position: progressive politics is always about envisioning better futures, and a call for challenging all orthodoxies – however conservative or radical – is something that might be applied to every area of global policy in order to extend further the boundaries of possibility. Channelling our inner Gramsci, what seems implausibly panglossian today can only become tomorrow's 'common sense' if we do extend those boundaries as far as they can be extended, even if our actual endeavours fall some way short of them. So, the sixth point is a simple one: any embryonic blueprint for reglobalization can never be too radical, because, even if there is a trade-off between vision and possibility, the realization of the latter will only ever occur in truly transformative ways by expanding the scope of the former.

Another broad area of agreement – and this is point number seven – is acknowledgment of just how partial our governance of globalization is and will remain if we do not determine otherwise. Many areas of the global political economy are, in fact, not adequately governed at all, with the result that our analysis of them is insufficiently extensive. The climate emergency and broader problem of environmental degradation represents the best illustration: despite the proliferation of institutions and initiatives (DeSombre, 2006), we still have no real consensus on how to understand and respond to what constitutes, within all areas of global policy, probably the most fundamental challenge to our way of life (Klein, 2014). Indeed, for some societies – especially the many small island states which are literally at risk of extinction, and whose interests are regularly transgressed by those of the powerful (Barnett & Campbell, 2010; Bishop & Payne, 2012; Scobie, 2019) – this is nothing less than an existential issue. The sheer gravity of the problem conceivably explains the intensity of anger amongst young people who, faced with an unremittingly bleak future on current trends, have driven the recent 'Extinction Rebellion' protests and challenged powerful business-as-usual inertia. All of this, as Hayley Stevenson (2020) points out, has been made much worse by the recent tendency of populist deglobalizers to decry and downgrade expert knowledge through the conscious deployment of 'political bullshit' – a particularly malign feature of the post-global-crisis interregnum, as, again, Gramsci (1971) would see it.

The eighth point is that global governance is not simply partial, but in many cases non-existent. This comes through clearly in Antoine Pécoud's (2020) analysis of migration: humans have always moved in huge numbers, and this is only likely to intensify; that we do not have an overarching framework to manage this – in a context where those migrating are amongst the most vulnerable on the planet – represents a shocking failure of politics. As is the case with many of the United Nations (UN) bodies that have been systemically under-resourced since the 1950s, especially those attuned to the developmental challenges facing poorer countries (Buzdugan & Payne, 2016), the International Organization for Migration (IOM) only has a fraction of the capacity (and prerogative) it requires to deal systematically with the myriad challenges faced by migrants and host countries alike. This is clearly a highly complex policy area in and of itself: from the millions living in refugee camps – or the refugees who have made it to rich countries only to be appallingly impoverished and effectively imprisoned (Mayblin, 2019) – to those engaging in clandestine forms of economic migration, or indeed those who are trafficked and then locked into dehumanizing forms of forced labour, legitimate public forms of governance are under-resourced, under-developed and, by providing the gaps into which such deleterious forces can seep, contributors to the problem (LeBaron & Phillips, 2019). The position of labour in general – from the continued decline of the bargaining power of trade unions vis-à-vis capital, to the proliferation of outright abuse at the bottom end of labour markets in rich and poor countries alike – is something that needs desperately to be addressed creatively. Again, existing UN bodies, like the International Labour Organization (ILO), simply do not have the resources to do so.

What is more, we have unavoidably missed many areas of global policy altogether from this special issue, some of which are genuinely novel and only just emerging. In all, global governance is even less developed and the governing power that does exist is frequently exercised by dominant private actors and forces of questionable legitimacy (and even outright illegitimacy and criminality), with grim implications for equity and democracy. These include, but are not limited to: the desperately precarious, increasingly financialized global food system in which many are exploited, hunger is rife, and all interests are far from represented (Clapp & Isakson, 2018; Thompson et al., 2020); the virtual world in general and the rise of 'big data' (Davies, 2017); the thorny challenge of the gigantic digital platforms and rapidly proliferating 'surveillance capitalism' (Zuboff, 2019); the longstanding incoherence of the 'prohibition regimes' (Nadelmann, 1990) underpinning proscribed commodities like weapons, narcotics and wild animals, which have regularly made the problems they purport to solve worse and have come under sustained opposition for the way their costs are often paid by the most vulnerable in society, especially in the 'war on drugs' (Bishop, 2016a). And so on … All are ripe for inclusion within the broad contours of a reimagined reglobalization in both theory and action. The gaps do not necessarily have to be filled by the creation of new institutions along the lines of, say, a 'World Big Data Organization', not least since many of these issues intersect and overlap with existing concerns around trade, finance, labour, environment and so on. But it does mean (point nine) that our existing panoply of global governance bodies needs to be upgraded and expanded and the overall architecture reconfigured in ways that embed a broader range of issues, permit a more penetrating set of interventions and support relentless democratic scrutiny.

A final point worth making here is that all of our authors acknowledge not only the partiality of global governance, but also its essential fragility and deeply fragmented nature. There is an irony here: dissatisfied progressives tend to offer the most penetrating critiques of contemporary neoliberal globalization and its management, thereby inadvertently providing ammunition to the most regressive forces of deglobalization. For all that, and notwithstanding their many faults, it is surely clear that something very precious will be lost if we allow the institutions that we do have to (continue to) atrophy. Our only gloss upon this analysis is that our emphasis draws attention to the special need for global bodies *beyond* the domestic level, capable of addressing the staggering collective-action problems which are only multiplying even as a retreat into regressive nationalisms is widely promulgated (Pisani-Ferry, 2019). As David Adler (2019) has suggested, it is remarkable that so much thinking on the left has been preoccupied with attempts to develop 'a slate of new institutions to reimagine and reconfigure their domestic political economies', with barely any consideration given to the international context in which these political economies are unavoidably enmeshed. Filling this vacuum, he argues, 'is strategically necessary, politically desirable and morally urgent'.

Moving beyond the interregnum: a post-Coronavirus political bargain?

We need now to move on to consider how this might happen and, in so doing, begin to confront some of the political problems that lie in the way of a turn towards a progressive reglobalization, whilst also simultaneously looking out for opportunities, even unexpected ones. As we were in the throes of completing this special issue, the Covid-19 crisis exploded. In the most immediate sense, this meant that one crucial policy arena that was missing from our collective deliberations in the special issue was public health. Many of the pathologies that we have discussed undoubtedly afflict global health, perhaps even to a greater extent: disease is the ultimate transboundary threat; it intersects dramatically with both processes of capitalist development and a changing climate; its governance is deeply fragmented, with its primary public institution, the UN World Health Organization (WHO), chronically under-resourced and constantly criticized; it is typified by massive inequalities of access to medicines, facilities and expertise, within and between countries, along with staggering resource misallocations causing the overproduction of non-essential healthcare in rich countries and for wealthy groups in poor countries to the detriment of the poor who are often excluded entirely from urgent medical interventions (see, *inter alia*: Davies, 2019; Davies et al., 2015; Harman, 2012; Muzaka, 2011, 2018; Rushton, 2019).

At the time of writing, the Covid-19 pandemic is still demonstrating daily, even hourly, just how woefully under-prepared the world has been for such a shock. It is, of course, far too early to speculate on how this crisis will ultimately play out, but, at least in its early stages, Western governments jettisoned parts of the neoliberal 'playbook' and, with it, the practical and discursive stranglehold of a decade of austerity (Tooze, 2020). Entire economies immediately ground to a halt as large numbers of people were forced to stay at home, with predictions of a global contraction of 30 per cent (annualized) or more in the second half of the year not seeming outlandish. Nouriel Roubini (2020) described it as the 'fastest, deepest economic shock in history' and predicted nothing less than 'The Greater Depression'. Larry Elliott (2020) likened its effects to those of war, rather than an economic shock: 'a neutron-bomb attack that targets the people but leaves the buildings unscathed'. The extent of its impact cannot therefore be overstated: even in the worst-affected Western countries, the 'Great Recession' only caused low single-digit contractions in 2009, and most had returned to growth again by 2010, even though they subsequently experienced a decade of deep political uncertainty and enduringly sluggish economic performance (Hay & Payne, 2013).

The irony – at least as seen from our proximate vantage point – is that 2008 was a full-blown capitalist crisis, yet it ultimately led only to rather tentative reforms *of* capitalism. In fact, in trying to keep the neoliberal show on the road, the deeper institutionalization of many of its most inequitable features actually paved the way for the deglobalizing tendencies we have discussed in this special issue. By contrast, the Covid-19 crisis appears, at least in the first instance, to be exogenous to broader economic processes. William Davies (2020) notes two distinguishing features of '2020 and its aftermath' in this regard: firstly, he suggests, although 'its transmission has followed the flightpaths of global capitalism … its root cause is external to the economy' as conventionally understood; and, secondly, the 'pandemic does not discriminate on the basis of economic geography', such that 'a striking feature … has been the universality of human behaviours, concerns and fears'.

Yet, also in contrast to 2008, the crisis rapidly prompted the most far-reaching economic reforms, almost overnight. Although their specific responses vary, many governments suddenly injected enormous amounts of capital into markets, underwrote (at least temporarily) the incomes of furloughed employees and essentially nationalized many strategic parts of the economy, especially in healthcare.

Framing health questions as 'external' to 'the economy' is potentially epistemologically problematic. The crisis demonstrated, with awesome immediacy, how a pandemic caused by a tiny micro-organism that can transcend borders in a faster and more malevolent way than just about anything else, has an uncanny ability to highlight brutally the shortcomings of existing economic institutions and practices. Although the disease itself is biological, as Davies (2020) further argues, the 'degree of devastation' will depend entirely on 'very basic features of global capitalism that almost no economist questions – high levels of international connectivity and the reliance of most people on the labour market'. These challenges are especially pronounced in the most neoliberalized states. By assuming a war footing, many of the assumptions that characterized late-era neoliberal governance in the West immediately went out of the window. From insufficient hospital intensive-care capacity and huge shortages of basic medical goods like masks and protective equipment, to atrophied public response systems and an inability to conduct sufficiently widespread disease monitoring and testing, the marketized states of the West – especially those of Britain and the US – seem to have been found the most wanting and have compared generally unfavourably to the decisive response of the Asian 'developmental states' (Bishop et al., 2018).

Going forward, the urgent question is the extent to which emergency shifts become more deeply institutionalized, coalescing into permanent and far-reaching change. As Barry Gills (2020), the editor of *Globalizations*, suggested recently, we may finally be moving from 'the great implosion to the great awakening' during which the intersection of Covid-19 with 'the systemic crisis of global capitalism and neoliberal economic globalization' and 'climate change and ecological breakdown' could produce 'radical systemic transformation'. This, he hopes, may generate a widespread realization that a different world is possible, 'where the collective being starts to take precedence over egoistic individualism'. As we write from locked-down northern England in May 2020, it is already difficult to imagine enthusiastically returning to a world where the 'gig economy' was rampant; healthcare was typified by spiralling waiting lists and below-inflation pay rises for nurses; those doing the crucial work of cleaning, cooking and caring were demonized as 'unskilled'; and a punitive social-security system vilified those without work and subjected them to enforced penury, overseen by parasitic profiteering firms. Much of what the left has argued for of late – rolling forward the state, universal basic incomes, nationalizing utilities and public goods – has, out of force of necessity, been placed on the table. In *The Great Leveler*, Walter Scheidel (2017) argues that waxing and waning inequality has only witnessed dramatic shifts towards greater equality in the aftermath of events in which people have made great sacrifice: war, pestilence, state collapse and revolution. With inequality at historically high levels and with the largest concentrations of wealth in the fewest hands since 1945, the Covid-19 pandemic may, ultimately, lead to just such a reckoning, especially because the patterns of winners and losers in respect of the virus have revealed starkly the unequal, and now deeply visible, fault-lines running through Western societies (with the losers paying the ultimate price with their lives).

In this respect, 2020 is probably going to be unlike 2008: the impact has been so universally comprehensive, affecting every single member of society and their families and friends instantaneously, that, literally, 'we are all in it together'. But some are more 'in it' than others, and this does not necessarily reflect existing hierarchies of power: the middle classes and wealthy cannot be fully insulated from 'the virus', as they were in 2008 and during the subsequent asset boom, and those with the widest networks of acquaintances – sportspeople, celebrities, politicians, even prime ministers – have found it especially difficult to avoid contracting it. Older, richer people have proven most vulnerable, as triage decisions over whom to save with acutely limited healthcare resources brutally privilege the young, and care homes have disastrously become repositories of infection. Moreover, those on the frontline, including those poorly-paid cooks, cleaners, carers (and couriers), will emerge the heroes of the crisis. They will not wish to go back to the pre-2020 world, nor should they, and over time they could become an important political constituency alongside the many middle-class people who have suffered the sudden shock of finding themselves in unanticipated, and previously unimaginable, precarity. Even the most basic neoliberal assumptions – for example, that punitive welfare regimes are required to 'incentivize' people to work – have been swiftly dispelled by the enormous mobilization in so many countries of volunteers prepared to put themselves in harm's way for the broader social good.

It is undeniably foolhardy to predict at this early moment the outlines of the post-coronavirus future of global politics. However, two things seem to be emerging already. First, we offer here a somewhat different analysis to that which we originally envisaged: this was to have been a discussion of the extent to which a turn towards reglobalization was subject, at least in part, to the exit from the political stage of deglobalizers like Trump, Putin, Erdoğan and, perhaps, Johnson too. We would also have lamented the fact that the energetic, yet inchoate opposition to the politics such leaders represent and the dysfunctions of late-era neoliberal globalization that can be identified throughout the world had not yet coalesced into generating the kind of social conditions that were central to forging the post-1945 'embedded liberalism' compromise that we discussed in our opening article (Bishop & Payne, 2020). Even today, the conventional wisdom remains that this is unlikely for good reason: the level of economic insecurity faced by many after coronavirus could lead to a further lurch rightwards and a retreat behind borders into even-darker nativist, xenophobic insularity. We do not discount this possibility for one moment in what is evidently an extremely febrile period of history.

Yet, equally, writing about the G20 summit in Osaka, Japan, in mid-2019, one of us (Bishop, 2019) sought to pose a counterpoint to the pervasive doom-laden narratives regarding the seeming permanence of the nationalist authoritarian turn by asking whether the 'multilateral fightback' may have actually already begun, albeit under the radar. This excessively optimistic analysis sought to be neither original nor conclusive: others have demonstrated the unheralded resilience of a liberal order which effectively prevented another depression after 2008 (Drezner, 2014), even though it struggled to stem the subsequent wave of populism, and the question was deliberately speculative. Rather, amid a preponderance of pessimism, it can be worth sketching out what an alternative account might look like, regardless of its ultimate veracity. There are, today, often-unacknowledged reasons for some degree of optimism. To cite two recent observations made in Britain: you cannot 'bullshit a virus' (North, 2020) and nor can you 'sing Rule Britannia' to it (Okwonga, 2020). The former references Boris Johnson's general approach to politics and the post-truth problem discussed at length by Stevenson (2020) in the special issue; the latter highlights the nationalist paroxysm of Brexit, which already seems a relic of a bygone era. We would not want to overstate the likelihood of a reglobalizing turn nor understate the possibility of a baleful reactionary nationalism emerging, but the deglobalizers do appear, for the first time in a while, to be demonstrably on the back foot, so cack-handed has been their response to Covid-19.

Consequently, the second suggestion we can now make is that, for the first time since 2008, we may be witnessing, at last, the dénouement of the period of neoliberal decay that became evident then, and the beginning of the end of the Gramscian 'interregnum' in which many 'morbid symptoms' – Trump *et al.* amongst them – could finally be transcended. This is, again, certainly not to say that this *will* happen. Borders have been presently reinforced all over the world and the very opposite may still prove to be true: some early analysis has explicitly questioned whether Covid-19 is actually a 'pandemic *of* deglobalization' (James, 2020, emphasis added) and expressed the fear that it could give rise to the kind of intensified 'mysticism, irrationalism, and xenophobia' that followed major pandemics in the (distant) past. However, this could also be read another way: if it is revealed beyond doubt that many rich countries were left seriously under-prepared to deal with coronavirus alone (emphasize: *alone*), it may signal the high point of deglobalizing neo-nationalism. States have evidently initiated highly nationalist policies in response to coronavirus, locking down populations and underwriting entire sectors of domestic economies. It is also true that – again, at the time of writing – the international response has been close to non-existent. Writing in mid-March, former British Prime Minister Gordon Brown – the man who drove the impressive response to the global financial crisis via the G20 at its high-point in 2009 – lamented the lack of leadership and the absence of a coordinated plan for addressing the pandemic, noting that 'one of the most disastrous weeks in the history of global medicine and global economics has ended with country after country retreating into their national silos'. In this 'divided, leaderless world', he argued, 'we are all suffering from the tendency to go it alone' and 'the very idea of global collaboration – and the convening of what would be a "virtual" G20 – sits uneasily with the "America first", "China first", "India first" and "Russia first" populist nationalism that has been subdividing our world' (Brown, 2020). This was followed in early April by a letter signed by over a hundred former world leaders demanding action, that only someone with Brown's network of contacts and commitment to multilateralism could plausibly organize (Berglöff et al., 2020).

Yet the reactions of many countries – closing borders, domestic lockdowns, even states of emergency – are not, in themselves, intrinsically national*istic*. They do not necessarily reflect conscious deglobalization; they are emergency responses to an urgent situation. Internationally, G20 governments did eventually convene a 'virtual' summit on 26 March 2020, but this could hardly have been less auspicious, led, as it was, by the unlikely figure of King Salman of Saudi Arabia, aged 80 and rarely seen in public, and comprising the least impressive cast of protagonists in recent memory. Nonetheless, it is the very contingency of these processes that offers some hope regarding the longer-term effects of the crisis. Four aspects of the situation are worth noting. First, alongside the evident need for investment in stronger national health and social security systems, there will inevitably be demands for more resources to be channeled to global institutions to prevent future pandemics, and actions such as Trump's suspension of funding to the WHO in mid-April will come to be viewed as little more than counterproductive vandalism and an embarrassing attempt to detract from domestic policy failings. Second, borderless threats in general are not going away; they are intensifying. Writing in *The Guardian* newspaper, George Monbiot (2020) described Covid-19 as 'nature's wake-up call to complacent civilisation'. The simultaneous economic shock and apparent improvement in air quality together arguably represent dry-runs for both the risks of tackling climate change *and* the potential for mitigating it. Achieving the latter inevitably requires a beefing up of multilateral institutions. Third, other global leaders who come to power after the pandemic – some of whom could do so rather sooner than anticipated – may have a very different attitude to truth, knowledge, public investment and global cooperation than those they succeed. Fourth, the response of many has already been characterized by a renewed internationalism: from calls for European 'coronabonds' to socialize the crisis across the Eurozone (Matthijs, 2020; Moschella & Quaglia, 2020), to demands for the IMF to transcend dollar hegemony and reduce global dependence on destabilizing US 'financial imperialism' (Adler & Arauz, 2020), not to mention China's widespread sharing of medical aid, there exist myriad forces pushing for greater cooperation.

For all of these reasons, it is at least arguable – if not, again, at this stage yet probable – that 2020 may be to 2008 what 1945 was to 1929. History suggests that it often takes a decade or more for a major crisis – properly defined as akin to a medical condition that could go either way – to be decisively resolved in one direction or another (Hay, 2011; Hay & Payne, 2013). So, it is possible that, over the next year or two, we may begin finally to see the necessary leadership coalesce around the kind of 'Bretton Woods II' that many hoped for, but was ultimately not realized, in the immediate aftermath of the global financial crisis (Helleiner, 2014a, 2014b). Just a few months ago, the historian Katrina Forrester (2019) crystallized the post-2008, pre-2020 era thus: 'we're living through a period of crisis' in which the crisis itself has 'become the new normal', and therefore a substantive 'rebuilding of … public institutions' is desperately required. This analysis was absolutely correct – the consequences of neoliberal decay were abundant – but the era it describes is surely now coming to an end. The vital rebuilding of the public realm is more necessary than ever, but with it must come a recognition – as Covid-19 evocatively demonstrates – that all politics is *both* local *and* global; the one cannot be reduced to the other; and that the kinds of interventions within, and improvements of, global governance in particular that were necessary after 2008 are even more pressing today, if we are genuinely to transcend the interregnum and inaugurate a new epoch of reglobalization.

This brings us full circle to the ten points we noted previously, distilled from the various articles in this special issue: (i) we *can* build a better globalization; (ii) it has to be predicated on a recognition that the inequalities inherited from the neoliberal era are indefensible and destabilizing to society as a whole; (iii) we *should* build a better globalization, since the extant problems do not constitute an argument for dispensing with it, but rather making it work more effectively; (iv) these can in turn only be overcome by thinking genuinely globally in terms of our response; (v) the compromises involved in developing the necessary policy and institutional innovations must be constructed on the basis of a shared social purpose; (vi) our ideas about what constitutes the boundaries of the possible can never be too radical, as they give our practical intentions something at which to aim; (vii) existing global governance is not only partial, but (viii) it is in many places non-existent, leaving the job of governing to undemocratic, illegitimate and often-malign forces; (ix) the existing architecture needs to be expanded, upgraded and relentlessly democratized; and (x) the extant multilateral order remains both fragile and deeply fragmented (but it is what we have, and we must work to improve it).

As a broad blueprint and guide for action, this is not bad. There is, evidently, much work to be done. However, for any wide-ranging process of reglobalization to work, it has to be coordinated. We have already discussed the political bargain that this requires, along with the kind of balance that needs to be struck between global rules (clearer, more transparent, equitable) and the necessary policy space for individual states, particularly poorer ones, to deviate to an extent from these rules in order to support genuinely progressive, developmental ends at the national level (Bishop & Payne, 2020). Yet we have said much less about how the range of issues facing us can be managed politically on some sort of institutional basis. This is the most difficult political issue to confront, because, as we know only too well, the sad reality of recent times is that the coordinating function serviced by the existing system of multilateralism has faced an onslaught from deglobalizers in almost every area of policy.

Back to the G20 … despite everything?

There is clearly an urgent need to break out of this deadlock, especially in the context of an ongoing full-spectrum political, social and economic crisis triggered by an epochal health emergency. The only way to chart an escape route is by means of politics and the highest of 'high politics' at that. The global order requires a renewed leadership that is willing and able to steer towards reglobalization step by step. Such leadership needs a vehicle and that again must be conceived and built (or rebuilt) politically. Although the many global technocratic bodies, whose options and policy debates have been considered in the articles in this special issue, will remain crucial to even partial achievement of such a goal, they cannot be expected to shape a solution without political direction from the top. This focuses attention upon the leaders, elected and otherwise, of the largest and most powerful states in the world and thereafter takes us quickly to further discussion of the role and ongoing potential of the G20, which is the only organization within which they all meet on any kind of regular basis.

We have mentioned the G20 already and its origins, early successes and unfolding history are by now well-known (Cooper, 2010, 2014; Cooper & Thakur, 2013; Kirton, 2016). So are its weaknesses. Much has been said – some of it by ourselves – about the many flaws in the design and failings in the operation of this organization. It is undeniably exclusionary, anti-democratic and enjoys much less popular legitimacy than a UN system that encompasses all countries and at least formally treats them equally (Narlikar, 2014). It is certainly the case that G20 members were selected quickly and in highly political fashion back in 1999 when the body was initially formed as a gathering of finance ministers following a conversation between the US Treasury and the German Finance Ministry; that too many other states just seem to be allowed to turn up and join in, with fuzzy membership criteria that lead to both questionable inclusions and exclusions; and that there are consequently real questions to be asked about the relationship of the G20 to the 'G172', namely, the 'marginal majority' that encompasses all other countries of the world (Payne 2010). It also evidently has not managed to successfully trade off one of 'legitimacy' or 'efficiency' against the other, as is generally the case with successful global governance bodies, and the extent of its 'success' in terms of financial re-regulation in the wake of the 2008 crash may even, perhaps, be somewhat less than is commonly perceived (Vestergaard & Wade, 2012a, 2012b).

But, as thorny as these problems may be, in institutional terms they all still ultimately add up, at best, only to a case for a bit more thought about, and then some adjustment to, the current membership and attendance procedures, as well as a clearer account of expectations regarding what the G20 can and should seek to achieve, along with the development of mechanisms to institutionalize and enforce it. In other words, by fiddling around the edges of the institution, its legitimacy could be improved – for example, maybe by inviting the regular participation of some regional bodies in lieu of the excluded smaller states that they represent – but it cannot, and should not, be turned into a mini-UN. A G20 (or a G21, or G22 ...), however selected, is always going to be an elite club for managing global affairs. That is its very raison d'être and there is no problem with it being so, granted that there exists a pressing need for precisely that governing capacity in managing the global political economy. As long as this role is clearly spelled out in terms of the shared social purpose we have already discussed, its benefits accrue widely, and, moreover, they are seen to do so by the global community as a whole, then this is potentially justifiable and desirable.

The deeper problem is that there has emerged an enduring tension at the heart of the G20's constitution and mission. On the one hand – and certainly since it came of age during the global financial crisis – it has plausibly been seen as a potential, if as yet not fully realized, 'premier forum for ... international economic cooperation', a claim it was bold enough to make about itself as early as its third summit in Pittsburgh in the US in September 2009 (G20 Leaders, 2009). In a context where substantial and necessary reform of the existing institutional paraphernalia inherited from the Bretton Woods era is badly needed but difficult to effect, the G20 is well-placed to help overcome the inertia within bodies that are either insufficiently representative (as in the case of, say, the IMF and World Bank) or too representative (as with the UN General Assembly) to pull off the necessary mix of consensus (i.e. legitimacy) and directional thrust (i.e. efficiency). Since the world is both characterized by a rapidly changing distribution of economic and political power, and the faltering, contested, but nonetheless ongoing expansion of a genuinely global political economy, this coordinating role is ever-more critical.

On the other hand, the G20 has often, and of late more frequently, been seen as little more than an expensive annual jamboree where world leaders, from an admittedly wider range of countries than in the past, and their entourages – but not usually their wives, who tend to be marginalized in an archaic display of 'hegemonic masculinity' (Dobson, 2012) – hobnob in front of the global media. Rather than offering serious policy development to manage the global economy, it has become a space in which the pressing diplomatic controversies of the moment provide the key storylines and points of intrigue. The global media paints and spreads this 'summit-as-circus' narrative, with personalities and gossip dominating the soap opera coverage (Bishop, 2018). In contrast, it could be argued that the summit is actually just the tip of an iceberg under which a huge amount of work goes on during the intervening months, with a wide range of ministerial and technocratic input from states themselves across a range of issue-areas, alongside intellectual and policy development by groups such as the 'Think 20' (T20) and pressure from civil society. Our argument is not that these networks are unimportant, rather that they lack for leadership that can tie their considerable output together coherently in a way that deeply penetrates, and has an unequivocally effective impact on, the making of global policy. Arguably, the summit, which should be a serious event that consolidates this work by producing communiqués of real heft and purpose that set the tone and direction for collectively managing the international order – rather than embodying trivial spats and vague, rhetorical allusions to satisfy the affectations of narcissistic leaders – has degenerated to such an extent that it may even undermine the work that goes on under the surface.

So, what is the G20, or, rather, what can it still become? Can it resolve the tensions that bedevil it to constitute something that at last lives up to the expectations raised when it was first proclaimed as that premier forum? Shortly after the 2008 shock and the G20's emergence into public and political consciousness as a body of leaders, Andrew Cooper (2010) characterized its essence as a 'crisis committee' or 'steering committee' for the global political economy. It was a highly insightful observation because 'steering' is what all forms of world order need if they are to function, both in and out of crisis. He noted, however, that this conceptualization was 'improvised' and 'contested' and that has undoubtedly remained the case, problematically so, over the last decade. Two other analysts, Mark Beeson and Stephen Bell (2009), also writing in the early days of the G20's existence, were more optimistic, cautiously identifying two processes of socialization at work within the G20 which they dubbed 'hegemonic incorporation' and 'collectivist cooperation'. The former involved the successful integration of emerging economies like China, India and Brazil into the structures and practices of neoliberal globalization; the latter highlighted the shift of economic power that was giving rise to these emerging economies and offered the prospect of a collective re-design of globalization broadly in their favour.

Much more recently, Tom Chodor (2017, p. 206) has offered a convincing explanation of why neither effective steering nor incorporation and more inclusive cooperation have occurred. He argues that the global political economy has altered structurally in two important ways since the global financial crisis: 'by accelerating the economic power shift – weakening the West and emboldening the South – and by undermining neoliberalism in the South'. In his view, these developments have stymied both of the processes identified by Beeson and Bell, 'as the US hegemon finds itself unwilling and unable to grant concessions necessary for incorporation while the emerging economies themselves become more confident in demanding a departure from the neoliberal consensus'. The result, in his view, has been gridlock. This, it would seem, is the major structural stumbling block to a fuller institutionalization of the G20, and indeed is a large part of the reason why the social purpose of other multilateral bodies has decayed. As China and other powers are still 'rising', how they are to be successfully accommodated within the existing global governance architecture as that process continues, let alone a reformulated one, remains an open question (see, *inter alia*, Bishop, 2016b; Bishop & Murray-Evans, 2020; Chin & Dobson, 2015; Cooper & Stolte, 2020). We only depart from this analysis in one small respect: as discussed previously (Bishop & Payne, 2020), it is the fact that neither the US nor any single state is truly hegemonic today, and that we have not yet found a mechanism for sharing and exercising such power collectively (between, say, the US, EU and China) that makes it so tricky to recast the regime as a whole.

This is, unfortunately, an accurate summation of the point that the G20 had reached by March 2020, as the inadequacy of the Saudi Arabian 'virtual' summit demonstrated yet again. As Chodor (2020) suggests, it has been 'missing in action' from the Covid-19 crisis. However, there is an underlying aspect to the situation which accounts of the serial failures of recent summits sometimes miss. After all, the G20 has been in existence long enough now for us to be able to see how and when it works, and also of course how and when it does not work, which has generally of late been an increasing proportion of the time. The truth is that it has become ever more apparent that the G20 suffers from a fundamental flaw in its structural design. This is not actually a matter of its membership, for reasons already articulated, but derives from the reality that, as presently set up, it is at heart only a vessel, largely empty of political direction until and unless it is periodically refuelled with new initiatives and priorities. Or, to adopt perhaps a more telling metaphor, it is in effect a parked-up car, sitting on the lot (between meetings) waiting for a new driver to come along and take over the steering wheel. President Putin rents the car out for a bit (in September 2013), then hands it back in (with nobody checking for or even less charging for damage); whereupon it is parked up again until Tony Abbott, then prime minister of Australia, presents himself, is given the keys and takes it back out on the road again (in November 2014). After him, the next driver is President Erdoğan of Turkey (in November 2015), then along comes Xi Jinping of China (in September 2016), and so the summits proceed on a bumpy road via Hangzhou, Hamburg, Buenos Aires, Osaka and, maybe in 2020, Riyadh, before carrying on.

The rental car analogy is no doubt exaggerated (for, as we have noted, a growing number of important G20 working groups do roll on between summits and commissioned studies are also always being researched). But it does, nevertheless, draw attention to the G20's fundamental lack of permanence, its 'occasionality', and the need for more sustained navigation. Indeed, one small element that symbolizes the problem is that G20 presidencies do not always align with the group's management, adding to the sense of drift: Germany, for instance, carried on running the G20 *after* its July 2017 summit for months until the conventional December handover to Argentina, which then oversaw the organization until its summit the following November. In short, the G20 was set up hurriedly amidst a crisis and was, naturally enough, modelled on the proclaimed informality and broad commonality of outlook of the member-states of the Group of Seven/Eight (G7/8). Yet this manifestly cannot be expected to work in the same way at the level of twenty (or more) states and other organizations, especially when their leaders, ministers and officials are inevitably drawn from diverse cultural and ideological backgrounds. It is, as a consequence, in need of urgent institutional reform. Part of the reason why the summit circus dominates is because, to the outside world, the G20 as a whole is reduced *to* those summits. What needs to happen is that, as the tip of the iceberg, they take full charge of the work going on under the water (which itself requires further expansion). In a nutshell, the G20 needs to be given the tools to do the critically important steering job towards reglobalization that we have argued is necessary.

Such a reform process should embrace three interlocking changes. First, the G20 needs at last to be properly institutionalized, with a more effective executive, composed like the present informal troika of the previous, current and next heads of government convening the summits, but toughened up considerably beyond current patterns of behaviour and supported by an influential Secretary-General heading a modest, but permanent, Secretariat. They should be a former head of state (or government), capable of talking as equals with current prime ministers and presidents, and chosen on merit for their political skills, range of connections and energy. Many potential figures could be identified without difficulty (an obvious one, to our minds, would be Gordon Brown, a man who commands respect internationally and evidently still has much to offer intellectually and politically). There should certainly be no national or regional 'grip' on this appointment, as still exists in relation to filling the leading positions in the IMF and the World Bank. The Secretariat should be located in an accessible state (probably outside North America and Europe) with good communications, an experienced diplomatic corps and as high a level of trust and competence as can be achieved. A strong candidate would actually be a non-G20 member, Singapore, which, as it happens, has attended most summits due to its hosting of the Asia-Pacific Economic Cooperation (APEC) Secretariat, and gained significant kudos from its role in creating the so-called Global Governance Group (3G), an informal grouping of some thirty smaller and medium-sized countries that collectively channels their views into the G20 process (Cooper & Momani, 2014; Slaughter, 2020). Singapore is, moreover, located outside the old 'West', not far from China (without of course being China), small enough not to be threatening to the larger G20 states, and well trusted due to its independent foreign policy and good governance. It is also possessed of outstanding diplomats who are especially well-versed in mediation, world-leading universities and technical capabilities, and a substantial amount of state capacity.

Second, the broad remit of the G20 should be widened to take an interest in all aspects of contemporary globalization, including every area of policy discussed in this special issue, plus many others too, of which health (in the context of the global spread of Covid-19) is only the most obvious. Importantly, this would take the organization's remit beyond a circumscribed definition of what constitutes 'international economic cooperation' to draw in as routine environmental issues (such as the greening of growth strategies), social matters (such as excessive levels of inequality) and human questions (such as the movement of peoples and the future of work). It makes no sense to seek to handle some aspects of globalization writ large inside the G20 and others outside. If that means creating new global organizations in some spheres of policy, or even seizing directional control of the politics of an issue like climate change from the UN system, then, in an era of emergencies, whether related to climate, health or migration, so be it. Climate change in particular is an issue of political economy, given its causation by the type of industrial growth that has been pursued all over the world for more than two centuries. Such a G20 agenda would necessarily be very broad, but with tight control of each summit's work-load it should be possible, certainly easier, to exclude passing diplomatic and security flare-ups of the sort that have forced several recent summits into a preoccupation with passing trivia (relatively speaking) and thereby effectively derailed them from their core job of steering the global political economy as a whole.

Third – and this is really the crucial reform that is required – the G20 needs at the same time to develop and then adhere strictly to an extremely narrow and highly focused view of what it can (or, rather, could) do better than any other existing body. This is to steer and coordinate all actions that necessarily have to take place across a large number of states to be effective. So, although its oversight remit should be wide in relation to issue-area (as above), it should be very specific, even shallow, in terms of the nature of its specific impact. We can debate the extent to which this role should be institutionalized: Cooper (2019) has recently argued, for example, that its role as a crisis committee is over, and it should instead be recognized as 'a hybrid focal point for global politics'. This perhaps implies something even shallower than what we are proposing. Either way, the key point is that the G20 cannot, and should not, risk doing nothing by trying to do everything. It should certainly seek to establish and manage clearly understood lines of influence over the major global economic institutions – the IMF, the World Bank, the WTO, the Organisation of Economic Cooperation and Development (OECD), the Financial Stability Board (FSB) and others – in order to give general direction to their work. But neither the summit nor the Secretariat should seek to undertake work that can be done better within other bodies possessed of specialist expertise. Above all, the G20 should endeavour to gather up all of the many, separate areas of policy into something approaching an overarching global agenda within which trade-offs take place between states and across issue-areas. The big hole at the heart of contemporary global governance is oversight of the whole phenomenon. Whatever a reformed G20 can achieve on this front will inevitably look messy and be incomplete. But it has a big hole to fill and it will not take much of substance to be poured into it to constitute an improvement on the absence of steering and lack of coordination that currently characterizes the governance of globalization.

Conclusion

What the G20 then did at its forthcoming summits in Saudi Arabia in November 2020, in Italy at some point in 2021 and in India at some point in 2022 would still depend on politics – on the balance of ideological positions asserted and deliberated upon in relation to all its activities (see Schirm, 2013). That is an inevitable limitation of what would remain, even if the reforms in its design suggested here were fully implemented, in essence an inter-governmental, rather than supranational, institution. Accordingly, the G20's varying package of leaders could still fail to steer, to chart a sensible way through the many crises of globalization. At times, there would still undoubtedly be impasse. But it would be more likely that there would also be more phases of pragmatic 'muddling through' and conceivably some periods when creative leaders were able to think big and set out, and then implement, at least to some degree, major programmes of global change and rescue. The core global political economic issue would remain the future of post-neoliberalism amidst grave climate change and fears of future pandemics and economic crises. But the crucial shift would be that the direction of this new reformed G20 would be worth fighting for politically, rather than just occasioning at intervals either good or bad, but ephemeral, headlines.

Does the Covid-19 pandemic offer such an opportunity? Directly, perhaps not, but indirectly it may well do. The broader intellectual point worth reiterating here is that our analysis in this article represents the 'structural' counterpart to the 'agential' account in our opening one regarding the kind of leadership necessary to develop a 're-embedded, post-neoliberal compromise' that can underpin reglobalization (Bishop & Payne, 2020). Put differently: the social conditions for such an epochal shift may, at last, be with us. This is not to say they definitely are, nor that a progressive future necessarily awaits us. The most regressive deglobalizing visions may prevail during the struggles of the early 2020s, especially as contestation over who should bear the costs of the coronavirus recessions become central to domestic politics in many countries. However, there is quite enough of that kind of pessimism dominating the airwaves and the academy alike, so there is little to be gained from us repeating it or contributing to what might become depressingly self-fulfilling received wisdom. Something better is at least plausible and our entire agenda in this special issue has been to envision and outline what it could be. The imperative of managing more effectively the global order is not going away: if anything, its urgency has been revealed decisively by the pandemic.

So, even if the post-coronavirus settlement leads to greater insular nationalism, this will only exacerbate the already-alarming incapacity of states to grapple collectively with transborder challenges, and, ultimately, provide yet further evidence for the desperate need for change. Moreover, the deglobalizers, especially the Anglo-American pairing of Trump and Johnson, have, at the time of writing, had a very bad crisis indeed, and the very people who are normally scapegoated in the aftermath of such upheavals – the poor, the foreign, those doing the under- and even un-paid caring work – are, for once, being recognized for their sacrifice. This potentially represents a period of disjuncture where popular connections might finally be made between unacceptable levels of inequality, the inability of supposedly advanced yet atrophied states to carry out the most basic role of protecting their citizens, and the wider disparaging of evidence, expertise and global cooperation.

Our broader contention, then, is not that the pandemic will necessarily induce change, but rather that it could at last represent the dénouement of a neoliberalism stagnant with decay specifically because it has decisively revealed, in ways not previously obvious to many, the pathologies that became evident during the global financial crisis as having degraded to the point that they require quite fundamental change. Indeed, the lack of an international response to Covid-19 – and the longer it goes on – only serves to demonstrate forcefully that it is needed more than ever. As much as they might try, even the most ardent deglobalizers may struggle to put that particular genie back in its bottle. We therefore need urgently, at a planetary level, to argue through, test out and ultimately shape a new global consensus that is both more appropriate to the changed balance of political power in the world and, above all, capable of initiating and delivering a beneficial process of reglobalization. The G20 is the only, and therefore the best, game in town when it comes to guiding global renewal. We all need to back it in order to imagine and negotiate a new global political settlement for a post-neoliberal, post-coronavirus era that steers decisively away from the rocky shores and false promises of deglobalization.

Disclosure statement

No potential conflict of interest was reported by the author(s).

ORCID

Matthew Louis Bishop http://orcid.org/0000-0001-6981-6241
Anthony Payne http://orcid.org/0000-0002-8151-9722

References

Adler, D. (2019). The international institutional turn: The missing ingredient in labour's new political economy. *Renewal: A Journal of Social Democracy*, *27*(4), 11–22.

Adler, D., & Arauz, A. (2020). It's time to end the Fed's 'Monetary Triage'. *The Nation*, March 23. https://www.thenation.com/article/economy/economy-fed-imf/

Baker, A. (2018). Macroprudential regimes and the politics of social purpose. *Review of International Political Economy*, *25*(3), 293–316. https://doi.org/10.1080/09692290.2018.1459780
Baker, A., & Murphy, R. (2020). Creating a race to the top in global tax governance: The political case for tax spillover assessments. *Globalizations*. https://doi.org/10.1080/14747731.2020.1774324
Banerjee, A. V., & Duflo, E. (2019). *Good economics for hard times*. Allen Lane.
Barnett, J., & Campbell, J. (2010). *Climate change and small island states: Power, knowledge and the South Pacific*. Earthscan.
Beeson, M., & Bell, S. (2009). The G-20 and international economic governance: Hegemony, collectivism, or both? *Global Governance: A Review of Multilateralism and International Organizations*, *15*(1), 67–86. https://doi.org/10.1163/19426720-01501005
Berglöff, E., Brown, G., & Farrar, J. (2020). A letter to G20 governments. *Project Syndicate*, April 6. https://www.project-syndicate.org/commentary/a-letter-to-g20-governments-by-erik-berglof-et-al-2020-04
Bishop, M. L. (2016a). *Negotiating flexibility at UNGASS 2016: Solving the 'World Drug Problem?'* SPERI Global Brief. http://speri.dept.shef.ac.uk/wp-content/uploads/2016/11/Global-Brief-5-Negotiating-Flexibility-at-UNGASS-2016-Solving-the-World-Drug-Problem.pdf
Bishop, M. L. (2016b). *Rethinking the political economy of development beyond 'The rise of the BRICS'*. Sheffield Political Economy Research Institute Paper No. 30. http://speri.dept.shef.ac.uk/wp-content/uploads/2016/07/Beyond-the-Rise-of-the-BRICS.pdf
Bishop, M. L. (2018). *The G20: Circus without a Ringleader?* Global Policy G20 Brief. https://www.globalpolicyjournal.com/sites/default/files/Matt%20Bishop%20-%20policy%20brief.pdf
Bishop, M. L. (2019). *Has the multilateral fightback begun?* Global Policy G20 Brief. https://www.globalpolicyjournal.com/sites/default/files/Has%20the%20Multilateral%20Fightback%20Begun_0.pdf
Bishop, M. L., & Murray-Evans, P. (2020). Five little B(R)ICS: Huffing and puffing, but not blowing your house in. *New Political Economy*, *25*(5).
Bishop, M. L., & Muzaka, V. (2018). Multilateralism. In K. Dingwerth & C. Weinhardt (Eds.), *The language of world trade politics: Unpacking the terms of trade* (pp. 64–79). Routledge.
Bishop, M. L., & Payne, A. (2012). Climate change and the future of Caribbean development. *Journal of Development Studies*, *48*(10), 1536–1553. https://doi.org/10.1080/00220388.2012.693166
Bishop, M. L., & Payne, A. (2019). The left and the case for 'progressive reglobalisation'. *Renewal: A Journal of Social Democracy*, *27*(3), 79–95.
Bishop, M. L., & Payne, A. (2020). The political economies of different globalizations: theorizing reglobalization. *Globalizations*. https://doi.org/10.1080/14747731.2020.1779963
Bishop, M. L., Payne, A., Sen, K., Breslin, S., Öniş, Z., Muzaka, V., Lindsay, C., & Yeung, H. W.-c. (2018). *Revisiting the Developmental State*. Sheffield Political Economy Research Institute Paper No. 43. http://speri.dept.shef.ac.uk/wp-content/uploads/2018/02/SPERI-Paper-No.-43-Revisiting-the-developmental-state.pdf
Brown, G. (2020). In the Coronavirus Crisis, Our Leaders Are Failing Us. *The Guardian*, March 13. https://www.theguardian.com/commentisfree/2020/mar/13/coronavirus-crisis-leaders-failing-gordon-brown
Buzdugan, S., & Payne, A. (2016). *The long battle for global governance*. Routledge.
Chin, G. T., & Dobson, H. (2015). China's presidency of the G20 Hangzhou: On global leadership and strategy. *Global Summitry*, *1*(2), 151–170. https://doi.org/10.1093/global/guw002
Chodor, T. (2017). The G-20 since the global financial crisis: Neither hegemony nor collectivism. *Global Governance: A Review of Multilateralism and International Organizations*, *23*(2), 205–223. https://doi.org/10.1163/19426720-02302005
Chodor, T. (2020). Missing in Action: The G20 in the Covid Crisis. *The Interpreter*, April 22. https://www.lowyinstitute.org/the-interpreter/missing-action-g20-covid-crisis
Clapp, J., & Isakson, S. R. (2018). *Speculative harvests: Financialization, food, and agriculture*. Fernwood.
Clift, B. (2018). *The IMF and the politics of austerity in the wake of the global financial crisis*. Oxford University Press.
Clift, B., & Robles, T.-A. (2020). The IMF, tackling inequality, and post-neoliberal 'reglobalization': The paradoxes of political legitimation within economistic parameters. *Globalizations*. https://doi.org/10.1080/14747731.2020.1774325
Cooper, A. F. (2010). The G20 as an improvised crisis committee and/or a contested 'steering committee' for the world. *International Affairs*, *86*(3), 741–757. https://doi.org/10.1111/j.1468-2346.2010.00909.x
Cooper, A. F. (2014). The G20 and contested global governance: BRICS, middle powers and small states. *Caribbean Journal of International Relations & Diplomacy*, *2*(3), 87–109.

Cooper, A. F. (2019). The G20 is dead as a crisis or steering committee: Long live the G20 as hybrid focal point. *South African Journal of International Affairs, 26*(4), 505–520. https://doi.org/10.1080/10220461.2019.1699855
Cooper, A. F., & Momani, B. (2014). Re-Balancing the G-20 from efficiency to legitimacy: The 3G Coalition and the practice of global governance. *Global Governance: A Review of Multilateralism and International Organizations, 20*(2), 213–232. https://doi.org/10.1163/19426720-02002004
Cooper, A. F., & Stolte, C. (2020). Insider and outsider strategies of influence: The BRICS' dualistic approach towards informal institutions. *New Political Economy, 25*(5). https://doi.org/10.1080/13563467.2019.1584167
Cooper, A. F., & Thakur, R. (2013). *The Group of Twenty (G20)*. Routledge.
Davies, S. E. (2019). *Containing contagion: The politics of disease outbreaks in Southeast Asia*. Johns Hopkins University Press.
Davies, S. E., Kamradt-Scott, A., & Rushton, S. (2015). *Disease diplomacy: International norms and global health security*. Johns Hopkins University Press.
Davies, W. (2017). How statistics lost their power – and why we should fear what comes next. *The Guardian*, January 19. https://www.theguardian.com/politics/2017/jan/19/crisis-of-statistics-big-data-democracy
Davies, W. (2020). The last global crisis didn't change the world. but this one could. *The Guardian*, March 24. https://www.theguardian.com/commentisfree/2020/mar/24/coronavirus-crisis-change-world-financial-global-capitalism#comment-139176234
DeSombre, E. R. (2006). *Global environmental institutions*. Routledge.
Dobson, H. (2012). Where are the women in global governance? Leaders, wives and hegemonic masculinity in the G8 and G20 summits. *Global Society, 26*(4), 429–449. https://doi.org/10.1080/13600826.2012.710594
Drezner, D. W. (2014). *The system worked: How the world stopped another great depression*. Oxford University Press.
Elias, J., & Roberts, A. (2016). Feminist global political economies of the everyday: From bananas to Bingo. *Globalizations, 13*(6), 787–800. https://doi.org/10.1080/14747731.2016.1155797
Elliott, L. (2020). The coronavirus is leading to a whole new way of economic thinking. *The Guardian*, March 22. https://www.theguardian.com/business/2020/mar/22/the-coronavirus-is-leading-to-a-whole-new-way-of-economic-thinking
Forrester, K. (2019). The crisis of liberalism: Why centrist politics can no longer explain the world. *The Guardian*, November 18. https://www.theguardian.com/books/2019/nov/18/crisis-in-liberalism-katrina-forrester
G20 Leaders. (2009). G20 leaders statement: The Pittsburgh Summit. http://www.g20.utoronto.ca/2009/2009communique0925.html
Gills, B. (2020). Deep restoration: From The great implosion to the great awakening. *Globalizations, 17*(4), 577–579. https://doi.org/10.1080/14747731.2020.1748364
Gramsci, A. (1971). *International journal of cultural policy selections from the prison notebooks*. International Publishers.
Hannah, E., Roberts, A., & Trommer, S. (2020). Towards a feminist global trade politics. *Globalizations*. https://doi.org/10.1080/14747731.2020.1779966
Hannah, E., Ryan, H., & Scott, J. (2017). Power, knowledge and resistance: Between co-optation and revolution in global trade. *Review of International Political Economy, 24*(5), 741–775. https://doi.org/10.1080/09692290.2017.1324807
Harman, S. (2012). *Global health governance*. Routledge.
Hay, C. (2011). Pathology without crisis? The strange demise of the Anglo-liberal growth model. *Government and Opposition, 46*(1), 1–31. https://doi.org/10.1111/j.1477-7053.2010.01327.x
Hay, C., & Payne, A. (2013). *The great uncertainty*. Sheffield Political Economy Research Institute Paper No. 5. http://speri.dept.shef.ac.uk/wp-content/uploads/2013/01/SPERI-Paper-No.5-The-Great-Uncertainty-389KB.pdf
Helleiner, E. (2014a). *Forgotten foundations of Bretton Woods: International development and the making of the postwar order*. Cornell University Press.
Helleiner, E. (2014b). *The status quo crisis: Global financial governance after the 2008 meltdown*. Oxford University Press.
Hobson, J. M. (2012). *The Eurocentric conception of world politics: Western international theory, 1760–2010*. Cambridge University Press.

Hobson, J. M. (2020). *Multicultural origins of the global economy: Beyond the western-centric frontier*. Cambridge University Press.
Hopewell, K. (2019). US-China conflict in global trade governance: The new politics of agricultural subsidies at the WTO. *Review of International Political Economy*, *26*(2), 207–231. https://doi.org/10.1080/09692290.2018.1560352
James, H. (2020). A pandemic of deglobalization? *Project Syndicate*, February 28. https://www.project-syndicate.org/commentary/covid-19-deglobalization-pandemic-by-harold-james-2020-02
Kaplinsky, R. (2013). What contribution can China make to inclusive growth in Sub-Saharan Africa? *Development and Change*, *44*(6), 1295–1316. https://doi.org/10.1111/dech.12059
Kirton, J. J. (2016). *G20 governance for a Globalized world*. Routledge.
Klein, N. (2014). *This changes everything: Capitalism vs. The climate*. Simon & Schuster.
LeBaron, G., & Phillips, N. (2019). States and the political economy of Unfree labour. *New Political Economy*, *24*(1), 1–21. https://doi.org/10.1080/13563467.2017.1420642
Matthijs, M. (2020). The right way to fix the EU: Put politics before economics. *Foreign Affairs*, *99*(3), 160–170.
Mayblin, L. (2019). *Impoverishment and asylum: Social policy as slow violence*. Routledge.
Milanović, B. (2016). *Global inequality: A new approach for the age of globalization*. Harvard University Press.
Monbiot, G. (2020). Covid-19 is nature's wake-up call to complacent civilisation. *The Guardian*, March 25. https://www.theguardian.com/commentisfree/2020/mar/25/covid-19-is-natures-wake-up-call-to-complacent-civilisation
Moschella, M., & Quaglia, L. (2020). The coronavirus is undermining Italy's economy. *The Washington Post*, March 25. https://www.washingtonpost.com/politics/2020/03/25/coronavirus-has-thrown-italy-into-an-economic-crisis-european-union-may-be-one-soon-too/
Muzaka, V. (2011). *The politics of intellectual property rights and access to medicines*. Palgrave Macmillan.
Muzaka, V. (2018). *Food, health and the knowledge economy: The state and intellectual property in India and Brazil*. Palgrave.
Muzaka, V., & Bishop, M. L. (2015). Doha stalemate: The end of trade multilateralism? *Review of International Studies*, *41*(2), 383–406. https://doi.org/10.1017/S0260210514000266
Nadelmann, E. A. (1990). Global prohibition regimes: The evolution of norms in international society. *International Organization*, *44*(4), 479–526. https://doi.org/10.1017/S0020818300035384
Narlikar, A. (2014). Unintended consequences: The G20 as global governance. *Caribbean Journal of International Relations & Diplomacy*, *2*(3), 61–71.
North, R. (2020). Coronavirus: You can't bullshit a virus. *EU Referendum Blog*, March 17. http://www.eureferendum.com/blogview.aspx?blogno=87549
Okwonga, M. (2020). You cannot sing 'Rule Britannia' to a virus. *Byline Times*, March 19. https://bylinetimes.com/2020/03/19/you-cannot-sing-rule-britannia-to-a-virus/
Payne, A. (2010). How many Gs are there in 'global governance' after the crisis? The perspectives of the 'marginal majority' of the world's states. *International Affairs*, *86*(3), 729–740.
Pécoud, A. (2020). Philosophies of migration governance in a globalizing world. *Globalizations*. https://doi.org/10.1080/14747731.2020.1774316
Phillips, N. (2009). Coping with China. In A. F. Cooper & J. Heine (Eds.), *Which way Latin America? Hemispheric politics meets globalization* (pp. 100–121). United Nations University Press.
Piketty, T. (2014). *Capital in the twenty first century*. Harvard University Press.
Piketty, T. (2020). *Capital and ideology*. Harvard University Press.
Pisani-Ferry, J. (2019). *Collective action in a fragmented world*. Brussels: Bruegel Policy Brief. http://aei.pitt.edu/100985/1/Bruegel_Policy_Brief-2019_05_1.pdf
Rodrik, D. (2017). *Straight talk on trade: Ideas for a sane world economy*. Princeton University Press.
Roubini, N. (2020). Coronavirus pandemic has delivered the fastest, deepest economic shock in history. *The Guardian*, March 25. https://www.theguardian.com/business/2020/mar/25/coronavirus-pandemic-has-delivered-the-fastest-deepest-economic-shock-in-history
Ruggie, J. G. (1982). International regimes, Transactions, and change: Embedded liberalism in the postwar economic order. *International Organization*, *36*(2), 379–415. https://doi.org/10.1017/S0020818300018993
Ruggie, J. G. (1992). Multilateralism: The anatomy of an institution. *International Organization*, *46*(3), 561–598. https://doi.org/10.1017/S0020818300027831
Rushton, S. (2019). *Security and public health: Pandemics and politics in the contemporary world*. Wiley.

Scheidel, W. (2017). *The great leveler: Violence and the history of inequality from the stone age*. Princeton University Press.
Schirm, S. A. (2013). Global politics are domestic politics: A societal approach to divergence in the G20. *Review of International Studies, 39*(3), 685–706. https://doi.org/10.1017/S0260210512000216
Scobie, M. (2019). *Global environmental governance and small states: Architectures and agency*. Edward Elgar.
Scott, J., & Wilkinson, R. (2020). Reglobalising trade: Progressive global governance in an age of uncertainty. *Globalizations*. https://doi.org/10.1080/14747731.2020.1779965
Slaughter, S. (2020). *The power of the G20: The politics of legitimacy in global governance*. Routledge.
Stevenson, H. (2020). Reforming global climate governance in an age of bullshit. *Globalizations*. https://doi.org/10.1080/14747731.2020.1774315
Thompson, M. S., Cochrane, A., & Hopma, J. (2020). Democratising food: The case for a deliberative approach. *Review of International Studies*, 1–21. https://doi.org/10.1017/S0260210520000017
Tooze, A. (2020). The normal economy is never coming back. *Foreign Policy*, April 9. https://foreignpolicy.com/2020/04/09/unemployment-coronavirus-pandemic-normal-economy-is-never-coming-back/
Vestergaard, J., & Wade, R. (2012a). The governance response to the great recession: The "success" of the G20. *Journal of Economic Issues, 46*(2), 481–490. https://doi.org/10.2753/JEI0021-3624460223
Vestergaard, J., & Wade, R. H. (2012b). Establishing a new global economic council: Governance reform at the G20, the IMF and the World Bank. *Global Policy, 3*(3), 257–269. https://doi.org/10.1111/j.1758-5899.2012.00169.x
Wilkinson, R. (2014). *What's wrong with the WTO and how to fix it*. Polity Press.
Zuboff, S. (2019). *The age of surveillance capitalism*. Profile.

Index

For Product Safety Concerns and Information please contact our
EU representative GPSR@taylorandfrancis.com Taylor & Francis
Verlag GmbH, Kaufingerstraße 24, 80331 München, Germany